DETERMINANTS OF INDIGENOUS PEOPLES' HEALTH IN CANADA

The **CSPI Series in Indigenous Studies** supports student development and academic inquiry by highlighting leading scholarship on Indigenous peoples. With an aim to offer innovative pedagogical resources and emphasize Indigenous intellectual traditions, the volumes in this series provide diverse approaches to Indigenous knowledges, histories, and politics.

Titles in the Series

A Recognition of Being: Reconstructing Native Womanhood by Kim Anderson

Determinants of Indigenous Peoples' Health in Canada: Beyond the Social edited by Margo Greenwood, Sarah de Leeuw, Nicole Marie Lindsay, and Charlotte Reading

Iskwewak Kah' Ki Yaw Ni Wahkomakanak: Neither Indian Princesses nor Easy Squaws by Janice Acoose-Miswonigeesikokwe

Sivumut—Towards the Future Together: Inuit Women Educational Leaders in Nunavut and Nunavik edited by Fiona Walton and Darlene O'Leary

Strong Helpers' Teachings: The Value of Indigenous Knowledges in the Helping Professions by Cyndy Baskin

Walking in the Good Way / Ioterihwakwaríhshion Tsi Íhse: Aboriginal Social Work Education edited by Ingrid Thompson Cooper and Gail Stacey Moore

DETERMINANTS OF INDIGENOUS PEOPLES' HEALTH IN CANADA

BEYOND THE SOCIAL

Edited by Margo Greenwood, Sarah de Leeuw,
Nicole Marie Lindsay,
and Charlotte Reading

Canadian Scholars' Press
Toronto

Determinants of Indigenous Peoples' Health in Canada: Beyond the Social
edited by Margo Greenwood, Sarah de Leeuw, Nicole Marie Lindsay, and Charlotte Reading

First published in 2015 by
Canadian Scholars' Press Inc.
425 Adelaide Street West, Suite 200
Toronto, Ontario
M5V 3C1

www.cspi.org

Library and Archives Canada Cataloguing in Publication

Determinants of indigenous peoples' health in Canada : beyond the social / edited by Margo Greenwood, Sarah de Leeuw, Nicole Marie Lindsay, and Charlotte Reading.

Includes bibliographical references and index.
Issued in print and electronic formats.
ISBN 978-1-55130-732-9 (paperback).—ISBN 978-1-55130-733-6 (pdf).—
ISBN 978-1-55130-734-3 (epub)

1. Native peoples—Health and hygiene—Canada. I. Greenwood, Margo, 1953-, author, editor II. De Leeuw, Sarah, author, editor III. Lindsay, Nicole Marie, 1975-, editor IV. Reading, Charlotte, 1959-, author, editor

RA450.4.I53D48 2015   362.1089´97071   C2015-902109-X   C2015-902110-3

Text design by BNTypographics West
Cover design by Em Dash Design

Printed and bound in Canada by Webcom

Canada

ABOUT THE COVER

The image on the cover of this book is a detail from "Me and My 2 Dead Brotherz," a 2003 totem pole designed and carved by Charles "Ya'Ya" Heit, a Gitxsan artist from northern British Columbia. This work, a five-foot-tall sculpture in red cedar, is the artist's response to the death of his brothers from HIV/AIDS. Ya'Ya shared the poem below to accompany his work.

Ya'Ya Mourns His 2 Dead Brothers

My bro Andy Clifton died in 1999
Am Hon wuz his real name
He wuz the first person I knew with AIDS
I wuz afraid back then
And so wuz he
Am Hon wuz afraid to live
So he went to die in Prince Rupert
And I wuz afraid of his AIDS
But I went to see him anywayz
I couldn't watch him die
So I went by the Skeena River
To fight my demons
There I watched his Rainbows
Taking him home
I almost missed seeing them
With giant steps they went soo fast
Am Hon and his Ancestors

On May 14, 2003 Yvon Micheal Starr died
 He wuz my bro
Now he no longer shares this world with me
This world has became smaller
And I cried for him to live again
To run thru the jungle with me
To live and laugh like we did when we were young
We had some crazy times
Wild crazy and free
Together we had known true pure freedom
Not a worry or a want
Those times past us years ago
Life took us far apart
But my brother stayed in my heart
And he crossed my mind often
Once in a while I worried about him
And wished he wuz near

Both of my brotherz had AIDS when they died
That made their deaths hurt xtra
I found my love for them again
With Native Pride

Charles Peter Heit
is
Ya'Ya

CONTENTS

Rethinking Determinants of Indigenous Peoples' Health in Canada

Sarah de Leeuw, Nicole Marie Lindsay, and Margo Greenwood

Indigenous peoples in Canada, and indeed around the world, have known for a long time something that non-Indigenous scholars, health care professionals, and decision makers are only recently embracing. Namely, that the well-being of individuals and communities is linked to much broader dynamics than typically assumed by the individualistic, biomedical approaches to health that have long dominated non-Indigenous medicine.[1] In the realms of mainstream medicine and public health, the acknowledgement that health is at least partially determined by social circumstances and contexts—as opposed to being solely dictated by individual biology—has gained traction and credibility only in the last decade. This credibility and traction have emerged as a burgeoning body of literature and research known broadly as social determinants of health (SDoH) work (see, e.g., Raphael, 2009; Commission on Social Determinants of Health, 2007; Kelly et al., 2007; Marmot, 2005; Anderson, Shinn, & St. Charles, 2002; Wilkinson & Marmot, 1998).

In Canada and beyond, social determinants of health approaches have made possible a more contextually nuanced analysis of the enduring health inequities experienced by Indigenous peoples relative to non-Indigenous peoples (see for instance, Richmond & Ross, 2009; Loppie Reading & Wien, 2009; Larson, Gillies, Howard, & Coffin, 2007; Baum & Harris, 2006; Adelson, 2005; Wilson & Rosenberg, 2002). In much of this work, SDoH approaches applied to Indigenous peoples have raised three important insights. First, within social and political domains, colonialism has yet to be fully and consistently accounted for as a significant determinant of health. This is despite the fact that Indigenous peoples—who globally experience the greatest disparities in health—identify colonialism as perhaps the *most* important determinant of their (ill) health (Loppie Reading & Wien, 2009; Richmond & Ross, 2009; Bourassa, McKay-McNabb, & Hampton, 2004; de Leeuw, Greenwood, & Cameron, 2010). Second, much of the literature and research about social determinants of Indigenous peoples' health remains a subsection or corollary to broader SDoH discussions instead of considering it as a unique area requiring sustained attention unto itself. Third, despite good efforts to the contrary, much of the literatures about social determinants of health, including that focused on Indigenous peoples' health, continue to be written by non-Indigenous peoples.

This book takes seriously the need to address and acknowledge these three points, both implicitly and explicitly. Firstly, all the contributing authors write with the understanding that colonialism is indeed the broadest and most fundamental determinant of Indigenous health and well-being in countries where settler-colonial power continues to dominate. Secondly, the chapters in this book consider Indigenous knowledges and ways of being in the world to be the primary frame of reference for understanding current health realities in Indigenous communities. Thirdly, and very relatedly, this text is comprised largely of Indigenous voices, voices that speak the truths and foreground the lived realities of being Indigenous in Canada in the twenty-first century.

Our approach in this book is premised on the observation that existing literature focused on determinants of health has been primarily concerned with how the "social" determines human (ill) health or (lack of) well-being, often to the exclusion of other forces that may not be considered strictly "social" in nature, including colonialism. We note that the concept of *social* determinants of health, by definition, tends to exclude or marginalize other types of determinants not typically considered to fall under the category of the "social"—for example, spirituality, relationship to the land, geography, history, culture, language, and knowledge systems. Many other important determinants of Indigenous peoples' health, while often considered to be part of the "social" realm—such as gender and sexuality, early childhood, economic and educational opportunity—tend to be subsumed under generalized SDoH approaches that do not fully account for the ways in which both historical and contemporary colonialisms continue to bear down on all aspects of Indigenous peoples' lives.

As a corrective to this tendency, this book begins with the basic assumption that colonialism is an active and ongoing force impacting the well-being of Indigenous peoples in Canada. Drawing upon insights from mostly Indigenous theorists, we argue that colonialism has impacted determinants of Indigenous peoples' health in Canada beyond what may typically be considered just "the social." This book therefore aims to expand health determinants discussions beyond the social in order to more fully account for the many forces bearing down on the health and well-being of Indigenous peoples in Canada. In this way, we hope to expand and refresh the growing literatures about social determinants of health in the Canadian context. Most importantly, however, we aim to broaden the ways Indigenous peoples' health is understood, harnessing new ideas and new voices that challenge theorizations about health inequities as being purely socially determined. Instead, the authors in this collection show that health is multiply and complexly determined by a myriad of factors that, although they invariably unfold within a colonial reality, are always unique to a specific time and place.

The argument advanced by all authors in this text is that there are a great variety of determinants of Indigenous peoples' health. These include, to name a few, geographic determinants, economic determinants, historical determinants, narrative and genealogical determinants, and structural determinants— most of which are not individually or biologically dictated, but all of which are unique because they interface with and are impacted by colonialism of the past and the present. This reconceptualization about how Indigenous peoples' health is determined in Canada and beyond (e.g., it is not solely "socially" determined, nor is "adding colonialism" to a social determinants of health framework sufficient to fully analyze and understand the realities of Indigenous peoples' health) is at the heart of this book, making it a unique text explicitly positioned to reconfigure the current state of knowledge and conceptualization about how Indigenous peoples' health is, and has come to be, theorized.

Having said this, however, we recognize that our contribution to discussions about the determinants of Indigenous peoples' health rests upon the foundations set by groundbreaking work in the field of social determinants of health. We turn next to a brief overview of the history of SDoH frameworks.

Social Determinants of Health Frameworks

In 1986, building on a rising tide of evidence suggesting a need for new models to address poor health and health inequalities around the world (see discussions in Commission on Social Determinants of Health, 2007, 2008), the World Health Organization (WHO) hosted the first International Conference on Health Promotion in Ottawa. The Ottawa Charter for Health Promotion

(OCHP) was subsequently signed, the action items of which included "re-orienting health care services toward prevention of illness and promotion of health." As an alternative to focusing on risk factors for illness or disease at an individual level, the Ottawa Charter stated that public health research and action should instead target "upstream" factors (determinants of health, including social determinants) like healthy environments and the social contexts in which people could be empowered to live healthy lives. Correspondingly, Health Canada proposed a population health promotion (PHP) model aimed at addressing the health of families, communities, and socio-cultural sectors as opposed to redressing ill health solely at the scale of the individual (Public Health Agency of Canada, 2013). Furthermore, the Ottawa Charter stated that population interventions—as opposed to individual interventions—should be based on an understanding about nine "determinants" of health (which have since grown to 12, as identified by the Public Health Agency of Canada), including income and social status, social support networks, education and literacy, working conditions, social and physical environments, child development, gender, and culture (see also Edwards, 2007).

In the years following the Ottawa Charter, a discourse about "social determinants of health" began to dominate in many conversations focused on public and population health. The dominance of SDoH approaches resulted in part from the increasing amount of evidence showing that poor health and health inequalities could not be solved by focusing solely on individual people's characteristics or their risk factors to the exclusion of underlying structural aspects of society that drive broad patterns of health. The evidence supporting SDoH has shown that upstream dynamics—such as income disparities, early childhood development, social inclusion/exclusion, existence of social safety nets, and employment and working conditions—figure significantly in shaping population health outcomes (Commission on Social Determinants of Health, 2007; Kelly et al., 2007; Marmot, 2005; Wilkinson, 2006; Wilkinson & Marmot, 1998). Partly in response to this increasing body of evidence, the WHO now very much privileges an SDoH approach, inside of which remains more biomedically inclined interventions such as vaccinations or disease prevention. As a result, the concept of SDoH has gained significant traction in global practices (and theoretical frameworks) focused on reducing health inequities. Indeed, the WHO has recently hosted two international forums—one in Adelaide, Australia, and one in Rio, Brazil—that were linked to the establishment of a WHO Commission on the Social Determinants of Health (CSDH).

Given this global focus, it is not surprising that social determinants of health approaches and perspectives have gained considerable attention and following. In the WHO's second edition of *Social Determinants of Health: The Solid Facts*, for example, leading global experts on social determinants of health analyzed "thousands of research reports" (Wilkinson & Marmot, 2003, p. 8) to conclude definitively that increased scientific attention corroborates "the remarkable sensitivity of health to the social environment and what have become known as the social determinants of health" (Wilkinson & Marmot, 2003, p. 7; see also Raphael, 2012). Although there is passing reference to genes and the human genome project as having profound and determining effects on human health, the authors nevertheless advance the case that it is "social" determinants of health that must be addressed if global health inequalities are ever to be resolved. With reference to the resilient inequities around the world between Indigenous and non-Indigenous peoples, the social determinants of health again have significantly more discursive space than health determinants that may fall less precisely into the category of the "social."

Among researchers and practitioners thinking about health inequities in Canada, "the social" has similarly gained traction and risen to a place of prominence (see, for example, Mikkonen & Raphael, 2010; Raphael, 2002). Key texts about Canadian health and health care, for instance, feature statements such as "[s]ocial determinants of health are the *primary* determinants of whether individuals stay healthy or become ill (a narrow definition of health)" (Raphael, 2009, p. 2; emphasis added). With specific reference to health disparities between Indigenous and non-Indigenous Canadians, social determinants of health have also risen to remarkable prominence—with the addition of colonization/colonialism as a unique (and yet still social) determinant in the lives and health of Indigenous peoples (Adelson, 2005; Carson, Dunbar, Chenhall, & Bailie, 2007; Smylie, Williams, & Cooper, 2006; Smylie, 2009; Loppie Reading & Wien, 2009; Wilson & Young, 2008).

Given, however, that the disparities between Indigenous and non-Indigenous peoples in Canada remain the most marked of any two groups (Reading, 2009), the question arises: How well are Indigenous ways of knowing and being served when the unacceptable health disparities lived by Canada's First Peoples are principally conceptualized through a social determinants of health framework? We wonder if, at times, the uptake of a social determinants of health framework has become so enduring and all-encompassing that it threatens to eclipse or subsume attention to other determinants of health. We wonder about the possibility of intervening into a social determinants of health framework without such interventions being simply enfolded into the very definition and fabric of the framework. Indeed, in health journals focused on applied practice (e.g., nursing), sentiments such as the following, drawn from the Public Health Agency of Canada, suggest the all-inclusive nature of an SDoH framework:

> [S]ocial determinants is both complex and *all-encompassing*, and depends heavily on a responsive, plentiful, and renewal natural environment. There are additional social determinants of health (such as peace, social support and family violence) that are not listed. (Public Health Agency of Canada, http://eco nurse.org/issues.html; emphasis added)

The subsuming of historic, geographic (perhaps even geological), environmental, economic, political, and even cultural drivers into a "social" determinants framework, we suggest, results in understandings about health that may not be nuanced enough to fully conceptualize the disparities and inequities lived by Indigenous peoples. This is particularly the case if it allows for only a single point from which to theorize colonialism and colonization.

Chapter Overviews

A determinants of health framework that is not purely "social" in nature but which is truly nimble and robust enough to respond to and address Indigenous peoples' health inequities in the twenty-first century must ensure complexity and nuance, must not lose sight of community utility, and must simultaneously never overlook the ongoing impact of colonialism. These are points honoured and considered by all the authors in this collection, whether they be Indigenous or non-Indigenous scholars, medical professionals, community advocates, or storytellers.

The book is divided into four sections. Part 1 sets the context by introducing several broad themes that run throughout the book. In Chapter 1, "Structural Determinants of Aboriginal Peoples' Health," Charlotte Reading highlights the importance of taking stock of historical legacies of colonialism and the lasting social, political, and legal structures that continue to position Indigenous communities at the margins of mainstream Canadian society, perpetuating relations of inequality that bear down on the health and well-being of First Nations, Inuit, and Métis individuals and communities. Reading draws from her past work on the proximal, intermediate, and distal determinants of Aboriginal health to lay the foundations for understanding how the "moving parts" of colonialism continue to exert control over health outcomes. While most standard public health interventions focus on the proximal determinants, or those determinants that are most easily identified as "social" or "individual" (such as early childhood, income and social status, education, social support networks, employment and working conditions), and some are beginning to address what she calls intermediate determinants (health promotion, education and justice systems, kinship networks, relationship to land and language, ways of knowing), too few public health researchers focus on the distal determinants: those deeply imbedded historical, political, ideological, economic, and social foundations from which all other determinants evolve. Using the metaphor of a tree to describe the relationships between the three levels of determinants (proximal determinants as the crown of the tree, intermediate determinants as the trunk, and distal determinants as the roots), Reading points out that "Just as maladies observed in the leaves are generally *not* the cause of unhealthy trees, inequities in human health frequently result from corruption or deficiencies in the unseen but critical root system" (p. 5). This insight echoes throughout many of the following chapters.

In Chapter 2, "Two-Eyed Seeing in Medicine," Mi'kmaw Elders Murdena and Albert Marshall (with the help of colleague and friend, Cheryl Bartlett) share their reflections on the role of traditional Indigenous knowledge and culture in navigating life in two worlds for Indigenous peoples: "that of their Native community and that of the newcomers, of the white people, whose ways are the ways of mainstream society" (p. 17). As Murdena and Albert Marshall point out, Two-Eyed Seeing is a "guiding principle" for walking in these two worlds, drawing from the strengths or the best of each and bringing together different ways of knowing for the benefit of all peoples—Indigenous and non-Indigenous. For virtually all of the authors writing in this collection, the challenge of walking in two worlds and maintaining a strong connection to Indigenous ways of knowing lies at the heart of health and well-being, whether through early childhood (Greenwood & Jones, Chapter 7), by honouring ceremony and Indigenous ways in the medical system (Makokis & Makokis, Chapter 19), in communities (Adam, Chapter 15), in medical professions (Caron, Chapter 20), or in the myriad other contexts covered by other authors in this collection.

In Chapter 3, "Inuit Knowledge Systems, Elders, and Determinants of Health: Harmony, Balance, and the Role of Holistic Thinking," Shirley Tagalik takes up the theme of holistic Indigenous knowledge systems in her exploration of *Inuit Qaujimajatuqangit* (IQ), or Inuit world view, through the words of Inuit Elders. As she points out, the core concepts of connectedness, belonging, and respectful relationship building are essential to Inuit understandings of well-being, or "living a good life." Inuit Elders interviewed by Tagalik confirmed the central role of holism—relationality and reciprocity—in all aspects of Inuit life. As she puts it, this holism is "intuitive, moral, spiritual, and represents a thorough integration of expectations and practices grounded in beliefs. . .called the *maligait*, or the big laws" (p. 26). These laws include working for the common good, respect for all living beings, maintenance of harmony and balance, and preparation for the future. Although processes of colonization have weakened and often disrupted the transmission of *Inuit Qaujimajatuqangit* from generation to generation, many Inuit are working to revitalize cultural teachings in order to equip their children with the knowledge they need to thrive in the present and into the future.

Marlene Brant Castellano takes up the importance of spirituality as an often-neglected component of holistic health in Chapter 4, "The Spiritual Dimension of Holistic Health: A Reflection." As she points out, spiritual health is as important to the well-being of Indigenous communities as cultural safety and physical wellness, and traditional knowledge about spirituality is an essential component of healing for many people. Castellano makes a powerful point that although spiritual health can be often sparked in a ceremonial setting, "it is lived outside the lodge." She goes on to say that:

> [Spiritual health] is expressed and sustained in relationships with family and friends. It is enlarged in reconnecting with the land that supports our feet. It is spread abroad in service to the community. It is inspired by the joy and energy of children. *Spiritual health is a communal affair and it is undermined by anything that assaults community vitality.* (p. 34; emphasis added)

Spiritual health is also crucial to the healing necessary to overcome the traumas of colonization that have manifested in a wide range of physical and mental health problems prevalent in Indigenous communities. Castellano argues that despite recent gains in Aboriginal health status, policy-makers and health practitioners face a daunting challenge in improving the efficacy of Indigenous health interventions by moving toward more holistic approaches based on cultural competence. She closes her chapter with the important point that "community leaders and professionals need to explore the feasibility of making cultural competence a standard of practice to which every person entrusted with the responsibility for enhancing Aboriginal health is expected to adhere, with access to appropriate preparation" (p. 37).

In Chapter 5, two poems by Métis poet Marilyn Iwama close Part 1 of the book by offering the grounded, felt experience of sickness and healing, birth and death. In "Take That Pain," Iwama explores the loss and longing that accompany physical illness and hospitalization, and the "special way / language is healing. . ." In a powerful recounting of an experience of hospitalization for a stroke, Iwama calls up the healing power of story and words: "So today I try again / to get Auntie to talk / about healing verbs." The second poem, "Medicine," opens with the smells brought home by the narrator's *nikāwiy*: "Cottage cheese and metal / mean birth. Death? / Violets and rotting plums." In this poem, the narrator invokes the names of medications— dilaudid, hydromorphone hydrochloride—given to her aging father as he approaches death. Both poems work the visceral images and sensations that powerfully connect illness and medicalization to the familial love and relationships that ground experiences of sickness and health.

In Part 2, authors explore determinants of Aboriginal health that push beyond the social. Many of these chapters recognize and touch on determinants of health falling within the realm of "the social," but they do so with a careful recognition about the chains of determinants that reach beyond this realm. Relationship to the land—which is arguably distinctly *not* social— figures powerfully in this section, and is intertwined with other important determinants that push the limits of "the social": culture and identity formation, gender, and the healing power of story also figure prominently in these chapters.

In Chapter 6, "The Relatedness of People, Land, and Health: Stories from Anishinabe Elders," Chantelle Richmond picks up on themes introduced in Chapter 3 (Tagalik) by highlighting the traditional knowledge and wisdom held by Elders. Where Tagalik's chapter focuses on Inuit knowledge, Richmond's interviews with Anishinabe Elders focus deeply on the vital connection to the land necessary for the health and well-being of Indigenous communities. As Richmond points out, reduced access to the land through encroaching development has compromised these special relationships, especially for younger generations of Indigenous peoples. The Anishinabe Elders cited in her chapter express concern about the impacts of this disruption, not only in terms of loss of culture and traditional knowledge, but in the sometimes devastating results in the health and well-being of young people in their communities.

Chapter 7, "Being at the Interface: Early Childhood as a Determinant of Health," by Margo Greenwood and Elizabeth Jones, focuses on the importance of cultural continuity and the roles and relationships of Indigenous children within the collective. As they point out, children play a vital role both as individuals and as members of the collective:

> In all of our considerations of the well-being of Indigenous children, we must take into account their experiences both as individuals and as members of collectives; it is not possible to separate the two. Indigenous children hold a unique place in our collective: they embody the past through our teachings, they experience the present, and they hold our dreams for the future. Their individual identities ensure collective cultural continuity. (p. 65)

Greenwood and Jones take up the concept of Two-Eyed Seeing to explore the processes and contexts through which Indigenous children become proficient at code-switching as they are socialized as "bicultural," living in both Indigenous and non-Indigenous worlds. Like many of the other authors in this text, Greenwood and Jones observed that relationships are central to identity formation and cultural survival for Indigenous communities. They point out that in learning to navigate "the complexity of the realities we find ourselves in, it is the relationships at the interface of cultures that offer possibilities for finding ourselves among competing pressures and potentials" (p. 70). Greenwood and Jones show how these practical, ethical spaces at the interface can be cultivated through culturally appropriate early education and child-care settings that engage the collective—including sometimes diverse families and communities—in program decision making regarding what is to be taught and how it is to be taught. They argue that honouring tribal and Indigenous knowledge in early childhood education settings requires conscious involvement and careful planning from the program planning level through to teacher education and credentialing, citing examples where these processes are being implemented with success.

Chapter 8, "Cultural Wounds Demand Cultural Medicines," continues the focus on culture and identity as crucial indicators of well-being among Indigenous communities and individuals. Building on their groundbreaking work about suicide in First Nations communities, authors Michael J. Chandler and William L. Dunlop advocate for a broader and more nuanced understanding of the important role of "cultural wounds" as root causes of the health inequities experienced by the world's Indigenous peoples. They argue that current suicide-prevention strategies fail to adequately address the community level and that it is cultural factors that act as true buffers against suicide: that is, "community-level efforts to achieve a high level ownership of their own cultural past, and an elevated level of success in controlling their own civic futures" (p. 87). In short, Chandler and Dunlop find that suicide rates are low to non-existent in communities characterized by self-government, active involvement in restoration of traditional land title, preservation of language and culture, and traditional roles for women in tribal governance, among other factors.

Chapter 9, "Activating Place: Geography as a Determinant of Indigenous Peoples' Health and Well-being," turns to another key theme running throughout many of the chapters in this collection—that is, the fundamental importance of understanding relationships to the land as crucial to the health and well-being of Indigenous peoples. Picking up on themes introduced in Chapter 6 and further explored in Chapter 11, among others, author Sarah de Leeuw argues for a reorientation of thinking about the determinants of health for Indigenous peoples that accounts for the important role played by geography—that is, physical place and space as experienced by Indigenous communities and individuals. As many Indigenous scholars and thinkers have powerfully noted, the physical and spiritual connections between Indigenous communities and the lands they have occupied from time immemorial are crucial both to their identities and to their sense of wellness—and colonial disruption of these important geographical connections has had devastating impacts on Indigenous individuals and communities alike. As de Leeuw points out, given this reality, it is crucial to think geographically about the social determinants of health to extended the scale of inquiry about health or health inequities "because for many Indigenous communities the inalienable connection with and right to specific ecologies, lands, water and soil systems, and other non-human wildlife is inseparable from human health, and yet not simply an extension of 'the social'" (p. 97).

In Chapter 10, "Embodying Self-Determination: Beyond the Gender Binary," author Sarah Hunt advocates thinking beyond the social in also examining the historical and political constructions of the colonial gender binary imposed on Indigenous peoples. In her exploration of gender as a determinant of health, Hunt highlights the erasure of traditional Indigenous transgender and two-spirit identities through the imposition of colonial norms. As she argues, this erasure is an ongoing form of violence rooted in colonial desires to impose normative gender categories on all Indigenous peoples—men, women, two-spirits, and children. As she points out, "gendered analyses of power in Indigenous communities tend to focus on men and women, reinforcing the gender binary and thereby erasing the realities of [trans] women like

Kellie Little" (p. 104). Hunt argues for an Indigenous gender analysis that displaces colonial norms in order to "make the lives of trans and other two-spirit people visible in conceptualizations of the health and self-determination of Indigenous communities" (p. 116). Despite the violence and erasure expe rienced not only by Indigenous women and girls, but also by their trans and two-spirit community members, the vibrant resurgence of two-spirit scholar-ship, organizing, and artistic expression points to "the potential to reclaim and re-story Indigenous gender roles and identities as part of broader efforts to create healthy, self-determining communities" (p. 116).

Chapter 11, "Take Care of the Land and the Land Will Take Care of You: Resources, Development, and Health," an interview with Carrier Sekani Tribal Chief Terry Teegee, returns to Indigenous relationships to the land in reference to the impacts of resource extraction and industrial development on Indigenous traditional territories. As a registered forester and a tribal chief, Teegee explains that although Indigenous communities are not always opposed to resource development, extractive and other industrial activities must be carried out with full participation and approval of the traditional owners of the affected territory. He points out that the history of colonization is also a history of resource extraction, and that this has had devastating re-sults for many Indigenous communities who have been sometimes violently separated from their traditional territories in order to make way for extractive activities and industrial and urban development. However, many Indigenous communities are starting to demand recognition and reclaim their roles as stewards of their lands and resources. Teegee points to court cases, interna-tional activism, and community solidarity as important strategies employed by many Indigenous groups struggling for greater control over their lands and resources. Ultimately, as Teegee points out, the priority for all Indigenous communities is to protect their land and resources for the health and well-being of future generations.

In Chapter 12, "Raven Healing," Roberta Kennedy (Kung Jaadee) tells her own story of becoming a teller of traditional Haida stories, emphasizing the importance of stories to health and healing. Writing from a place of remark-able resiliency and cultural strength, Kung Jaadee reminds us of the centrality of stories as a way for Indigenous peoples to come to know their history, traditions, and identities. She also points to the healing effect of stories. She describes the effect both on her son and on herself the first time she told a traditional story in her son's kindergarten classroom:

When I told this story, I noticed a positive effect on my son's face. Once his classmates commented on how lucky he was, he really lit up! He had the biggest smile. I realized I was telling stories for him, to help him. I only learned a few years ago while telling this story to an audience of storytellers that this really was the beginning of my own healing. (p. 135)

In Part 3, "Wellness Is Knowing Who We Are: Culture, Language, Identity," authors expand on the centrality of these important themes in Indigenous health and wellness. In these chapters, language and education feature strongly as determinants of health for Indigenous communities and individuals insofar as they are two crucial paths for understanding who we are as distinct peoples. In Chapter 13, "*atikowisi miýw-āyāwin*, Ascribed Health and Wellness, to *kaskitamasowin miýw-āyāwin*, Achieved Health and Wellness: Shifting the Paradigm," Madeleine Dion Stout draws on her knowledge of the Cree language to demonstrate a poly-vocal approach to understanding health and wellness rooted in Indigenous knowledge and world views. In accessing and sharing the complex and nuanced understanding of health and well-being offered through Cree concepts, Dion Stout shows how Indigenous language and world conceptualizations can be understood as powerful health determinants. She uses the Cree language to illustrate the resilience and strength of Indigenous communities as they move toward reclaiming responsibility for their health and well-being and agency in determining the policies and processes that impact them, in the process offering non-Cree readers a valuable window into the world views and perspectives of Cree peoples concerning their own health and well-being.

In Chapter 14, "*miyo-pimâtisiwin* 'A Good Path': Indigenous Knowledges, Languages, and Traditions in Education and Health," authors Diana Steinhauer and James Lamouche describe how Indigenous knowledge about health is being formalized through an innovative Indigenous Health Sciences Program (IHSP) at Blue Quills First Nations College in northeastern Alberta. The Blue Quills program is designed by and for Indigenous communities, based on *nehiyawak* (Cree) concepts, philosophies, and teachings about health, healing, and wellness. The Blue Quills program places the primary themes of land, language, and relationships at the centre of its curriculum, building on the strengths and values of the communities its graduates will serve.

Chapter 15, "Reshaping the Politics of Health: A Personal Perspective," by Warner Adam, reflects on the interconnections between the cultural, political,

and historical drivers of health and well-being, and especially on the important role Elders play in bridging the past with the present and helping orient
First Nations communities and individuals to the values that guide them.
Drawing from his personal experiences, Adam's reflections about language,
identity, and racism demonstrate the quiet resilience that characterizes so
many Indigenous communities and individuals as they navigate the complex
legacies of colonialism. As he points out, however, this resilience is also a
powerful force that draws on the voices of our ancestors and Elders: "Their
voices echo in my mind: to be respectful of this land, to be mindful of the
temptations of the world, to be smart enough to use systems to rebuild our
nations with pride and dignity, and to become self-sufficient" (p. 167). Adam's
reflections remind readers that efforts to decolonize the health of Indigenous
peoples must be holistic and built on the foundations of Indigenous governance and values.

Chapter 16, "Aboriginal Early Childhood Development Policies and Programs in British Columbia: Beyond the Rhetoric," by Karen Isaac and Kathleen Jamieson, returns the focus to early childhood, picking up on many
themes introduced in Chapter 7 by Margo Greenwood and Elizabeth Jones.
Focusing on current early childhood development (ECD) practice in British
Columbia, Isaac and Jamieson show how government policy and programs are
falling short in providing the necessary supports to Indigenous children and
families. While they acknowledge that many well-meaning policies have contributed resources to ECD program development, the authors point out that
the constant political flux of changing priorities has resulted in a patchwork of
programs that served "a few fairly well and others not at all" (p. 169). Instead,
they argue, a reinvigorated system of Aboriginal ECD programs and policies
must be developed and directed by Aboriginal communities in order to truly
meet the needs of all Aboriginal children and families in Canada.

In a humorous applied example of intergenerational connectedness and
knowledge sharing, Chapter 17 features a story by Richard Van Camp titled
"Grandma and Grandpa and the Mysterious Case of Wolf Teeth in the
House!" This amusing story, featuring the author's grandparents, a set of false
teeth, and a surprising twist ending, displays the playful humour characteriz-
ing so many Indigenous cultures.

Van Camp's story perfectly sets the stage for Chapter 18, "Knowing Who
You Are: Family History and Aboriginal Determinants of Health," wherein
Métis scholar Brenda Macdougall carefully and methodically charts the impor-
tance of stories and narrative genealogy—both of which were systematically

erased by colonial expansion, although both can be resurrected with care—to the health and well-being of Indigenous peoples. Beginning with a well-known story about the woman who married Beaver, Macdougall charts the lessons of stories and the lifeblood of narrative for Indigenous peoples, arguing that genealogical stories are material and ontological forces by which Indigenous peoples knew and know place, relationality, and each other as individuals and communities. Stories also explained Indigenous navigation of settlers, making sense of a new world and providing points of reference about identity and by which to live well. According to Macdougall, "It is important to know how a people conceive of themselves—who they are and where they come from—in order to understand how they fashion relationships with the world around them—which is, of course, fundamental to health and well-being" (p. 188).

The five chapters in Part 4, "Revisioning Medicine: Toward Indigenization," represent various engagements with medical paradigms, encouraging readers to rethink the medical system through Indigenous eyes. In Chapter 19, "*miyo-pimâtisiwin*: Practising 'the Good Way of Life' from the Hospital Bed to Mother Earth," mother and son Patricia and James Makokis share their stories of honouring and upholding their Indigenous values in a Western medical system. They describe their personal experiences as Cree individuals navigating Western medicine as a patient and a medical student, respectively, reflecting on the challenges and rewards of bringing their Indigenous knowledge, world views, and traditions to bear within the medical system.

In Chapter 20, "Reflections of One Indian Doctor in a Town up North," Nadine Caron relates stories of her experiences as one of still very few Indigenous medical doctors, highlighting both the rewards of acting as a role model for Indigenous youth and the challenges of standing alone as a "first" in her field. She raises the important unresolved question asked in various ways by others in similar roles: "as a First Nations person and a physician, the never-ending challenge is the question: In which world should one place one's feet? Western? Indigenous? Why do we have to choose? How often can we move between these worlds?" (p. 221).

Chapter 21, "Type 2 Diabetes in Indigenous Populations: Why a Focus on Genetic Susceptibility Is Not Enough," takes readers into the complex world of medical research and science, providing an accessible overview of the limitations of genetic studies in understanding fully the high rates of diabetes among Indigenous peoples. Authors Fernando Polanco and Laura Arbour advocate for a broader understanding of the determinants of Type 2 diabetes susceptibility in Indigenous populations, pointing out that the expression of genetic factors cannot be understood as separate or isolated from the environments in which individuals live.

The health determinants of Indigenous peoples living with HIV and AIDS, some of whom also experience gender in different ways, is the topic of Sherri Pooyak, Marni Amirault, and Renée Masching's Chapter 22, "Determining Life with HIV and AIDS." In this chapter, the authors reflect on the realities faced by Indigenous peoples affected by HIV and AIDS, highlighting their resilience, strength, knowledge, and humour. As the authors point out, however, the high and rising rates of HIV infection among Indigenous communities is rooted in the history of colonialism: "For the Aboriginal community as a whole, we have a framework to understand the roots of the HIV and AIDS epidemic within the broader context of the living legacy of colonization and how our collective healing journey is linked to the end of the epidemic" (p. 241). They end on a positive note, stating that "the end of AIDS will come when our circle is strong again. . . . In understanding the roots of disease, we also discover the roots of healing—as individuals, as families, as communities, nations, and as proud Aboriginal peoples" (p. 242).

Chapter 23, "Medicine Is Relationship: Relationship Is Medicine," by Leah May Walker and Danièle Behn-Smith, closes Part 4 and the book with a reflection on how medical professionals and educators are working to honour Indigenous health knowledge in the context of a Western medical system.

Together, the chapters in this collection urge a complex and unbounded understanding of what determines the well-being of Indigenous peoples in Canada and beyond. The authors are not satisfied with a biomedical or even a strictly "social" determinants framework; instead, they urge for theorizations that extend more broadly to include Indigenous ways of knowing and being. At the heart of what all authors are arguing here, either implicitly or explicitly, is that despite the acknowledged benefits of the recent turn to social determinants of health frameworks, these frameworks must respectfully be broadened in order to account for more and multiple and complex determinants of Indigenous peoples' health. This intervention must, very importantly, place the voices and experiences of Indigenous peoples front and centre.

The authors in this text have thus focused on the broad, complex, and varied determinants of Indigenous peoples' health in Canada, taking seriously the impressive contributions of SDoH theories and frameworks as means of understanding well-being and/or inequities, while pushing them forward and particularizing the concepts to the realities of Indigenous peoples (inclusive of a foregrounding of colonialism's role). Their work and words are timely, needed, and appropriate—they remind us to reconsider and redirect the burgeoning field of social determinants of health so that it becomes even more relevant to the lives of Indigenous peoples in this country. The authors individually and collectively remind us of where a social determinants of health framework comes from, and the importance of its role in theorizing and understanding health inequities, while also tapping impressively into both a changing world and a changing set of ideas of what determines the lives and health of Indigenous peoples in Canada and beyond.

NOTE

1. We are conscious of risks involved in oversimplifying either "non-Indigenous" or "Indigenous" ways of knowing and being: both groupings are extraordinarily heterogeneous, complex, varied, and dynamic. It is with this understanding that we are writing, although often for ease of discussion we do revert to referencing "Indigenous" or "non-Indigenous," sometimes even making reference to "Western" or to "traditional" ways of knowing and being.

REFERENCES

Adelson, N. (2005). The embodiment of inequality: Health disparities in Aboriginal Canada. *Canadian Journal of Public Health, 96*, S45–S61.

Anderson, L. M., Shinn, C., & St. Charles, J. (2002). Community interventions to promote healthy social environments: Early childhood and family housing—a report on recommendations of the Task Force on Community Prevention Services. *Morbidity and Mortality Weekly Report, 51*, 1–8.

Baum, F., & Harris, L. (2006). Equity and the social determinants of health. *Health Promotion Journal of Australia, 17*, 163–165.

Bourassa, C., McKay-McNabb, K., & Hampton, M. (2004). Racism, sexism and colonialism: The impact on the health of Aboriginal women in Canada. *Canadian Woman Studies, 24*, 23–29.

Carson, B., Dunbar, T., Chenhall, R., & Bailie, R. (Eds.). (2007). *Social determinants of Indigenous health*. Crows Nest, NSW: Allen & Unwin.

Commission on Social Determinants of Health. (2007). *Achieving health equity: From root causes to fair outcomes*. Geneva, Switzerland: World Health Organization.

Commission on Social Determinants of Health. (2008). *Closing the gap in a generation: Health equity through action on the social determinants of health: Commission on Social Determinants of Health final report*. Geneva, Switzerland: World Health Organization.

de Leeuw, S., Greenwood, M., & Cameron, E. (2010). Deviant constructions: How governments preserve colonial narratives of addictions and poor mental health to intervene into the lives of Indigenous children and families in Canada. *International Journal of Mental Health and Addiction, 8*, 282–295.

Edwards, P. (2007). The social determinants of health: An overview of the implications for policy and the role of the health sector. Ottawa, ON: Health Canada.

Kelly, M. P., et al. (2007). *The social determinants of health: Developing an evidence base for political action.* The World Health Organization and the Measurement and Evidence Knowledge Network. Retrieved from http://www.who.int/social_determinants/resources/mekn_final_report_102007.pdf

Larson, A., Gillies, M., Howard, P. J., & Coffin, J. (2007). It's enough to make you sick: The impacts of racism on the health of Aboriginal Australians. *Australian and New Zealand Journal of Public Health, 31*, 322–329.

Loppie Reading, C., & Wien, F. (2009). *Health inequalities and social determinants of Aboriginal peoples' health.* Prince George, BC: National Collaborating Centre for Aboriginal Peoples' Health.

Marmot, M. (2005). Social determinants of health inequalities. *Lancet, 365*, 1099–1104.

Mikkonen, J., & Raphael, D. (2010). *Social determinants of health: Canadian facts.* Toronto, ON: York University School of Health Policy and Management.

Public Health Agency of Canada. (2013). *What is the population health approach?* Ottawa, ON: PHAC. Retrieved from http://www.phac-aspc.gc.ca/ph-sp/approach-approche/appr-eng.php

Raphael, D. (2002). *Social justice is good for our hearts: Why societal factors—not lifestyles—are major causes of heart disease in Canada and elsewhere.* Toronto, ON: Centre for Social Justice Foundation for Research and Education.

Raphael, D. (Ed.). (2009). *Social determinants of health: Canadian perspectives* (2nd ed.). Toronto, ON: Canadian Scholars' Press Inc.

Raphael, D. (2012). *Tackling health inequalities: Lessons from international experiences.* Toronto, ON: Canadian Scholars' Press Inc.

Reading, J. (2009). *The crisis of chronic disease among Aboriginal peoples: A challenge for public health, population health, and social policy.* Victoria: Centre for Aboriginal Research.

Richmond, C. A., & Ross, N. A. (2009). The determinants of First Nation and Inuit health: A critical population health approach. *Health & Place, 15*, 403–411.

Smylie, J. (2009). The health of Aboriginal peoples. In D. Raphael (Ed.), *Social determinants of health: Canadian perspectives* (2nd ed.) (pp. 280–301). Toronto: Canadian Scholars' Press Inc.

Smylie, J., Williams, L., & Cooper, N. (2006). Culture-based literacy and Aboriginal health. *Canadian Journal of Public Health, 97*, S21–S25.

Wilkinson, R. (2006). *The impact of inequality: How to make sick societies healthier.* New York, NY: The New Press.

Wilkinson, R., & Marmot, M. (1998). *Social determinants of health: The solid facts.* Geneva, Switzerland: World Health Organization.

Wilkinson, R., & Marmot, M. (2003). *Social determinants of health: The solid facts* (2nd ed.). Geneva, Switzerland: World Health Organization.

Wilson, K., & Rosenberg, M. (2002). Exploring the determinants of health for First Nations peoples in Canada: Can existing frameworks accommodate traditional activities? *Social Science & Medicine, 55,* 2017–2031.

Wilson, K., & Young, K. (2008). An overview of Aboriginal health research in the social sciences: Current trends and future directions. *International Journal of Circumpolar Health, 67,* 179–189.

PART 1

SETTING THE CONTEXT

CHAPTER 1

Structural Determinants of Aboriginal Peoples' Health

Charlotte Reading

The *Oxford Dictionary* (n.d.) defines "structure" as "the arrangement of and relations between the parts or elements of something complex." In order to understand the challenging realities of Aboriginal health—specifically, the persistent disparities between the health of Aboriginal peoples and non-Aboriginal people in Canada—it is necessary to examine the interrelated features and relationships of the structural (historical, political, societal, and economic) determinants that shape Aboriginal health.

There is increasing consensus that the oppressive colonial structure within which Aboriginal peoples live produces social and material inequities that result in health disparities that persist over several generations (Waldram, Herring, & Young, 2006). Diminished life expectancy, disproportional burden of chronic disease and communicable illness, addictions, and social violence have all been linked to an overarching colonial structure (Butler-Jones, 2008).

This chapter explores this structure and how its "moving parts" influence the observable health burden experienced by Aboriginal peoples in Canada. I begin with an overview of structural determinants of health before moving to a discussion of how the historical structure of colonialism is connected to disproportionate rates of disease, disability, violence, and early death experienced by Aboriginal peoples. I also examine contemporary ideological and political structures in order to trace the pathways through which they exert control over the determinants of Aboriginal health. Although it is challenging to establish an empirical connection between the ideological, political, economic, and social structures of Canadian society and the health inequities experienced by Aboriginal peoples, this undertaking is essential in order to create lasting change in the health trajectories of Aboriginal children, youth, and future generations.

Structural Determinants of Health

Understanding the intricacies and interconnections between proximal, intermediate, and distal determinants of Aboriginal health (Loppie Reading & Wien, 2009) is a critical first step in appreciating how these determinants influence the socio-economic trajectories for children and youth that often predict their health status during adulthood. Within an Indigenous paradigm, the metaphor of a tree is perhaps most appropriate for exploring the social determinants of health. Similarly, and within the context of diverse cultures, the tree is a familiar part of the natural world. We typically think of trees as possessing three interconnected elements: the crown (leaves and branches), the trunk, and the roots. Each part of the tree is dependent not only upon the other parts for sustenance and support, but also upon the environment that nourishes and sometimes damages them.

Like the crown of a tree, proximal determinants influence health in the most obvious and direct ways. Within a determinants of health model, proximal determinants include early child development, income and social status, education and literacy, social support networks, employment, working conditions and occupational health, the physical environment, culture, and gender (Krieger, 2008). There is overwhelming evidence that disadvantage and inequity within this stratum (e.g., poverty, discrimination, lack of education, unemployment, poor working conditions, and inadequate or harmful physical environments) give rise to all manner of physical, emotional, mental, spiritual, and social challenges (Marmot, 2005).

Like the trunk or core of a tree, intermediate determinants facilitate or hinder health through systems that connect proximal and distal determinants. These determinants include health promotion and health care, education and justice, social supports, labour markets, as well as government and private enterprise (Loppie Reading & Wien, 2009). Within an Indigenous framework, intermediate determinants might also include kinship networks, relationship to the land, language, ceremonies, as well as ways of knowledge sharing (Loppie Reading & Wien, 2009). At this stratum, determinants have a less direct impact on the health of individuals, yet profoundly influence proximal determinants. For instance, we know the following: there are inadequate federal/provincial resources available to support healthy development for all Aboriginal children (Blackstock & Trocmé, 2005); lack of economic development opportunities leads to poverty in many Aboriginal communities (Backhouse, 1999); inaccessibility of health care services for many First Nations peoples living on-reserve leads to diminished screening, late diagnosis, and negative health outcomes (Cardinal, 2004), a problem that is compounded when many of the health care programs and services that are accessible to these communities fail to consider the cultural safety of Aboriginal peoples (Smye & Browne, 2002).

Although there is an undeniable need to explore the processes and health impacts of inequitable proximal and intermediate determinants, the focus of this chapter is on the distal or root (or structural) determinants of Aboriginal peoples' health. Like the roots of a tree, these deeply embedded determinants represent the historical, political, ideological, economical, and social foundations (which includes Indigenous world views, spirituality, and self-determination) from which all other determinants evolve. Just as maladies observed in the leaves are generally *not* the cause of unhealthy trees, inequities in human health frequently result from corruption or deficiencies in the unseen but critical root system.

In much the same way that all domains of health (physical, mental, emotional, and spiritual) are intimately interconnected, so too are the proximal, intermediate, and distal determinants of health. Similarly, within each of these strata of determinants, elements of influence combine to create synergies of advantage and/or disadvantage. In the sections that follow, I discuss the historical and contemporary structures that have formed the distal determinants of health for Aboriginal peoples.

HISTORICAL STRUCTURES

In order to fully appreciate the current health disparities facing Aboriginal peoples, we must first explore the historical roots upon which current structures have evolved. Over the past 400 years, Indigenous societies across North America have experienced similar patterns of colonial oppression. While the details of distinct historical colonial encounters may have differed, the impacts of colonization, conquest, and attempted or successful assimilation into the dominant society are nearly universal. Few Indigenous groups have been spared the dramatic alteration of economic, political, and social structures, nor the drastic changes in disease patterns and general health brought about by colonialism (Klein & Ackerman, 1995).

Given that engagement in subsistence activities represents a critical determinant of health (Marmot, 2005), it is clear that interrupted access to land, food, and water is intimately linked to the drastic post-colonial changes in health among Indigenous peoples in Canada and elsewhere. Prior to colonization, many Indigenous groups travelled regularly to access resources and maintain social networks. Through the Indian Act of 1876,[1] the imposition of a reserve system in Canada prevented seasonal migration of small family groups, who instead became confined to one location year-round (Kelm, 1998). In general, reserve lands were, and continue to be, insufficient to sustain food production through either agriculture or ranching.

Further, these relatively small tracts of land are frequently very remote and lack access to potable water (Waldram, Herring, & Young, 2006). Historically, water rights and services were developed to meet Euro-Canadian needs with little regard for the consequence to Aboriginal communities. As a result, when combined with widespread water contamination resulting from colonial development of surrounding lands, lack of access to clean water facilitated the spread of communicable illness on many reserves. Ironically, although decisions about resource allocation were primarily made by federal and provincial governments, high rates of illness in Aboriginal communities were perceived as the result of resistance to adopting "healthy" (i.e., Western) modes of living (Waldram et al., 1995).

The intrusion of European settlers and the conversion of traditional hunting territories to pasture land severely restricted Indigenous peoples' access to food and other resources. Encroachment and increasing mechanization frightened game away, while unscrupulous trappers stripped traditional lands of fur-bearing animals. Further, many forms of Indigenous hunting and fishing were banned in the interests of expanding capitalist ventures (Waldram et al., 1995). In fact, most government regulations appear to have been designed to support industry at the expense of Indigenous self-sufficiency. The demise of the fur trade and ever-increasing restrictions to reserve land compelled many Indigenous peoples to engage in wage labour. However, racially discriminatory hiring and wage practices meant that they operated on the margins of Euro-Canadian society, often resulting in widespread poverty (Kelm, 1998; Lemchuk-Favel, 1995; Waldram et al., 1995).

Prior to and during the processes described above, European diseases devastated Indigenous populations. According to Kunitz, "[c]ontact induced diseases were as much a prelude as an aftermath of European domination" (1994, p. 8). Indigenous peoples had never been exposed to European diseases such as smallpox, measles, whooping cough, tuberculosis, diphtheria, typhus, yellow fever, influenza, and dysentery, leaving them defenseless through either immunological or medical means. Epidemics decimated entire populations, spreading through trade routes or in advance of the colonizers, often carried by people fleeing before them (Oakes et al., 2000; Kunitz, 1994).

Early Western medical aid to Indigenous peoples was immersed in an agenda that sought to justify and sustain Canada's colonial activities (Kelm, 1998). The Indian Act directed the minister of Indian Affairs to enforce regulations regarding the suppression of communicable disease, reserve sanitation, as well as the provision of medical treatment and health services. However, the Act was more permissive than directive with respect to obliging Indian agents to appoint doctors or the federal government to assume financial responsibility for health services. In fact, the federal government refused to accept legal obligation to provide health care to First Nations peoples, despite the widespread, albeit capricious and substandard, practice of providing on-reserve care by government doctors (Waldram et al., 1995).

Western medicine played a key role in the colonization of Indigenous peoples by virtue of the rationale given for its involvement in their lives and its intrusion into their bodies (Kelm, 1998). For the most part, early Indigenous health policy was based on notions of "white" racial superiority, assimilation goals, and an irrational fear of "interracial" contagion. Disease prevention initiatives sought only to minimize the colonial burden of sick Indigenous peoples and to contain disease, thereby protecting Euro-Canadians (Kelm, 1998).

Medicine was instrumental in not only shaping ideas about Indigenous peoples and their communities but in perpetuating a medical discourse that described them as inherently pathological, making the provision of health care a colonial obligation. The prevailing belief that health could only be guaranteed through assimilation meant that Indigenous bodies became sites of colonization by missionary doctors (Kelm, 1998). Medicine was seen as "one of the most effective agencies in spreading the glorious Gospel of the Blessed God" (Thomas Crosby, nineteenth-century Methodist missionary) (cited in Waldram et al., 1995, p. 104). Moralizing and humanitarianism became the framework upon which the colonial project was fashioned and missionaries were granted the right to rule through good deeds, with medicine symbolizing humanitarian domination (Kelm, 1998).

The colonial partnership between religion and government was formalized in 1867, when churches were given control over education and residential schools became the primary instrument of assimilation. The racist ideology that rationalized these schools also promoted the notion that Indigenous peoples required physical as well as spiritual healing. Colonial education was designed to facilitate and support economic and social transformation as well as to eradicate Indigenous family and kinship structures (Kelm, 1998; Miller & Churchryk, 1996). Children were forcibly removed from their home communities for extended periods of time, thereby disrupting social networks and cultural learning. Attempts were made to indoctrinate them into a system that stripped them of their Indigenous identity and transformed them into second-class Canadian citizens and low-wage labourers (Kelm, 1998).

With few exceptions, residential schools were underfunded and understaffed, which meant that children were often poorly fed, ill-clothed, and overworked. Tuberculosis (TB) was rampant in many schools, its spread often facilitated by overcrowding. Children frequently returned to their home communities infected with TB, spreading the disease to others. In 1907, the Department of Indian Affairs (DIA) reported that in the previous 15 years, between 25 and 35 percent of students in residential schools had died, mostly from TB (Waldram et al., 1995). In the early 1900s, then DIA Deputy Minister Duncan Scott admitted that 50 percent of Indian students never lived to "benefit" from the education they received. While many parents objected to the absence of their children from home (sometimes for as long as 10 months a year) and the harsh conditions children were subjected to in residential schools, they risked imprisonment if they attempted to withhold their children from school (Assembly of First Nations, 1994; Kelm, 1998).

Within the walls of residential schools, Indigenous languages, customs, and dress were forbidden and children often paid a terrible price in the form of harsh physical punishment for small or unwitting infractions. The legacy of sexual abuse still impacts many Aboriginal men and women who were forced to attend residential school as children. This federal effort to re-educate, convert, and assimilate Aboriginal children caused unimaginable physical, emotional, mental, spiritual, and sexual harm to thousands of Aboriginal peoples, spanning 100 years (Assembly of First Nations, 1994). Perhaps the greatest loss was to entire Indigenous cultures, languages, stories, and spiritualities— some are lost forever, but many are in the process of being restored (Kelm, 1998; Knockwood, 1992). Unfortunately, the practice of apprehending Aboriginal children and placing them within non-Aboriginal living and learning environments did not end with the closing of the last residential school. Rather, the practice continued with the "sixties scoop" (Johnston, 1983) and the current overrepresentation of Aboriginal children who are apprehended and placed in the child welfare system, in which no distinction is made between neglect due to parental poverty and neglect resulting from parental disregard (Trocmé, Knoke, & Blackstock, 2004).

CONTEMPORARY STRUCTURES

Ideally, the structures (social, political, economic) of any given society facilitate cohesion among its members, as well as create systems through which all people can access resources and derive benefit from opportunities. Instead, Canadian society has, by and large, engaged in systemic discrimination *against* Aboriginal peoples, manifested as inequitable structural determinants that detrimentally impact the health and well-being of individuals, families, communities, and nation-states.

Contemporary relations between Aboriginal peoples and the Canadian state are founded on a racialized ideology, which continues to support the tenets of colonialism. The historical records of early explorers and clergy generally describe the Indigenous peoples of North American as, first and foremost, not white (Red Men), often preceded by adjectives such as "primitive" or "savage" and thus intellectually, morally, and socially inferior to white Europeans. The generosity and tolerance of early Indigenous peoples toward Europeans was reconstructed through the colonial gaze into racialized stereotypes of apathy and submissiveness, thus providing a rationale for discriminatory policies, appropriation of lands, generalized violence, and the exploitation of Indigenous women. These groundless stereotypes also provided the ideological foundation upon which the Indian Act was written into Canadian law.

The Indian Act includes several sections that define the identity of Indigenous peoples; the lands upon which they can live, fish, hunt, and harvest food; governance over community decision making; services and resources available to community members; and the political relationship they have with the Canadian state. The health-related, systems-level determinants resulting from this policy document are far-reaching and influence almost every aspect of First Nation peoples' lives. Ironically, the exclusion of Métis and Inuit peoples from the colonial identity of "Indian" created a separate but similarly pernicious trajectory of health for these groups (Royal Commission on Aboriginal Peoples, 1996).

Within the context of social justice, systematic discrimination from resources and opportunities may well be interpreted as a form of structural violence. Examples can be found in the exclusion of Aboriginal peoples from social goods such as inadequate housing on First Nation reserves, insufficient funding for Aboriginal programs and services, in addition to improper infrastructure in Aboriginal communities and health systems that fail to provide prompt and adequate care (Reading & Halseth, 2013). The exclusion of Aboriginal peoples from social reproduction[2] is manifest in an historical record that neglects to accurately or fully report the colonial challenges they continue to face, failure to acknowledge the important cultural contributions made by Aboriginal peoples, and denial of opportunities for them to actively participate in Canadian society (Galabuzi, 2004). Economic exclusion is likewise revealed when Aboriginal peoples are denied equitable educational and employment opportunities, particularly in remote communities, where economic development is crucial to community health (Human Resources and Social Development Corporation, 1999; Standing Committee on Aboriginal Affairs and Northern Development, 2007).

Research dating back to the Whitehall study of 1966 clearly links health status to a socio-economic gradient across populations (van Rossum, van de Mheen, Grobbee, & Marmot, 2000). Moreover, this type of disadvantage has cumulative effects, not only over the life of an individual, but also across generations (Reading, 2009). Socio-economic stratification creates a gradient of disparities in health-promoting conditions, which contribute to health damage among those who are relegated to increasingly disadvantageous living conditions (Diderichsen, Evans, & Whitehead, 2001). The 1996 *Report of the Royal Commission on Aboriginal Peoples* concluded that "Aboriginal people are at the bottom of almost every available index of socioeconomic well being, whether [we] are measuring educational levels, employment opportunities, housing conditions, per capita incomes or any of the other conditions that give non-Aboriginal Canadians one of the highest standards of living in the world" (n.p.).

In describing the influence of structural determinants on health, Gehlert, Sohmer, Sacks, Mininger, McClintock, and Olopade (2008) employ a descending causal model that describes structural determinants as "upstream" forces, creating conditions that flow *down* to affect population health. Within the tree metaphor, however, resources from the surrounding environment are taken up by the roots (distal determinants) and travel up through the systems of the trunk (intermediate determinants) and into the crown (proximal determinants). Two excellent examples of the "trickle-up" effect of structural determinants on Aboriginal health can be found in diabetes and HIV.

Few Canadians are unaware of the widespread crisis of diabetes among Aboriginal peoples, with rates between three and five times those of non-Aboriginal Canadians (Oster et al., 2011). If we hope to appropriately address diabetes, we must first understand what determinants are influencing the development and persistence of this debilitating and life-threatening illness. Yet, if we limit our analysis to its proximal determinants, as is often the case, we will continue to focus our attention on obesity, poor diet, and sedentary lifestyle. If, however, we explore further, we will likely encounter additional determinants such as economic (lack of resources to afford healthy food) and/or geographic (remote locations with expensive shipping costs) barriers to accessing healthy market or country foods, as well as physical environments that do not always support health-promoting exercise (crowded housing, lack of sidewalks or walking trails, cold weather, lack of accessible recreational infrastructure or programs) (Butler-Jones, 2008). If we search deeper still for the determinants responsible for shaping these conditions, we discover the root of the problem—a colonial structure—fashioned from the centralization of Aboriginal peoples into remote communities and reserves, the oppressive nature of the Indian Act, the damaging legacy of residential schools, racial discrimination in social environments and the labour market, as well as lack of public or private investment in economic development for Aboriginal communities (Royal Commission on Aboriginal Peoples, 1996).

HIV provides another example of how structural determinants are linked to current health issues facing Aboriginal peoples. Although Aboriginal peoples represent just over 4 percent of the Canadian population, in 2008 they accounted for 12.5 percent of all new HIV infections and 8 percent of its prevalence in Canada, with women representing half of all Aboriginal peoples infected (Public Health Agency of Canada, 2010). We also know that the majority of Aboriginal peoples become infected with HIV through injection drug use. In addressing this epidemic, most health promotion programs look for ways to reduce drug use or the harms associated with it. In attempting to understand HIV among Aboriginal peoples, several researchers have explored the experiences of people who contracted HIV through injecting drugs. Most of them report a personal history of violence and abuse, which is often intergenerational in nature and frequently began in foster care and/or resulted from the residential school experiences of their parents and/or grandparents. Once again, structural determinants are revealed as the foundation upon which successive trauma, sometimes over generations, leads to coping through drug use and the current epidemic of HIV among Aboriginal peoples.

Conclusion

Research exploring the relationship between stress and health has clearly demonstrated that individuals experience increased stress when they are exposed to systemic disadvantage, when they face barriers to control over their lives, and when they encounter dehumanizing treatment (Clark, Anderson, Clark, & Williams, 1999). Beyond the acute stress brought about by overt personal discrimination, chronic stress, in this case linked to systemic oppression, has been shown to diminish immunity and resiliency to disease (Avitsur, Powell, Padgett, & Sheridan, 2009). Likewise, social problems such as interpersonal violence and substance misuse represent reactions to and a means of coping with unrelenting stress (Walters, Simoni, & Evans-Campbell, 2002). Perhaps most importantly, physical, emotional, mental, and spiritual harm caused by cumulative stress can decrease an individual's capacity to address health problems by diminishing one's sense of agency (Roddenberry & Renk, 2010).

Disparities in Aboriginal health cannot be understood in isolation of structural determinants such as historical and contemporary political contexts, social structures, and resource distribution. Despite a plethora of evidence supporting a structural approach to redressing inequities in Aboriginal peoples' health, policy-makers continue to focus on proximal determinants. This is clearly irrational and counterproductive. Instead, policy should be aimed at (1) ensuring that no Aboriginal child is denied the basic resources for healthy development; (2) creating fair employment opportunities and work environments for Aboriginal peoples; (3) supporting Aboriginal peoples to maximize their capacities and self-determination; (4) facilitating the development of healthy and sustainable Aboriginal communities; (5) decreasing exposure of Aboriginal communities to industrial toxins and development pollutants; (6) ensuring that policy decisions are based on balancing social stratification; and (7) preventing the consequences of differential exposure to harmful environments.

If we neglect to consider the most profoundly influential determinants of Aboriginal health, we are not only ignoring what is now a critical mass of evidence (Commission on Social Determinants of Health, 2008), but we are complicit in the perpetuation of structural inequities that will impact the health and well-being of future generations of Aboriginal peoples. In a country that distinguishes itself on principles of equity and social justice, this lack of attention to the root determinants of Aboriginal health is conspicuous and suspect.

NOTES

1. Enacted by the Parliament of Canada in 1876, the Indian Act grants the federal government authority over First Nation lands, First Nation governance, and First Nation identity (Constitution Acts, 1867).

2. Processes that sustain the characteristics of a given social structure or tradition over time (Darvill, 2008).

REFERENCES

Adelson, N. (2005). The embodiment of inequality: Health disparities in Aboriginal Canada. *Canadian Journal of Public Health, 96*: S45–S61.

Assembly of First Nations. (1994). *Breaking the silence: An interpretive study of residential school impact and healing as illustrated by stories of First Nations individuals.* Ottawa, ON: Native Tribal Health Consortium—Cancer Program.

Avitsur, R., Powell, N., Padgett, D., & Sheridan, J. (2009). Social interactions, stress, and immunity. *Immunology Allergy Clinics of North America, 29*, 285–293.

Backhouse, C. (1999). *Colour-coded: A legal history of racism in Canada, 1900–1950.* Toronto, ON: The Osgoode Society.

Blackstock, C., & Trocmé, N. (2005). Community-based child welfare for Aboriginal children: Supporting resilience through structural change. *Social Policy Journal of New Zealand, 24*, 1–22.

Butler-Jones, D. (2008). *The Chief Public Health Officer's report on the state of addressing health inequalities.* Ottawa, ON: Public Health in Canada.

Cardinal, J. (2004). *First Nations in Alberta: A focus on health service use.* Edmonton, AB: Alberta Health & Wellness.

Clark, R., Anderson, N., Clark, V., & Williams, D. (1999). Racism as a stressor for African Americans: A biopsychosocial model. *American Psychologist, 54*, 805–816.

Commission on Social Determinants of Health. (2008). *Closing the gap in a generation: Health equity through action on the social determinants of health. Final Report of the Commission on Social Determinants of Health.* Geneva, Switzerland: World Health Organization.

Constitution Acts. (1867). *The Indian Act.* Retrieved from Laws.justice.gc.ca

Darvill, T. (2008). *Oxford concise dictionary of archaeology.* Second edition. Oxford: Oxford University Press.

Diderichsen, F., Evans, T., & Whitehead, M. (2001). The social basis of disparities in health. In T. Evans, M. Whitehead, F. Diderichsen, A. Bhuiya, & M. Wirth (Eds.), *Challenging inequities in health: From ethics to action* (pp. 12–23). New York, NY: Oxford University Press.

Dussault, R., & Erasmus, G. (1994). *The high arctic relocation: A report on the 1953–55 relocation.* Ottawa, ON: Canadian Government Publishing.

Galabuzi, G. (2004). Social exclusion. In D. Raphael (Ed.), *Social determinants of health: Canadian perspectives* (pp. 235–252). Toronto, ON: Canadian Scholars' Press Inc.

Gehlert, S., Sohmer, D., Sacks, T., Mininger, C., McClintock, M., & Olopade, O. (2008). Targeting health disparities: A model linking upstream determinants to downstream interventions. *Health Affairs, 27*, 339–349.

Human Resources and Social Development Corporation. (1999). *Aboriginal social and economic development: Lessons learned summary report.* Retrieved from http://www.hrsdc.gc.ca/eng/cs/sp/hrsdc/edd/reports/1999-000376/page05.shtml

Johnston, P. (1983). *Native children and the child welfare system.* Ottawa, ON: Canadian Council on Social Development.

Kelm, M. (1998). *Colonizing bodies: Aboriginal health and health in British Columbia.* Vancouver, BC: UBC Press.

Klein, L., & Ackerman, L. (1995). *Women and power in Native North America.* London: University of Oklahoma Press.

Knockwood, I. (1992). *Out of the depths: The experiences of Mi'kmaw children at the Indian residential school at Shubenacadie, Nova Scotia.* Halifax, NS: Roseway Publishing.

Krieger, K. (2008). Proximal, distal, and the politics of causation: What's level got to do with it? *American Journal of Public Health, 98,* 221–230.

Kunitz, S. (1994). *Disease and social diversity: The European impact on the health of non-Europeans.* New York, NY: Oxford University Press.

Lemchuk-Favel, L. (1995). *Rights of First Nations, issues, and impact of the planned changes to federal funding: A discussion paper for the First Nations Health Commission.* Ottawa, ON: First Nations Health Services.

Loppie Reading, C., & Wien, F. (2009). *Health inequalities and social determinants of Aboriginal peoples' health.* Prince George, BC: National Collaborating Centre for Aboriginal Health.

Marmot, M. (2005). Social determinants of health inequalities. *Lancet, 365,* 1099–1104.

Miller, C., & Churchryk, P. (1996). *Women of the First Nations: Power, wisdom, and strength.* Winnipeg, MB: University of Manitoba Press.

Oakes, J., Riewe, R., Koolage, S., Simpson, L., & Schuster, N. (2000). *Aboriginal health, identity, and resources.* Winnipeg, MB: Departments of Native Studies and Zoology and Faculty of Graduate Studies, University of Manitoba.

O'Hara, P. (1998). *Action on the ground: Models of practice in rural development.* Galway, Ireland: Irish Rural Link.

Oster, R., Johnson, J., Hemmelgarn, B., King, M., Balko, S., Svenson, L., Crowshoe, L., & Toth, E. (2011). Recent epidemiologic trends of diabetes mellitus among status Aboriginal adults. *Canadian Medical Association Journal, 183,* 803–808.

Oxford Dictionary. (n.d.). *Structure.* Retrieved from http://oxforddictionaries.com/definition/english/structure

Public Health Agency of Canada. (2010). *HIV/AIDS epi updates—July 2010.* Retrieved from http://www.phac-aspc.gc.ca/aids-sida/publication/epi/2010/8-eng.php

Reading, J. (2009). *A life course approach to the social determinants of health for Aboriginal peoples.* Ottawa, ON: The Senate Sub-Committee on Population Health.

Reading, J., & Halseth, R. (2013). *Pathways to improving well-being for Indigenous peoples: How living conditions decide health.* Prince George, BC: National Collaborating Centre for Aboriginal Health.

Roddenberry, A., & Renk, K. (2010). Locus of control and self-efficacy: Potential mediators of stress, illness, and utilization of health services in college students. *Child Psychiatry & Human Development, 41,* 353–370.

Royal Commission on Aboriginal Peoples. (1996). *Report of the Royal Commission on Aboriginal Peoples.* Ottawa, ON: Supply and Services Canada.

Smye, V., & Browne, A. (2002). "Cultural safety" and the analysis of health policy affecting Aboriginal people. *Nurse Research, 9,* 42–56.

Standing Committee on Aboriginal Affairs and Northern Development. (2007). *No higher priority: Aboriginal post-secondary education in Canada* (p. 4). Ottawa, ON: 39th Parliament, 1st Session.

Trocmé, N., Knoke, D., & Blackstock, C. (2004). Pathways to the overrepresentation of Aboriginal children in Canada's child welfare system. *Social Service Review, 78,* 577–600.

van Rossum, C., van de Mheen, H., Grobbee, D., & Marmot, M. (2000). Employment grade differences in cause specific mortality: A 25-year follow-up of civil servants from the first Whitehall study. *Journal of Epidemiology & Community Health, 54,* 178–184.

Waldram, J., Herring, A., & Young, T. (1995). *Aboriginal health in Canada: History, culture, and epidemiological perspectives.* Toronto, ON: University of Toronto Press.

Waldram, J., Herring, D., & Young, K. (2006). *Aboriginal health in Canada: Historical, cultural, and epidemiological perspectives* (2nd ed.). Toronto, ON: University of Toronto Press.

Walters, K., Simoni, J., & Evans-Campbell, T. (2002). Substance use among American Indians and Alaska Natives: Incorporating culture in an "Indigenist" stress-coping paradigm. *Public Health Reports, 117,* S104–S117.

CHAPTER 2

Two-Eyed Seeing in Medicine

Murdena Marshall, Albert Marshall, and Cheryl Bartlett

We (Murdena and Albert) are two old Mi'kmaw people from our Traditional Territory of Mi'kma'ki on the east coast of Turtle Island. These are our thoughts. We offer them to you. Sometimes Murdena has the best way of saying things. Other times, Albert does. So, in the written text below, we try to make it clear who is saying what words. Also, we've asked our old friend and colleague Cheryl (who is of newcomer lineage and grew up in southern Alberta, within the Traditional Territory of the Siksika of the Blackfoot Confederacy) to help write our thoughts and weave them together. We three have worked and walked and talked and laughed together in Unama'ki (Cape Breton, Nova Scotia) for over 20 years. We hope to continue to do the same for many more years.

As Elders (Cheryl wrote that last word and you can tell because we would just continue saying "two old Mi'kmaw"), we know all too well that First Nations across Canada are constantly and painfully being reminded that our health depends on us. We also know that our pathways to better health lie within our own cultures. We have these understandings forever embedded within us, but because of the history of domineering and dismissive attitudes of European culture toward our First Nations' cultures, toward our Indigenous methods, and toward our Traditional Knowledges, we have been unable to utilize them.

MURDENA: TRADITIONAL KNOWLEDGE AND TWO-EYED SEEING

Our Traditional Knowledge teaches us that there are four components involved in human wholeness: spiritual, emotional, physical, and intellectual.

But it is more than that. We must realize that when these four components are not in harmony, we are in jeopardy of having poor health. We need to understand this in a deep way. That's why Albert repeatedly says, "When you force people to abandon their ways of knowing, their ways of seeing the world, you literally destroy their spirit and once that spirit is destroyed, it is very, very difficult to embrace anything—academically or through sports or through arts or through anything—because that person is never complete. But to create a complete picture of a person, their spirit, their physical being, their emotions, and their intellectual being. . .all have to be intact and work in a very harmonious way."

As Elders, we also know that today First Nations peoples all have to be able to walk in two worlds: that of their Native community and that of the newcomers, of the white people, whose ways are the ways of mainstream society. We cannot overemphasize how important this ability is for the recovery and health of our communities and our community members, and especially for the nurturance of our children and youth in grade schools and for the "wholistic" (Murdena says, "Spell that last word with a *w* to remind us of "whole," not "hole") health and professional capabilities of our older students studying in mainstream institutions of higher learning such as, for example, the professional schools of health sciences. This is why Albert coined the phrase "Two-Eyed Seeing" as a guiding principle for walking in two worlds.

Two-Eyed Seeing can help us understand how our traditional teachings, our Traditional Knowledges, can work together with the knowledge of the newcomers for a better and more healthy world. Two-Eyed Seeing grew from the teachings of the late Mi'kmaw spiritual leader, Healer, and chief, Charles Labrador of Acadia First Nation, Nova Scotia, especially with these words: "Go into a forest, you see the birch, maple, pine. Look underground and all those trees are holding hands. We as people must do the same." Two-Eyed Seeing is, therefore, the gift of multiple perspective treasured by many Aboriginal peoples. The phrase was coined when Albert felt that audiences hearing Chief Labrador's words could benefit from additional encouragement toward the "it's us" consciousness of the "trees holding hands." For today's times, Two-Eyed Seeing is a guiding principle for bringing together different world views, different paradigms.

ALBERT: LEARNING TO SEE FROM TWO EYES

Two-Eyed Seeing refers to learning to see from one eye with the strengths of (or best in) Indigenous knowledges and ways of knowing, and learning to see from the other eye with the strengths of (or best in) Western knowledges and ways of knowing. . .and, most importantly, using both of these eyes together for the benefit of all. Two-Eyed Seeing adamantly, respectfully, and passionately asks that we bring together our different ways of knowing to motivate people, Aboriginal and non-Aboriginal alike, to use all our understandings so we can leave the world a better place and not compromise the opportunities for our youth (in the sense of Seven Generations) through our own inaction.

Two-Eyed Seeing is hard to convey to academics as it does not fit into any particular subject area or discipline. Rather, it is about life: what you do, what kind of responsibilities you have, how you should live while on Earth. It is a guiding principle that covers all aspects of our lives: social, economic, environmental, etc. The advantage of Two-Eyed Seeing is that you are always fine-tuning your mind into different places at once, you are always looking for another perspective and better way of doing things.

We need to utilize Two-Eyed Seeing to determine the benefits both in the modern medical science knowledges and in our Indigenous knowledges. It can help teach Aboriginal students in medical school and other health sciences about the validity of our Indigenous sciences within Traditional Knowledges. In fall 2010, we heard the profound despair in the voices of young Aboriginal medical students deprived of any such opportunity within current medical school curricula. We heard the spiritual anguish in their quiet sobs as they asked the assembled group of Traditional Healers and Elders to consider working with the medical school personnel and administrators to find ways to enable inclusion of Traditional Knowledges within the curricula. As Elders, we also know that we must allow other (non-Aboriginal) medical school and health science students to learn and to see the validity in our Indigenous sciences. We must act on our belief that Indigenous ways of knowing concerning health and well-being are vital and can help all people to live better. Two-Eyed Seeing encourages that we draw upon both new technologies and traditional practices to lead to better health outcomes for everyone. In including our Indigenous knowledges, we would also be providing the opportunity for students to learn about alternative medicines and to document their effectiveness.

In appropriate circumstances, while working within a Two-Eyed Seeing approach, we could also choose to use words that resonate more closely with traditional ways of knowing. For example, rather than talking about "positive psychosocial outcomes" for child development, we could talk about how storytelling can nurture a child's spirit of interconnectivity. . .one that is well prepared for lifelong learning, seeks to be in harmony with all of his or her relations, and works toward balance within his or her experiences over the entire life journey. We need also to use our Aboriginal stories to pinpoint possible solutions and to study the plant world, to relearn to use the proper herbs, plants, and trees for our good health and well-being.

Moreover, as Elders we maintain that when we as First Nations peoples recover from cultural starvation, we can again become conduits of Traditional Knowledges for our children. We can start this recovery by using our language and spirituality; in our Traditional Territory of Mi'kma'ki this means we must use our Mi'kmaw language and our Mi'kmaw spirituality. We need to recapture our stolen spirits, revitalize our broken methods, and map anew our journey toward healthy communities. Standards introduced by another culture push out our own knowledge, our own language, our own spirituality . . . and weaken the will. If we have learned anything from Two-Eyed Seeing, it is to appreciate the wisdom in our Traditional Mi'kmaw Knowledge—to remember it, to honour it, to cherish it, and to claim it.

Where do understandings that nourish our traditional teachings, our Traditional Knowledges, come from? Mother Earth provides for us, shelters us, feeds us, nourishes us. So, we then must look to her good example for guidance. Our actions toward her must be actions of gratitude. We, too, must be humble, and provide for other living things. We must provide shelter for the vulnerable, medicine for the sick, and nourishment for the hungry. We must always look to Mother Nature to inform us how to live. We do not inform her. For example, as we watch the birds consume food and then regurgitate it into the mouths of young, we also chew our food so that babies can accept it and then place it in their mouths. As we watch the animals of the forest construct their homes out of the materials nature provides, so do we honour them by imitating their examples. As we see the species of the fish swimming along the warmer shoreline in the early spring so they may grow and develop, so we forbid our children to swim in the waters until after this vulnerable time for the fish has passed, so that they will respect these fish, which will later give their lives for them. Our seasons are adjusted to the cycles of the Earth and her species, so that our children may always be reminded of the integrity and beauty of creation, and of our dependence upon her. We watch . . . and in so doing we learn.

MURDENA: LANGUAGE, TEACHING, AND RELATIONSHIP

Our traditional teachings were and remain very subtle. No one ever sits you down and says, "Do this." For example, when children say, "Where is the baking powder?" there is no lesson that teaches "Over there." And no mother puts her child down and says, "Look at me while I go for the baking powder." The children learn themselves by watching, and when they get a bit older— three or four years old—they start doing it. And so you see them, when they are playing house, they start using their mouths, they start pinch-puckering their lips to point out directions or instructions, just as they've seen the adults doing. Children watch . . . and in so doing they learn.

The role of language within our social structure and our world view must also be emphasized and it must be understood that they are intimately connected—the language provides the "hard wiring" for understanding relationships within the family, the community, and the culture. For example, let's consider parenting: our Mi'kmaw language allowed us to teach respect and since we come from a collective thought, a child knew that he or she could not get away with anything. Every adult in the community had the right to forbid wrongdoing by children when the parents were absent. Then along came standards from outside (e.g., Children's Aid) and convinced us that discipline and punishment were solely a parental right—that only biological parents could administer any form of child rearing. As a result, our right to parenting was distorted. So now we find ourselves being monitored by organizations to prove that we are parents, but that process then excludes all other interested parties who may be of some assistance as we try to recover from cultural disarray. We need to recover from cultural starvation for healthy parenting to return. We need our language and spirituality to recover. We need to recapture our spirits and our methods on our journey toward healthy parenting. We need to develop our own priorities and utilize those that work best. We need to reintroduce our traditional teachings in parenting. They may seem ancient and out of touch to some, but it instills pride in our children.

As further illustration of strengths in traditional ways, we offer the example of how our Mi'kmaw world view and its traditional social structure nurture a healthy spirit of connectivity and interconnectiveness. The clan system within our Mi'kmaw Nation has existed since time immemorial. Clans are named after animals that lived year-round within our Traditional Territory of Mi'kma'ki. Thus, a person might belong to the Bear Clan, another to the Moose Clan, a third to the Muskrat Clan, someone else to the Lobster Clan, and another to the Squirrel Clan (these are just a few examples). The clan line is passed down via the mother, so a child is a member of the same clan as her or his mother. Each clan has a matriarch whose role is as overall Grandmother to those in her clan. Some clans have annual gatherings to weave the circles of interconnectiveness even more richly; it is a time to celebrate belonging to a clan, learning culture, and feeling collective identity, and also a time to reconfirm interconnectiveness with the natural world. Moreover, the clan helps reinforce a person's connections to members of his or her family, no matter where he or she is living or how distant the connection. Clan members are family in a dynamic circle that continues to grow. This expanding sense of wholeness and interconnectivity provides understandings about kin and all of one's relations.

Our relations extend to all on our Earth Mother. In our stories, in our language, it is okay to talk to birds. It is okay to talk to trees. So, you see, it is okay to talk to all beings in our language and sometimes the trees and birds or others even answer you. If you are downhearted or depressed, go into the forest and listen to the trees. You will hear them whisper, hear the sap running. Just try to interrupt the gentle breezes blowing through the boughs! You can actually make yourself feel better through meditation and intensify your traditional beliefs. We believe our Mother Earth is a living example of wise principles, a life-giving Mother, and a healing bounty. This is the consciousness of our Elders.

Like me, you may love and admire a tree, or you may feel sorry for it because it has to give up its life for my accommodations, for keeping me warm, or giving me a roof. I feel sorry because someone's life has to end for my benefit. It serves me and never complains. It is not unusual for a First Nations person to go out into the park or the yard and talk to trees. It is absolutely normal, but only on Indian reserves. If I do it out in the town of Truro, Nova Scotia, or if I do it in Halifax, or if I do it anywhere that is a non-Native community, I will be arrested for being nuts. I am here to thank the trees. But when you walk down the street and you start talking to trees and ducks, and you get these queer looks: "She is talking to animals. They do not answer her back." It will not take long for them to declare that you are not normal at all, that there is something wrong with you. And thus, we need to remember the wholesome, healthy consciousness in the teachings from our Elders.

Traditionally, teachings such as the above would begin very early in one's life and would have been conveyed in the form of story. This is also imperative today because children need to know their ancestral teachings before *jumping without a parachute into another culture*. Stories are the main vehicle of instruction and guidance and thus a vital tool at all stages of life development, but especially during the early years of childhood and adolescence where such guidance affects life choices. Stories are everywhere, they are all the time. As a child, if someone else is there with you, they would be telling a story. Stories are not merely narratives to fill time or lull a child to sleep; they are vehicles of cultural transmission that allow spiritual knowledge transfer . . . along with the emotional (feelings conveyed by the story's narrative), physical (sound vibrations), and intellectual (a traditional teaching).

CONCLUSION

Traditionally, nothing was taught as black and white. Rather, everything was story . . . where you have the responsibility to listen and reflect. This is a much more profound way of learning because you have the opportunity for relationship with the knowledge. And, furthermore, because you can return again and again to the story or you can hear it over and over, and each time you will find new and richer understandings relevant to your own personal journey, to your growing sense of wholeness and interconnectiveness. And thus Two-Eyed Seeing is needed to help us understand how Traditional Knowledges from an ancient culture can work for a better and healthier world.

Traditional Knowledges were never meant to stay static and stay in the past. Rather, we must bring them into the present so that everything becomes meaningful in our lives and in our communities. As humans, we have responsibilities—yes, to ourselves, but also to all the other species. They have rights. We humans have responsibilities.

We offer our thanks to all who have helped, and also to our Earth Mother and all our relations. *Msit No'kmaq.*

These are our words.

RECOMMENDED RESOURCES AND READINGS

Bartlett, C. M., Marshall, M., & Kavanagh, S. (2004). How Rabbit got his long ears. *HorizonZero Issue 17(2): TELL: Aboriginal Story in Digital Media.* Banff New Media Institute and the Culture.ca gateway. Retrieved from http://www.horizonzero.ca

Bartlett, C., Marshall, M., & Marshall, A. (2012a). Two-Eyed Seeing and other lessons learned within a co-learning journey of bringing together Indigenous and mainstream knowledges and ways of knowing. *Journal of Environmental Studies and Sciences, 2,* 331–340.

Bartlett, C., Marshall, M., & Marshall, A. (2012b, March). *Moving forward with Elders' recommendations from APCFNC Elders Research Project "Honouring Traditional Knowledge"—considerations from Two-Eyed Seeing and co-learning for "Honouring Traditional Knowledge in Academia."* Presentation for AAEDIRP's (Atlantic Aboriginal Economic Development Integrated Research Program's) university partners and others; organized by AAEDIRP and APCFNC (Atlantic Policy Congress of

First Nations Chiefs) Secretariat, Cole Harbour, NS. [PowerPoint slides]. Retrieved from http://www.integrativescience.ca/uploads/articles/2012-AAEDIRP-Bartlett -Marshall-Aboriginal-Elders-Recommendations-Two-Eyed-Seeing.pdf

Harris, P., Bartlett, C., Marshall, M., & Marshall, A. (2010, October). Mi'kmaq night sky stories: Patterns of interconnectiveness, vitality, and nourishment. *Communicating Astronomy to the Public Journal (CAPjournal), 9*, 14–17.

Harris, P., Marshall, M., Denny, D., Young, F., Marshall, S., & Bartlett, C. (2013). *Nkij'inen teluet Kina'matnewe'l telimuksi'ki we'wkl atukwaqnn / Our grandmothers' words—traditional stories for nurturing.* [Children's storybook in Mi'kmaw and English]. Sydney, NS: Cape Breton University Press.

Hatcher, A., & Bartlett, C. (2010, May). Two-Eyed Seeing: Building cultural bridges for Aboriginal students. *Canadian Teacher Magazine,* 14–17.

Hatcher, A., Bartlett, C., Marshall, M., & Marshall, A. (2009a). Two-Eyed Seeing: A cross-cultural science journey. *Green Teacher, 86,* 3–6.

Hatcher, A., Bartlett, C. M., Marshall, A., & Marshall, M. (2009b). Two-Eyed Seeing in the classroom environment: Concepts, approach, and challenges. *Canadian Journal of Science, Mathematics, and Technology Education, 9,* 141–153.

Hatcher, A., Kavanagh, S., Bartlett, C., & Marshall, M. (2009). Traditional legends: Meanings on many levels. *Green Teacher, 86,* 14–17.

Institute for Integrative Science & Health. (n.d.). Retrieved from http://www.inte grativescience.ca

Iwama, M., Marshall, A., Marshall, M., & Bartlett, C. (2009). Two-Eyed Seeing and the language of healing in community-based research. *Canadian Journal of Native Education, 32,* 3–23.

Iwama, M., Marshall, M., Marshall, A., Mendez, I., & Bartlett, C. (2007). *I got it from an Elder: Conversations in healing language.* Devil's Whim Occasional Chapbook Series, no. 20. Kentville, NS: Gaspereau Press.

Marshall, A. (2005). The science of humility. In *New horizons of knowledge section: Proceedings for: Te Tol Roa—Indigenous Excellence, World Indigenous Peoples' Conference on Education.* Hamilton Aotearoa, New Zealand, November 27–December 1, 2005. Retrieved from http://www.integrativescience.ca/uploads/articles/2005 November-Marshall-WIPCE-text-Science-of-Humility-Integrative-Science.pdf

Marshall, A., Marshall, M., & Iwama, M. (2010). Approaching Mi'kmaq teachings on the connectiveness of humans and nature. In S. Bondrup-Nielsen, K. Beazley, G. Bissix, D. Colville, S. Flemming, T. Herman, M. McPherson, S. Mockford, & S. O'Grady (Eds.), *Ecosystem based management: Beyond boundaries.* Proceedings of the Sixth International Conference of Science and the Management of Protected Areas, May 21–26, 2007, Acadia University, Wolfville, NS. Science and Management of Protected Areas Association, Wolfville, NS.

Marshall, L., Marshall, M., Harris, P., & Bartlett, C. (2010). *Muin Aqq L'uiknek Te'sijik Ntuksuinu'k - Mi'kmawey Tepkikewey Musikiskey A'tukwaqn / Muin and the seven bird hunters—a Mi'kmaw night sky story.* [Children's storybook in Mi'kmaw and English]. Sydney, NS: Cape Breton University Press.

Marshall, M. (2005). On tribal consciousness—the trees that hold hands. In *New horizons of knowledge section: Proceedings for: Te Tol Roa—Indigenous Excellence, World Indigenous Peoples' Conference on Education.* Hamilton Aotearoa, New Zealand, November 27 –December 1, 2005. Retrieved from http://www.integrative science.ca/uploads/articles/2005November-Marshall-WIPCE-text-On-Tribal -Consciousness-Integrative-Science.pdf

Marshall, M. (2008). *Health and healing—death and dying: Women's roles within.* Workshop training materials for cultural sensitivity and cultural humility; for health organization. Retrieved from http://www.integrativescience.ca/uploads/ articles/2008-Marshall-cultural-sensitivity-humility-module-aboriginal-health .pdf

Marshall, M. (2011). *L'nuita'si*: Mi'kmaw tribal consciousness. In T. Bernard, L. M. Rosenmeier, & S. L. Farrell (Eds.), *Ta'n Wetapeksi'k: Understanding from where we come* (pp. 173–177). Proceedings of the 2005 Debert Research Workshop, Debert, NS. Eastern Woodland Print Communications, Truro, NS.

CHAPTER 3

Inuit Knowledge Systems, Elders, and Determinants of Health

Harmony, Balance, and the Role of Holistic Thinking

Shirley Tagalik

Indigenous knowledge systems are holistic in nature. This integrated, inclusive, holistic view of the world is a natural and intuitive view implying connectedness, reciprocity, and relationality—the big picture perspective. Over the past several years, I have been honoured to explore *Inuit Qaujimajatuqangit* (IQ) or Inuit world view with Inuit Elders. From this work, the core concepts of connectedness and belonging, based on respectful relationship building, have been described to me as essential to the Inuit intention of living a good life. Relationality and the rules that govern how one interacts, both with others and within the natural world, require a holistic perspective because no one thing can be separated from its other relational aspects. Successfully negotiating a holistic approach in life is entrenched in the need to continually maintain harmony and balance in all things. The interconnection of these concepts is an indicator for collective and personal well-being.

Elder Louis Angalik explained the difference in holistic/non-holistic thinking through the analogy of giving directions when travelling. We Western thinkers tend to travel off toward a destination with a specific direction in mind. If asked how to get to a place, we narrowly describe a directional route or just use GPS points. Louis presents directions from the perspective of looking down on the land to be travelled through. He describes geographical features, including links to unusual land forms, flora, snowdrift patterns, animal trails, and atmospheric conditions. He uses place names that carry information about the way the land looks or the way it has been used over generations. His directions paint a mind picture that enables the traveller to build relationships with this environment. Once connected in this way, these relationships will last through a lifetime (L. Angalik, personal communication, September 28, 2008). For Elders, the loss of this holistic perspective leaves one disconnected, with a diminished sense of belonging and wellness. The holistic perspective is understood to be a protective factor for Inuit well-being.

Inuit knowledge systems are grounded in this all-encompassing holistic view of an interconnected world—a world that is imbued with and defined through relationship and interactivity. Everything is known by its relationship to everything else—there is a universal wholeness of relationship and no one thing can be separated from the view of the whole (NCCAH, 2009a). World view is gained through lived experiences, embedded in observations, reflections, and interactions. It is highly contextualized and very personal. The following illustrative analogy of Indigenous knowledge is provided by Barnhardt and Kawagley:

> For Indigenous people there is a recognition that many unseen forces are at play in the elements of the universe and that very little is naturally linear, or occurs in a two-dimensional grid or a three-dimensional cubic form....Through long observation they have become specialists in understanding the interconnectedness and holism of our place in the universe (Barnhardt and Kawagley 1999; Cajete 2000; Eglash 2002). . . . Indigenous people have long recognized these interdependencies and have sought to maintain harmony with all of life. Western scientists have constructed the holographic image, which lends itself to the Native concept of everything being connected. Just as the whole contains each part of the image, so too does each part contain the makeup of the whole. The relationship of each part to everything else must be understood to produce the whole image. (Barnhardt & Kawagley, 2005, p. 12)

RELATIONAL AND RECIPROCAL WAYS OF BEING

Holism is relational and reciprocal in every dimension. It is intuitive, moral, spiritual, and represents a thorough integration of expectations and practices grounded in beliefs. These beliefs apply to every aspect of life and in Inuktitut are called the *maligait*, or the big laws. These include working for the common good, being respectful of all living beings, maintaining harmony and balance, and continually planning and preparing for the future (NCCAH, 2009a). Indigenous world views also describe cultural concepts of ways of knowing and ways of doing. These are symbiotic processes in Indigenous systems underlying the expectation that individuals will live a good life, contributing their skills and knowledge to the common good. The development of skills and knowledge are understood to occur when the individual applies new understanding through direct experience with the natural world, thus encountering an iterative and complementary process of knowledge construction through direct application (NCCAH, 2009b).

Inuit Elders confirm this and assert there is no value to knowing something if the knowledge is not used to improve the common good, that knowledge without application has no purpose. Knowledge—not just the knowing of something, but the ability to understand and predict the consequences of things—comes from being grounded in a continuum to time, relationship, and collectively lived experiences (NCCAH, 2009b). The ultimate use for knowledge is to make good decisions that will lead to an improved future. Making good decisions requires understanding and respecting the past, being critically observant and intuitive about the present, and striving toward a better future.

LIVING A GOOD LIFE

Inuit knowledge systems hold this core expectation of living a good life. In our interviews, Elders describe this concept in the following terms: "In Inuit belief it is a good thing to live a contented life. When you do not know this peace of mind, it is very difficult to get motivated in life. People who experience this peace on the land will always seek it" (B. Nirlungajuq, personal communication, August 21, 2012). Another Elder, Alice Ayalik, states that "a good life comes from sharing the good that you have and staying clear of the bad that is out there. This is wisdom" (A. Ayalik, personal communication, August 21, 2012). The concept of a good life is heavily reliant on living respectfully—being in close relationship to everything and everyone. In another Elder's words, the concept of a good life includes:

> The need to focus on the initial teachings such as respecting everything—people, land, tools, animals, teachings—in order to have peace and contentment, you need to have good relationships. People are wrestling just to have the basics. They are not equipped with the teaching our parents gave to us so that we could build a good life for ourselves. (N. Attungala, personal communication, August 21, 2012)

The pursuit of a good life enables you to experience harmony. Elders describe a key goal in life as the ability to overcome obstacles. The late Donald Suluk, who wrote extensively about the concept of living a good life, states that "We have always heard that a person who strives for happiness, even when it doesn't seem attainable, will always reach that goal sooner or later. Likewise, a person who gave up would always reap what he sowed" (Bennett & Rowley, 2004, p. 110). Other Elders concur: "My mother would tell me that I would not have harmony all day so to be prepared for problems. I was to do my best to have peace within myself" (J. Tattuinee, personal communication, August 22, 2012). Being in harmony and continually promoting harmony within the group was and continues to be a cultural expectation. Children were specifically taught to seek solutions when faced with obstacles, to never demonstrate anger, to avoid conflicts, and always restore good relationships. Elders see the impacts of colonization as diminishing both the teachings and the cultural expectations, but insist that the significance of these teachings remains strong and needs to be reinforced by returning to cultural parenting practices.

INUNNGUINIQ—MAKING A HUMAN BEING

The Inuit concept of parenting—*inunnguiniq*—is directed at making a human being. Elders describe a process of preparing a child to develop abilities to overcome obstacles and to avoid creating obstacles. In order to attain this better life, it was essential to get rid of the things that caused discord— through avoiding conflict or else through confession of wrongdoing, seeking forgiveness, and returning to harmony with others. Teaching children to continually build strong, respectful relationships and to avoid conflict was foundational to living a good life (Briggs, 1970, 1998). Joe Karetak describes it like this:

> When you are a child, you will not be told everything at the same time, but will be given small bits to practice. The person who instructs always has the bigger, holistic picture in mind, but breaks it down for the child. Without the foundation of respect, the child is unable to apply the laws to have a good life. Learning to become a human being, to be a good person, to live a good life—cannot be set aside. (J. Karetak, personal communication, August 22, 2010)

Inunnguiniq teaching was very intentional. As Elder Joanasie Muckpa relates:

> My uncle also used to admonish and discipline me but they did it with such love that it immediately made you want to obey them. If you discipline harshly, the child will be resistant and will not want to listen or be able to listen because

they are already too upset. Even discipline can be administered in a calm way that builds connection and confidence and promotes harmony within the family. There were always some situations that led to anger. This anger would be diffused so that harmony was restored. (J. Muckpa, personal communication, August 21, 2012)

Aiyola Takolik adds, "With harmony it is important not to be easily offended. This is something that we were taught and that our children now do not understand" (A. Takolik, personal communication, August 22, 2012). Elders are concerned with changes in their children's and grandchildren's experiences. They attribute the high incidence of alcohol, drug abuse, and youth suicide as evidence that harmony is harder to attain in today's world.

Colonization of Inuit resulted in many broken or damaged cultural systems. Norman Attungala poignantly shares his experience:

We agreed to this life because we thought it would be better. Today we should be weeping with contentment rather than with anger if those promises had been kept. In this new life, it is more difficult to find contentment today. We used to live a life where everything was connected. Today's life is tangled and without clear purpose. (N. Attungala, personal communication, August 21, 2012)

Mary Muckpa explains that "Today everything is so much easier, but we are lacking something—direction and harmony within families" (M. Muckpa, personal communication, August 21, 2012).

Harmony Requires Balance

Elders recognize the much greater challenge of equipping children with skills to live harmoniously today. Louis Angalik summarizes it like this:

Our children's way of life is so different. But, in spite of all these changes, we still need to pass along the teaching about a good life because these basic things do not really change. Many of our children are led into addictions because they are looking for the good life. They look in the wrong places because they think life should be easy. (L. Angalik, personal communication, August 21, 2012)

Elders see hope through their work to revitalize cultural teachings. Joanasie Muckpa sees possible solutions:

Relying on IQ [Inuit world view] again will make everything easier for all. Having a good life and living in harmony is very important. We need strong leaders grounded in these beliefs to be able to get our communities back on track. The leadership of Elders has been disregarded, but if the younger generation would listen again and understand the wisdom that can be gained from Elders, this would help bring the communities back into harmony and balance. (J. Muckpa, personal communication, August 21, 2012)

The need to regain harmony and balance is a common concern for Elders because they see a stark contrast between the lives they once lived where these concepts were central and the lives of the next generations where they perceive significant imbalance. Bernadette Utuq points out that "Our lives are out of balance. Today, life is too materialistic. All the different aspects of life need to be in balance—the physical, intellectual, social, emotional, and spiritual" (B. Utuq, personal communication, August 22, 2012). Cultural researcher Joe Karetak emphasizes the importance of balance, saying:

We are simply trying to talk about life in balance and the ways to maintaining a balanced life, no matter what you are going through. It was noticed, or became noticeable, when someone went through difficulties—not being able to maintain harmony and losing their balance. It is just so obvious—seeking solutions and solving problems is so necessary to maintaining harmony and balance. Simply said, there are too many things we just don't control—that influence and affect us all the time—the only thing we really can control is ourselves. So, we are in control of our own harmony, balance, and maintaining a good life. (J. Karetak, personal communication, August 22, 2012)

Concluding Thoughts: The Need for Healing

Harmony and balance in life are indicators for social and personal well-being. Wellness can be framed through interconnectivity and relational supports, which enable each person to live a good life, following and applying the big laws. For Inuit, this provides the basis for the cultural concepts of wellness and wisdom. When there is an imbalance in a person's life, healing is required. As Ituksamajaq shares from his experience:

Being honest within the family and speaking openly is very important. This is key to maintaining peace. We need to confront problems right away. We need to seek them out and be careful to sense when someone is having difficulty or the family harmony is slipping away. Following the rules such as sharing your catch is very important to this. It is essential for healing to obey these ways of living a good life. Healing needs to start from home. How Inuit looked after each other and how they practiced caring for each other lead to contentment. Individually we cannot stand on our own, that has always been the Inuit expectation. It was always recognize that we must help each other. (T. Ituksamajaq, personal communication, August 21, 2012)

Another Elder, Atuat Akittirq, highlights the importance of healing: "Maintaining harmony and balance was accomplished through healing. Back then, *anniatpalauqmataajuq* [to let out]—people would (let it out) to regain harmony" (A. Akittirq, personal communication, October 12, 2012). Healing was supported through *aajiiqatigiiniq*, a process that Hubert Amrualik further describes in the following way:

They all would talk about what was wrong and what was expected. Everyone had a chance to express his or her side of the story [*aniaslutik*]. Once this was over, they were able to restore harmony and strengthen their mutual bonds and family kinship ties. Everyone felt better afterwards. (Bennett & Rowley, 2004, p. 99)

To think holistically is to be in respectful relationship with all that is around you. With the holographic image, you must adjust and balance the various elements until a harmonious image appears. Elders describe harmony as a blessing—a wellness of spirit and a sense of being personally centred and connected. They describe a good life as being content with your place, feeling competent to face the future, and sharing what you possess with others. Inuit knowledge systems identify maintaining harmony and balance as one of the four big laws (NCCAH, 2009a). It is not optional; it is an expectation precisely because it was known as a source of happiness and good living, and as the ultimate determinant of health.

REFERENCES

Barnhardt, R., & Kawagley, O. (2005). Indigenous knowledge systems and Alaska Native ways of knowing. *Anthropology and Education Quarterly, 36*, 8–23.

Bennett, J., & Rowley, S. (2004). *Uqalurait: An oral history of Nunavut*. Montreal, QC: McGill-Queen's University Press.

Briggs, J. (1970). *Never in anger: Portrait of an Eskimo family.* Cambridge, MA: Harvard University Press.

Briggs, J. (1998). *Inuit morality play: The emotional education of a three year old.* New Haven, CT: Yale University Press.

NCCAH. (2009a). *Inuit Qaujimajatuqangit: The role of Indigenous knowledge in supporting wellness in Inuit communities in Nunavut.* Retrieved from www.nccah.ca/44/Fact_Sheets.nccah

NCCAH. (2009b). *Inunnguiniq: Caring for children the Inuit way.* Retrieved from www.nccah.ca/44/Fact_Sheets.nccah

NCCAH. (2010). *Framework for Indigenous school health: Foundations in cultural principles.* Retrieved from www.nccah.ca/docs/nccah%20reports/NCCAH_CASH_report.pdf

CHAPTER 4

The Spiritual Dimension of Holistic Health

A Reflection

Marlene Brant Castellano

The invitation from the editors of this volume to contribute a brief reflective piece on the determinants of health stimulated a trip down memory lane, starting with my first encounter with Indigenous knowledge on the subject.

In 1980–1981, I undertook to apply my concurrent studies in adult education to assist the Health Steering Committee of the Union of Ontario Indians to prepare on-reserve leadership for transfer of selected responsibilities from Health Canada to community administration. I was excited about international developments endorsing primary health care, which incorporated many of the features we now call determinants of health, and reaffirming the World Health Organization's definition that "Health is a state of complete physical, mental and social well-being and not merely the absence of disease or infirmity" (World Health Organization, 1948/2006, p. 1). I spoke to the Health Steering Committee about the convergence of these developments with First Nations' understandings of health. The most incisive comment in the meeting came from the Elder, a tiny Anishinabe woman, who said: "This is good, but they have left out the spiritual part of health." Thirty years later, I am still learning about "the spiritual part of health" and questioning how it can be integrated in health systems throughout the continuum, from prevention and promotion to cure and rehabilitation. And I am still in awe of the insight of Elders who can evaluate and enhance the knowledge of the most prestigious professionals.

Holistic health, encompassing physical, mental, emotional, and spiritual dimensions, has become a mantra in the discourse on Aboriginal well-being. Still, what we mean by "spiritual health" is largely left to the interpretation of

33

the patient, practitioner, or researcher without distinguishing the concept within the complex and various forms of culture, tradition, ceremony, healing, and Healers with which it is associated. It is not surprising, then, that healing the spirit is predominantly left to the initiative and resources of individuals seeking out Elders, Healers, and medicines outside formal health systems. I don't propose in this commentary to offer definitions or prescriptions for spiritual health. I do suggest that it is possible to find convergences among different paradigms of knowledge.

"The Spiritual Part of Health"

Spiritual health has various names among different peoples—"being alive well," peace, balance, awareness, faith. I recently watched an interview with a young man who had escaped life on the street and gang membership and found a home in an urban community, practising traditional ceremonies. He said of his experience in the sweat lodge: "It's like love or something." Spiritual health may be sparked in a ceremonial setting, but it is lived outside the lodge. It is expressed and sustained in relationships with family and friends. It is enlarged in reconnecting with the land that supports our feet. It is spread abroad in service to the community. It is inspired by the joy and energy of children. Spiritual health is a communal affair and it is undermined by anything that assaults community vitality. In a 2006 conference presentation, Madeleine Dion Stout illustrated the pileup of risks imposed on her people by multiple poverties over generations, and the resilience with which they have adapted, all conveyed in Cree terminology (see also Castellano & Archibald, 2007, pp. 74–78; and Chapter 13 in this book).

My brother, the late Dr. Clare Brant, spoke eloquently about the risks of isolating spiritual healing from determinants of health or ill health in the surrounding environment. In a presentation to the Royal Commission on Aboriginal Peoples (RCAP), he told about his findings as a psychiatric consultant in the 1991 inquest into a series of suicides at the Prison for Women in Kingston. Inmate survivors whom Clare interviewed expressed the view that their peers killed themselves "because they were ashamed." On further investigation, he concluded that one of the precipitating factors in the suicide epidemic was the self-awareness fostered by an Aboriginal cultural program, including outside medicine people, sweat lodges, and sweetgrass ceremonies. In the RCAP Round Table report, *The Path to Healing*, Clare was quoted as saying:

Some of these women, who had lived anti-social lifestyles to the point where they had to be locked up for their own safety and the safety of others became aware that life had meaning, purpose and direction, but when they returned to the cells and the ranges and were confronted with the harsh realities of the oppressive and cruel prison structure, the change was too abrupt and over-whelming. Suicide was their escape from this mind-splitting discrepancy between the inner peace they had acquired and the unspeakable cruelties of the prison system. (Royal Commission on Aboriginal Peoples, 1993, p. 62)

Roland Chrisjohn made a complementary point in his report for RCAP, in which he passionately argued that "residential school syndrome" should properly be seen as a disorder of the people and systems that perpetrated the many abuses of residential schools instead of a failure of those who survived them (Chrisjohn & Young, 1997).

SUPPORTING CONVERGENCES

From 1998 to 2012, the Aboriginal Healing Foundation (AHF) assembled a body of research that makes an extraordinary contribution to our under-standing of community-based health initiatives that go beyond the conventional definition of determinants of health to acknowledge historical, cultural, and political influences on health, as well as relationship with the land.[1] Although the focus of projects and research is residential school experience, the AHF collection is relevant to enhancing Aboriginal health in every domain. In its 2006 final report on the first seven years of its mandate, the AHF identified three fundamental characteristics of successful healing programs: (1) they reflect the underlying philosophy and world view of the Aboriginal peoples who design and benefit from them; (2) they establish physical, emotional, and cultural safety for participants; and (3) they engage healing teams comprised of skilled Healers, therapists, Elders, and volunteers, most often using a combination of traditional and Western professional approaches (Castellano & Archibald, 2007, pp. 85–86; Aboriginal Healing Foundation, 2006).

Physical and emotional safety is a well-established prerequisite for healing physical or emotional trauma. For peoples whose lives and identities have been under threat for generations, cultural safety is equally necessary. My brother Clare, who was highly successful as a therapist with First Nations youth in conflict with the law, told me that the first real communication from such patients was usually in the form of a challenge: "You killed the buffalo; you stole our land. You can't help me!" In the face of anger and defensiveness, Clare was able to establish a climate of safety. That Clare's ancestors had suffered comparable loss was a starting point, but the compassion he communicated was grounded in his own struggle for balance. He said that it took five years at Queen's University to turn him into an M.D. and it took years more of psychoanalysis to regain his identity as a Mohawk (Brant, personal communication, n.d.). When he learned how to use his biomedical knowledge and skills in concert with his innate Mohawk knowledge and intuition, he began to realize his lifetime goal of being a Healer—not only of his own Iroquoian people, but also of Aboriginal peoples across Canada (Wieman, 2000).

Research into the trauma of residential schools has deepened our understanding of historic trauma and the accumulation of stresses affecting Aboriginal individuals, families, and communities over generations without respite to regroup and devise new, effective coping strategies (Castellano, 2010; Wesley-Esquimaux & Smolewksi, 2004). Ongoing research continues to reveal the disastrous effects of chronic stress on the functioning of all body systems. The relationship between stress and the incidence of diabetes, heart disease, obesity, and other ills is being explored. The stress of acculturation has been enforced on all Aboriginal peoples over generations by schooling that devalues our languages and traditional wisdom; history that ignores our existence as competent, self-determining peoples; and institutions that claim authority for healing. The challenge of creating change in all those systems is daunting, even with the significant gains that we have made in the past 50 years. For health workers, researchers, and readers of this volume on determinants of health, the salient question is this: How do we move forward toward holistic health among Aboriginal peoples?

In its hearings and research, the RCAP heard persuasive testimony about the value of traditional healing in restoring spiritual, as well as physical, balance. The Commission also heard concerns about abuses of vulnerable patients and communities by people claiming sacred authority. RCAP noted that "Forms of self-regulation and community control that once operated through religious, spiritual or medicine societies or simply through local reputation are, in some places, weakened or non-existent" (RCAP, 1996, p. 355). To advance recognition of traditional healing and Healers, the RCAP recommended that four critical issues should be addressed at the levels of policy and program: (1) access to the services of traditional Healers; (2) protection and extension of the existing skills and knowledge base; (3) self-regulation by existing practitioners; and (4) the need for dialogue between traditional Healers and biomedical (and related) personnel (RCAP, 1996, pp. 290–293, 360).

For the necessary dialogue with policy-makers and health practitioners, we need language that is clear and accessible to all players. I found Gaye Hanson's (2009) exposition of "cultural competence" very enlightening. She defines cultural competence as "the human relational capacity to seek and find compassionate connection within, between and among people of differing cultural backgrounds and perspectives" (Hanson, 2009, p. 243). Cultural competence is a relational skill that can be acquired, starting with awareness of one's own experience, sensation, thoughts, and cultural environment, so that these influences do not become a distorting lens through which one sees others (Hanson, 2009, p. 250). Cultural competence thus defined is congruent with culture-based pedagogies and ethics of research that have been articulated elsewhere (Williams, 2000; Castellano & Reading, 2010). Cultural competence was also a hallmark of Clare Brant's practice and teaching.

Beyond dialogue, community leaders and professionals need to explore the feasibility of making cultural competence a standard of practice to which every person entrusted with responsibility for enhancing Aboriginal health is expected to adhere, with access to appropriate preparation. We also need to attend to our own spiritual health, taking time for our own growth and renewal, hanging out with people of good mind, and learning from many streams of knowledge.

CONCLUSION

Thirty-five years have passed since I first heard an Elder articulate her people's definition of health, not rejecting the WHO concept but enriching it. Health systems in Canada and around the world have adopted the language of social determinants of health in the context of prevailing biomedical approaches. Indigenous practitioners, among others, including those cited in the foregoing reflection, have emerged as influential voices affirming the importance of holistic healing and "the spiritual part of health" in maintaining *human* well-being, not just the health of Indigenous peoples. It is my hope that my words and the chapters in this collection contribute to broadening that vision.

Nia:wen. Thank you for your attention.

NOTE

1. Note that the research collection of the Aboriginal Healing Foundation has been donated to Algoma University and the Children of Shingwauk Alumni Association as of 2012.

REFERENCES

Aboriginal Healing Foundation. (2006). *Final report*, vol. III: *Promising healing practices in Aboriginal communities*. Prepared by L. Archibald. Ottawa: Aboriginal Healing Foundation.

Castellano, M. B. (2010, November). Healing residential school trauma: The case for evidence-based policy and community-led programs. *Native Social Work Journal*, 7, 11–31. Retrieved from https://zone.biblio.laurentian.ca/dspace/handle/10219/378

Castellano, M. B., & Archibald, L. (2007). Healing historic trauma: A report from the Aboriginal Healing Foundation. In J. P. White, S. Wingert, D. Beavon, & P. Maxim (Eds.), *Aboriginal policy research, moving forward, making a difference*, vol. IV (pp. 69–92). Toronto, ON: Thompson Educational Publishing Inc.

Castellano, M. B., & Reading, J. (2010). Policy writing as dialogue: Drafting an Aboriginal chapter for Canada's Tri-Council policy statement: Ethical conduct for research involving humans. *International Indigenous Policy Journal*, 1. Retrieved from ir.lib.uwo.ca/iipj

Chrisjohn, R., & Young, S., with Maraun, M. (1997). *The circle game: Rethinking the Indian residential school experience*. Penticton, BC: Theytus Books.

Hanson, G. (2009). A relational approach to cultural competence. In G. G. Valaskakis, M. Dion Stout, & E. Guimond (Eds.), *Restoring the balance, First Nations women, community, and culture* (pp. 237–264). Winnipeg: University of Manitoba Press.

Royal Commission on Aboriginal Peoples (RCAP). (1993). *The path to healing*. Ottawa. Minister of Supply and Services.

Royal Commission on Aboriginal Peoples (RCAP). (1996). *RCAP report*, vol. 3: *Gathering strength*. Chapter 3: Health and healing. Retrieved from www.aadnc -aandc.gc.ca/eng/1307458586498

Wesley-Esquimaux, C., & Smolewksi, M. (2004). *Historic trauma and Aboriginal healing*. Ottawa, ON: Aboriginal Healing Foundation. Retrieved from http://www.ahf.ca/downloads/historic-trauma.pdf

Wieman, C. (2000). A simple country doctor: Remembering Dr. Clare Brant. *Canadian Journal of Psychiatry*. Retrieved from ww1.cpa-apc.org:8080/Publications/Archives/CJP/2000/Sep/Brant.asp

Williams, L. (2000). Urban Aboriginal education: The Vancouver experience. In M. B. Castellano, L. Davis, & L. Lahache (Eds.), *Aboriginal education, fulfilling the promise* (pp. 129–146). Vancouver, BC: UBC Press.

World Health Organization. (1948/2006). Constitution. Retrieved from www.who.int/governance/eb/who_constitution_en.pdf

CHAPTER 5

Two Poems

Marilyn Iwama

Take That Pain
from a story told by Murdena Marshall

For instance, take the one that drills
your skull just behind your ear. Take that
burning where your supper sits
every night reminding you
Loser
you tell yourself
of every stupid way
you screwed up again today.
And that numb patch on your foot
that makes you itch and trip
and wish for days you could—

for once take it to the aunties
like that day we wanted to
talk about talking. About how
there's a special way
language is healing and this
auntie had one hour between the last
meeting and minding
her grandson. He's a dog

this week. Call him Scrappy
says Auntie as he crawls through the gap

he tore in the screen yesterday
with his paws. When they thought
he still had hands.

Hi Scrappy. Ruff
barks Scrappy to Auntie's terrier.
Ruff ruff. Wagging their tails.

Like it was the first time
Auntie tells me about taking
the bus to Restigouche.
I was so dizzy my girl
said you gotta stop driver
my mother is sick.

The driver said ten minutes
at the next Irving not one
more but the earth kept swirling
into the sky like marble
cake and Auntie only made it
as far as the steps.

The smokers were happy
until the driver said nice try
and herded them back on the bus.

At Restigouche the ambulance was
waiting. Do you think
the driver called ahead?
And they made the hospital
in record time but didn't
Auntie have another stroke
in Emerge. I made it

to Quebec City like I always
wanted she said and the old
man was waiting for me except
I was out like a light my arms

tied to the bed rails for
the breathing tube up my nose
and the I.V. and one for peeing so
I never got to see
the place. Dammit
Auntie—but I don't say it—
what about language?

So today I try again
to get Auntie to talk
about healing verbs.
To say if
this last bit is true
to the tense. We need
Auntie's okay about that paper
so we can send it off like
they say in the business
and Auntie starts in
on Restigouche again.

She told the bus driver
please stop. My mother's sick.
Maybe if she got some air. . . .
And the driver says I'll give you ten
minutes but I was so dizzy I went
back to my seat and the smokers
they were happy until the driver told them
get in folks it's time to move. At Restigouche

the ambulance was waiting. I think
the driver called ahead. So
they got me to the hospital
right away and I had another
stroke in Emergency.

For the first time
I got to Quebec City
and Albert was waiting

except I didn't know.
I was unconscious.
My arms were
tied down. I guess
for the breathing
tube up my nose
and the I.V.
and one for peeing.

This sounds like Auntie's story
about the paper about healing
needing fixing and us wanting
her go ahead.

Medicine

Nohkôm Bella delivered babies
and laid out the dead. No
not me Mom said but I knew
which one *nikāwiy* had done
by the smells she brought home
with her. Cottage cheese and metal
mean birth. Death?
Violets and rotting plums.

Say you're old and back
having your heart checked
or your bowels and you
get up in the night to go
because that's what you do
and you fall and you crack
your head and start
bleeding into your wasting
brain and all you ever wanted
for the last ten years is someone
please take my shadow
into the field and shoot.

Dilaudid.
Hydromorphone hydrochloride.
A real workhorse.

Dilaudid makes roadblocks
no pain can smash.
Dilaudid makes brains
forget to breathe. Turns out

none of us had what it took
so Dad's brain has been
shrinking for years.

Dilaudid is a runner too.
Half a chance and it'll race
blood flooding
the stem of any brain.
Last soldier standing.

Saying it is easy.
Like making a wish
or confessing.

Lips and tongue working
round *hydromor*
phone hydrochlo
ride. Easy pea
sy break it
down

       water

             sound

                  salt—

Now
and then
and then a nurse
will add these bits
to Dad's dear blood.

We only have to
see it first then say
he hurts.

Why remember
we say
anything now?

Each two hours
says the nurse.
A twitch. A sign.
Just tell us.

Pat pat the blanket
padded knurls here
and there. Climb
that long slope
to thin still
brown hair. Lift
the mask that feeds
him air. Stroke
cream on tracks
the mask
leaves on chin
and nose. Stroke.
Stroke. Sniff.

PART 2

BEYOND THE SOCIAL

CHAPTER 6

The Relatedness of People, Land, and Health

Stories from Anishinabe Elders

Chantelle Richmond

A wide body of research demonstrates a special, multifaceted relationship between Indigenous peoples and their local lands and traditional territories (LaDuke, 1999; Adelson, 2003; Richmond & Ross, 2009; Parlee, Berkes, & Gwich'in, 2005; Durie, 2005). The health-supporting role of the land has been defined as inseparable from that of their cultures, social relationships, and traditional ways of living. This relationship is characterized by a deep spiritual relatedness between people and the land (Deloria, 2003), which has been sustained for generations through the acquisition, sharing, and practice of Indigenous knowledge (Berkes, 2012; Battiste & Henderson, 2000).

Since the onset of colonialism in North America, Canada's First Nations have endured centuries of environmental dispossession and cultural upheaval. Environmental dispossession refers to the processes through which Indigenous peoples' access to the land and resources of their traditional environments is reduced or fundamentally altered (Richmond & Ross, 2009). The results of these processes are understood to be related to, or at least distant causes of, many of the health and social statistics we see in the First Nations population today (Reading & Wien, 2009).

Reduced access to traditional lands and territories following colonization has significantly altered the special relationship between Indigenous peoples and the land. The results of these changed relationships have had cascading effects on the acquisition and practice of Indigenous knowledge, which has in turn affected the quality of social relationships—many of which are nurtured through time spent on the land—and compromised abilities to find and consume traditional foods (Turner et al., 2013). As processes of environmental dispossession continue in the modern day to displace First Nations peoples from their traditional lands and territories, we can expect to see continued shifts in the cultural identities of First Nations, with important consequences for social relationships and overall health.

Drawing on interview data with Anishinabe Elders from the north shore of Lake Superior, the purpose of this chapter is to push the limits of critical thinking about what determines First Nations health (Richmond & Ross, 2009) and, more specifically, to engage First Nations health and policy research to consider how fundamental land, in all of its various meanings, is for the health and cultural identity of First Nations peoples. This chapter seeks to widen the dialogue regarding critical population health thinking in both research and policy worlds about the important role that land plays for the cultural identities, social relationships, and overall health and well-being of First Nations. Further, this chapter asks how and why it is that processes of environmental dispossession, particularly in the form of industrial development, have had such devastating consequences for the current realities of First Nations communities, and what role researchers and policy-makers can play in drawing greater public attention and awareness to these inequities.

The chapter is organized into the following sections. First, the process of environmental dispossession is characterized, with specific attention paid to the ways that land, cultural identity, knowledge, and health are interrelated, particularly in the context of the north shore of Lake Superior, where the Elders who contributed to this chapter come from. The next section will detail stories from Anishinabe Elders about how they understand their health, the ways that land influences health, and the important role that social relationships foster links for shared knowledge and cultural identity. The final section of this chapter challenges health researchers and policy-makers to consider the sufficiency of current models of health, and current framings of Indigenous health research more generally, for meeting the needs of Anishinabe people.

People, Land, and Health:
The Anishinabe Context of Lake Superior

The health effects of environmental dispossession are of considerable concern among the Anishinabe communities on the north shore of Lake Superior (Davidson-Hunt, 2003), just as they are among Indigenous communities in Canada and elsewhere (Parlee & Furgal, 2012; Richmond et al., 2007; Luginaah, Smith, & Lockridge, 2010; Windsor & McVey, 2006; de Leeuw et al., 2012a). This body of research highlights the deep and consequential impacts of environmental dispossession among Indigenous communities. Despite the fact that affected communities represent a diversity of cultures and geographies, these processes have similarly compromised the practice and transfer of Indigenous knowledge across generations, and negatively affected community health, well-being, and cultural identity (Green, King, & Morrison, 2009; Rigby et al., 2011; Garnett et al., 2009; Berrang-Ford et al., 2012; Turner et al., 2013).

In the time since the Hudson's Bay Company (HBC) set up a post at the mouth of the Pic River in the 1800s, Anishinabe communities have endured centuries of environmentally exploitative resource development. The establishment of the HBC post was followed by the construction of both the Canadian Pacific Railway and the Trans-Canada Highway; the introduction of white fur-trappers; the commercialization of the Lake Superior fishery; and the settlement of towns, cities, and other industry in Anishinabe traditional territories. This early exploration and the subsequent settlement of townships and cities along the north shore have significantly changed the Anishinabe's relationship with the lands, lakes, and rivers. And too often industrial development in this natural resource–rich area has led to contamination of traditional lands and waters, resulting in little economic benefit for the communities themselves. Today, the political ecology of the north shore is such that pulp-and-paper mills are closing down in historic proportions, and the federal and provincial governments are supporting unprecedented mining exploration and windmill development. Across Canada, similar forms of economic, industrial, and tourism development are occurring in the traditional territories of First Nations, while many land claims remain unsettled and highly contested (McGregor, 2011; Natcher et al., 2009; O'Bonsawin, 2010; Takeda & Røpke, 2010). These concerns are paramount for many communities located on the shore of Lake Superior, including the Ojibways of the Pic River First Nation and the Batchewana First Nation of Ojibways.

Pic River is located roughly midway between the cities of Sault Ste. Marie and Thunder Bay, Ontario, and Batchewana is located 20 kilometres east of the city of Sault Ste. Marie. In both communities, there is considerable angst among the local population toward industrial development in their traditional territories, particularly concerning the various ways these industries have negatively affected the quality of local lands and environmental resources. For example, community members from Pic River explain how a burst tailings line at Hemlo Gold Development (located 40 kilometres upstream) contaminated their groundwater supply, forcing the community to rely on bottled water for several years in the 1990s. Another common narrative from Pic River revolves around the creation of a nearby national park during the late 1970s, and the limitation this has had on the community's ability to practise traditional hunting and harvesting activities within the boundaries of the park, which consumes a considerable portion of their traditional territory.

Individuals from Batchewana First Nation speak with concern about the steel industry in the neighbouring city of Sault Ste. Marie, raising questions about water and air quality, and the safety of consuming fish and mammals from these waterways. Batchewana residents are also expressive about wind turbine development on the shore of Lake Superior and the effect of ground vibration on migrating animals. With regard to local health concerns, the two communities are anxious about issues such as diabetes, mental health, and loss of culture and spirituality. They also speak about unprecedented social issues, including alcohol and drug addictions, abuse, and family break-down, many of which they link back to the residential school legacy.

Despite the geographic distance between them, and the fact that the processes of environmental dispossession they each endured has been different, the two communities speak with remarkably similar concern about the consequences of these industrial threats to the health and well-being of their communities. Limited control over and reduced quality of their local environmental resources has led to decreased access to the cultural determinants of health, such as participation in hunting, fishing, and trapping, and other activities (e.g., ceremonies, traditional medicines, language). In particular, Elders in the two communities expressed concern about a growing disenchantment they see in local youth with regard to learning and practising Anishinabe culture, language, and traditional ways of connecting with the land. On a more pragmatic level, Elders worry about what this growing disenchantment means for the future preservation of their Indigenous knowledge, local culture, resolution of community land claims, and the health of future generations of Anishinabe.

THE WORDS OF THE ELDERS

The data presented here come from the voices of Anishinabe Elders from Batchewana First Nation and Pic River First Nation. This chapter is just one piece of writing from a larger multi-year, community-based research (CBR) study that involved 46 Elders from these two communities. The larger objective of this study was to preserve Elder knowledge to protect health for future generations. The Elders' stories have been preserved in various forms, including a documentary (www.giftsfromtheelders.ca). Over the summer months of 2011, five youth from the two First Nation communities were hired and trained to undertake these interviews. Tobias, Richmond, and Luginaah (2013) present a more in-depth look at the larger study, including greater detail about the interview process, and a focused description of our CBR approach. The narratives of the Elders provide the substantive basis of this chapter; their words are provided verbatim, with pseudonyms and community name attached to each quote.

In the broadest sense, these interviews focused on meanings that Anishinabe Elders associate with the land, the goal being to better understand the ways that Anishinabe identity is formed through connection to land, to examine the ways that connection to land forms the basis for social relationships, and to understand what this means for health more generally. At the most basic level, Elders conceived of themselves as distinctly related to the land, often referring to themselves as being "of the land." In defining this interrelatedness to the land, many of the Elders turned to the Ojibway language to describe the connection. As one Elder describes it:

> That word "Anishinabe" covers a lot. When you think of that word "Anishinabe," [it means] we are always from the land. "Anishinabe." That's what "nabe" means, where we come from. So you're speaking and saying "I am from this land." That's what Anishinabe means, that what we call ourselves. We don't go around saying "I'm Ojibwa," "I'm Chippewa," we use "Anishinabe," we use our term to describe who we are, where we come from, from this land here. We're not from anyplace else. (Louise, Batchewana)

This tie to land was described by many through a deep spiritual connection, wherein the Anishinabe naturally conceive of themselves as part of the land, and with strong moral responsibilities as its protector:

> We are the land—there is a strong spiritual connection, everyone has their role in life, including the land and people. There is a respect that we need to show the land and it's relatedness to us. We are the land. If the land is sick, then it isn't going to be very long before we're going to get sick. How we take care of the land is important and we always have to recognize and give thanks to the land. Everything that's below the earth and on the earth and the earth itself, always remembering that those particular elements continue to do the responsibilities that they set out to do and how we have some responsibilities to make sure they

are able to do that and that we help them do those kinds of things. I've learned that over time the power of *sema* [tobacco] is really integral to how I am related now with the land. (Henry, Batchewana)

There is a strong symbiotic relationship between the Anishinabe and the land, meaning that the land is central to the way the Anishinabe understand their own selves and, at the same time, that the Anishinabe have responsibilities to the land. In this sense, there is a give and take with the land, and a strong belief that actions taken on the land will have important repercussions for the wellness of the Anishinabe. In this regard, the relationship between the Anishinabe and the land is not just a spiritual connection, but a sentient relationship, with direct physical connection:

> The land means a lot to me because that's where we live and we have to treat it good because man has ruined it with all this technology, with all the knowledge they use today. They cut all the forests down, they do a lot of blasting, they don't take care of Mother Earth, and Mother Earth reacts. If I did something to you, you'd react. If someone did something to me, I'd react. You have to treat Mother Earth with respect in everything you see, just like the animals you have to respect, like that fire you have to treat it with respect, or else it will hurt you. If you don't treat something with respect, it will hurt you, it will come back at you. That's why the land is very important to the Anishinabe people because that's where we live on Mother Earth and that is why we're here. We have to look after Mother Earth, that's where we live. (Gordon, Pic River)

Several of the interviewees spoke about the strong spiritual connection between the Anishinabe and the land, and traditional ceremony was identified as a critically important practice through which these identities are merged, and wherein people come together to collectively share and celebrate this special relationship:

> The ceremonies play a big part with—within, within our spiritual self. The full moon ceremonies that we do back at the lodge—it's for our people to come to be together so we can share because if we don't share what we're feeling inside, then a lot of sickness happens and we just keep it—keep it within. And we've been doing the ceremonies for many, many, many moons, many, many, many years, and our Elders that have come in that circle and shared their life, their

pain, their hurts—they've all talked and shared so much which is very, very sacred. And it's always about love, love of the family, love of their loved ones, and they continue on to pray. (Tammy, Pic River)

As noted above, this spiritual connection to land, practised through ceremony, is the foundational strength upon which the Anishinabe build and sustain the power of their social relationships, which are critical for health and well-being. Participation in these ceremonies enables a sense of belonging, both in the natural and spirit world, and a renewed sense of purpose and identity in these spaces of belonging. By participating in and being part of ceremony, Elders talked about ceremony as crucial for maintaining a collective sense of wellness in the community, strengthening family ties and relationships, and reinforcing social and moral responsibilities to the land.

Several of the Elders spoke about the innate connection between water and the health of the Anishinabe. Water was referred to as a Healer, with cleansing properties:

I think health is very important, important part of our being and I think with, with the water and the healing within the water to, to pick up that water each day and again to be thankful for, for the water and the berries that are here on the land for us to use and the blueberries within to help cleanse ourselves, the healing with inside. And it plays a big part of our whole being and our whole life. (Pamela, Pic River)

Just as the water was described as a healing resource, Elders spoke about the critical healing property of being connected with one another out on the land:

How does someone heal? They go back to the land. They go back to the land and you sit with people that really care. You just sit and you be, and you listen. It's all within the spirit within that guides—that guides with caring ears, with a caring heart, with a caring being and you listen with all your heart, to listen to somebody that actually will go inside themselves to talk about their pain, the pain within. There's no time factor when you want to come to heal. We can't say, I need 15 minutes or I need an hour. Only they know. And the love is the greatest teacher, the love of the eagle, the eagle fan and to want to, to come to people. (Tammy, Pic River)

The idea of what health means, then, is bound in significant ways not just in one's physical body, but it extends to intimate, spiritual relationships with the land—and all of the medicines the land provides—and also to the social relationships one has with family members and the wider community:

> Well, what health means to me is that—for looking after yourself the best way possible, taking care of your body for as they say, you know, your body is your temple. And trying to live a balanced life and a healthy life, you know, to the best of your ability and for looking after your family the best way, you know, to try to—try to make sure that everything is balanced, you know, and in, in our family circle or in your—in your life circle. (Pamela, Pic River)

The strong conceptual framework that the Elders have provided of the linkages between people and the land illuminates the incredible vulnerability of the Anishinabe people's health and way of life as a result of processes of environmental dispossession, including colonial policy and regulations such as the Indian Act, and differing forms of industrial development that have fundamentally altered the relationship between the Anishinabe people and their lands:

> The land is what we live on and if we don't look after it, there will be nothing for the next generation. Actually there's three generations left. Everything will be gone. You can tell now things are changing. Even with the big windmills, you can see across there the big windmill. Our fishing has changed since I've been here. We used to fish on that shoreline. Now we don't fish over there because there are no fish in there. We used to go across the bay to fish, but now there's a big windmill and the vibration from that windmill is driving the fish away from that shoreline. There's a big change in our land because of what the white man is doing to our land, putting up windmills. (Clayton, Batchewana)

In the past century, the Anishinabe have been dispossessed of their traditional lands due to a number of environmentally exploitative industries, including the arrival of white trappers, the development of the Canadian Pacific Railway, logging along the Pic River and St. Mary's River, the production of steel at Sault Ste. Marie, and the mining of the Hemlo gold deposit. Among many other colonial developments, these particular industries have significantly undermined the Anishinabe's traditional use of the land. Perhaps the most direct link between the health of the Anishinabe people and the land comes in the form of water, food, and medicines:

> Health means eating the right food. The right food is what we get from Mother Earth—that is how we grew up—wild meat, fish, and berries. Not all that greasy stuff like McDonald's or fries. I know I am guilty of all of that I eat today. That's why the Anishinabe people are hit badly with diabetes, the sugar. Our Elders have a lot of sugar. That's why you have to watch what you eat. That's why you have to eat healthy. . . . To be healthy for me is to eat good. (Dan, Pic River)

These extreme changes in the eating patterns of the Anishinabe have not occurred without significant health impacts, including high rates of obesity, early onset diabetes, and other chronic diseases:

> And, you know there's so much sugar diabetes happening right now in our people. Before talking to our Elders, you know, they didn't have that before— sugar diabetes—because they had good food. They were eating right off the land and healthy food and that and then, boom, the next thing you know all this, you know, commercial food and chemicals that came in, you know, kind of destroyed, our eating habits. Then we got into bad eating habits, and right now today sugar diabetes has just rocketed, you know. And I think that's happening to every First Nation out there. (Dan, Pic River)

As alluded to in the previous quote, the dietary change experienced in these communities is a result both of a shift to market foods and because of the potential risks posed to human health as a result of eating traditional foods, the quality of which is affected by industrial development:

> There are cautions put out in regards to moose and kidneys, particularly for older moose, especially the organs, particularly the liver and kidneys. But for animals other than that, there's nothing that I am aware of. Fish is another matter altogether. Not inland fish, I understand, the fish in Lake Superior because of all the pollution draining into Superior. Small fish are supposedly not an issue; just the bigger fish because they accumulate all the chemicals. That's another thing that restricts people from having a good diet. Not to mention that there's not that many fish out there anymore. It's pretty hard to feed your family just from fishing. At one time that lake was full of lake trout. But now it's

pollution. I guess you don't want to eat it. I still eat it. I'm old. I'm not going to accumulate too much chemical in my body before I kick the bucket. That's not what's going to kill me. (Brian, Pic River)

In spite of these vast changes in their ways of life and the potential risks associated with consuming traditional foods, many of the interviewees demonstrated a strong resilience and continued desire to eat traditional foods. They expressed worry that by not doing so, the important knowledge they hold will be lost over time. In the interviews, many of the Elders took time not only to sit and share their knowledge about their lives, but many made the incredible effort—in spite of their own physical ailments—to go out on the land and demonstrate the special places and medicines they were talking about.

In Indigenous communities across the globe, there is a deep and growing concern that the special ties linking youth and Elders within the context of Indigenous knowledge is becoming eroded over time, and Elders claim that processes of environmental dispossession are at the root of this troubling pattern (Ermine et al., 2005; Deloria, 2003). As demonstrated in the following quote, the Elders are the knowledge keepers, and there is a critical need to find ways of preserving this knowledge for the sustained cultural identities of future generations:

You know, that's the Elders. You need Elders, you know. There's not very many Elders. I grew up with Elders. I think, that's a gift, you know, that's why I see a lot of different things that happen in the land. I guess before even that was mentioned of culture, I still went hunting, you know, hunting and trapping with my uncle and that guy didn't have no dollar. Yeah, he had the welfare that came in at the end of the month. . . . But he didn't need that—he didn't need that to live. He lived right off the land. He got everything off the land and I think that's what happened. But, you know, people they don't go trapping, hunting no more. I think if you're around it long enough, you're going to know what that plant is. That's fireweed there, you know [he speaks in Ojibwa]. You'll know the names of the trees, but in order for it to work, you've got to practise. (Gordon, Pic River)

An important point made in the above quote is that this knowledge cannot be learned only by talking about it, but that to really understand this knowledge, it must be practised. And while reduced access to land means that fewer people in these two communities possess this knowledge today, these spiritual ties to land and the special knowledge connecting them to the land remain strong:

> But if we were to go back to our old ways of, you know, trying to eat the best that we could off the land, and hunting and fishing and, you know, growing our own gardens and that, I think it would be a lot healthier in those ways for us. (Louise, Batchewana)

While the changes First Nations communities have endured over the past 150 years have significantly changed their relationships with the land, their Indigenous knowledge has not been lost. The Elders who took part in this research were adamant that this knowledge still exists today, and that by practising these old ways of doing, and making efforts for younger generations to experience the life on the land, there is great hope for the continued health and well-being of the Anishinabe people.

PEOPLE, LAND, AND HEALTH:
DIRECTION FOR RESEARCH AND POLICY

In Canadian academic and policy worlds, the idea of "connectedness to land" as a determinant of health among First Nations has received very little attention (Wilson, 2003; Richmond & Ross, 2009; Parlee & Furgal, 2012). Perhaps it is the highly politicized nature of First Nations' relationship with the federal government—one fuelled by a limited public education about the deep, historic roots underlying this relationship—that serves as a distraction from focusing on what the land means for the health and well-being of First Nations (Wotherspoon & Hansen, 2013). Or perhaps it is the ongoing crises that we see in so many First Nations communities today, including outbreaks of infectious diseases, a desperate need for housing, and ongoing water contamination events, that direct research and policy emphasis away from issues related to land. Nor can we discount the significant role the media plays in shaping the ways contemporary First Nations realities are portrayed.

Indeed, there are myriad reasons why health research and policy have not engaged in more meaningful debate about the fundamental causes of poor health in the First Nation context. Some would suggest the most significant problem lies in a stagnant preoccupation with the biomedical model, an approach that takes comfort in addressing acute outcomes, and views the work of identifying and thinking about ways to tackle the original causes of those health problems as insurmountable (Bryant et al., 2011; Czyzewski, 2011).

And as the stories and messages relayed in this chapter demonstrate, it is important that we not focus our research and policy efforts solely on the sensationalized stories of the day, but rather that we begin to open the dialogue about how these modern-day crises are in fact outcomes of the historic and ongoing cultural and environmental dispossession of First Nations peoples (Marmot, 2007; Durie, 2005; LaDuke, 1999; Hunting & Browne, 2012). The relationship between First Nations peoples and the land is a multifaceted one, and formative for countless social determinants of health, including social relationships, spirituality, and access to foods and medicines.

In this chapter, the Elders challenge the ways that land may be considered in the most positivist, academic sense—for example, as parcels of space that are devoid of meaning—and to reconsider how indelibly and intricately the land is linked with the practice of everyday living, including the acquisition and sharing of Indigenous knowledge(s), and how this interaction with the land and with one another can strengthen the cultural identities of First Nations peoples. Here, I argue that it is time to think more critically about dispossession from land as a root cause of these ongoing crises (Baum et al., 2013), and to uncover—or at least begin to conceptualize—the multiple meanings and functions that the land holds for First Nations peoples (Ermine et al., 2005; Adelson, 2003; Parlee et al., 2005). At both the research and policy levels, there needs to be a greater appreciation of the powerful systemic forces that are represented by processes of environmental dispossession, and how these forces shape the contemporary social and material determinants of First Nations' health (Richmond & Ross, 2009; Marmot, 2007; O'Neil, 1995).

There are a number of ways forward. The use of community-based participatory research (CBPR) is a promising research practice for research with Indigenous communities. A CBPR approach represents a way of doing research whereby both researchers and community work together to set the research questions, identify the methodology, participate in data collection and tool development, interpret findings, and disseminate the research results (Israel et al., 2005; Minkler, 2005). Who, other than the community itself, best knows its health needs?

In a recent chapter (Tobias et al., 2013), we highlight the ways we worked with Anishinabe communities on the north shore of Lake Superior and the protocols we followed. For many community organizations and Indigenous scholars, this approach is not a new one—many researchers who work with and for their own communities have endorsed this approach to ensure that research has benefits for both researchers and the researched (Wallerstein &

Duran, 2006; Macaulay et al., 1998). When done right, CBPR research can produce policy-relevant data that communities can use to meet their specific needs and desires. However, as many have cautioned (Castleden, Morgan, & Lamb, 2012; de Leeuw, Cameron, & Greenwood, 2012b; Wallerstein & Duran, 2006), a CBPR approach to Indigenous research must not be taken lightly; at the community and institutional levels, these research relationships must be built upon a foundation of trust, reciprocity, and—perhaps most significantly—a shared philosophical understanding of both the research problem and the envisioned outcome.

The overarching objective of this chapter is meant to highlight the incredible relationship between Anishinabe people and the land, and to draw on this example as a way to overcome some of the most pressing health issues in Canada today. As stated earlier, one of the key objectives of this chapter is to direct the Indigenous health research focus back to questions of land; to encourage researchers to work with communities to identify the multiple meanings and functions of the land for health and cultural identity; and to use this research to develop community-led strategies that will get people, including youth, back on the land.

This chapter also challenges researchers to conceptualize the wider body of "Indigenous health research" from a resource-centred paradigm rather than from the current redundant, deficits-based model (Richmond, Ross, & Egeland, 2007). Though we cannot expect to see rapid changes in the social, economic, and health conditions of First Nations communities, as researchers we can take control over the ways we approach health research with Indigenous peoples and communities, for instance, by making a conscious effort to outline the successes we have witnessed in Indigenous health over the years, and to challenge other researchers to draw from similar models in their work.

There is much to be said about community resilience and the role of human agency in initiating social movements that mobilize Indigenous communities to move from suffering and dispossession to equality and health. For example, the Nuu-chah-nulth and Cowichan peoples of British Columbia report that assuming jurisdiction over the medical services of their communities has served a decolonizing agenda, defined as increasing community self-esteem, enhancing skills, and allowing for revitalization of their own healing traditions (Read, 1995; Modeste et al., 1995). The challenge, of course, remains making such successes a possibility for the Indigenous population as a whole. In a research area that has historically centred on disparity, inequity, and difference with non-Indigenous populations, an approach focused on success, healing, and happiness should provide a refreshing and hopeful direction for Canadian Indigenous health researchers.

Perhaps most importantly, however, there needs to be recognition that investments in activities like this will need time to take root at the community level and commitment to this work for the long term as the health benefits of these activities will not manifest quickly (Bryant et al., 2011; Reading & Wien, 2009; Durie, 2005; Marmot, 2007). The consequences of environmental dispossession on the health of First Nations peoples have been ongoing for several centuries now. In attempts to repossess land and cultural traditions, we need to be patient, to trust in the stories and wisdom of the Elders, and have faith that the burden of the inequitable fight for improved health will not be for First Nations communities to carry alone.

References

Adelson, N. (2003). *Being alive well: Health and the politics of Cree well-being.* Toronto, ON: University of Toronto Press.

Battiste, M., & Henderson, J. (2000). *Protecting Indigenous knowledge and heritage: A global challenge.* Saskatoon, SK: Purich Publishing.

Baum, F. (2007). Cracking the nut of health equity: Top down and bottom up pressure for action on the social determinants of health. *Promotion & Education, 14,* 90–95.

Baum, F. E., Laris, P., Fisher, M., Newman, L., & MacDougall, C. (2013). "Never mind the logic, give me the numbers": Former Australian health ministers' perspectives on the social determinants of health. *Social Science & Medicine, 87,* 138–146.

Berkes, F. (2012). *Sacred ecology: Traditional ecological knowledge and resource management.* Philadelphia: Taylor & Francis.

Berrang-Ford, L., Dingle, K., Ford, J. D., Lee, C., Lwasa, S., Namanya, D. B., . . . & Edge, V. (2012). Vulnerability of Indigenous health to climate change: A case study of Uganda's Batwa Pygmies. *Social Science & Medicine, 75,* 1067–1077.

Berry, H. L., Butler, J. R., Burgess, C. P., King, U. G., Tsey, K., Cadet-James, Y. L., . . . & Raphael, B. (2010). Mind, body, spirit: Co-benefits for mental health from climate change adaptation and caring for country in remote Aboriginal Australian communities. *New South Wales Public Health Bulletin, 21,* 139–145.

Bryant, T., Raphael, D., Schrecker, T., & Labonte, R. (2011). Canada: A land of missed opportunity for addressing the social determinants of health. *Health Policy, 101,* 44–58.

Castleden, H., Morgan, V. S., & Lamb, C. (2012). "I spent the first year drinking tea": Exploring Canadian university researchers' perspectives on community-based participatory research involving Indigenous peoples. *Canadian Geographer, 56,* 160–179.

Czyzewski, K. (2011). Colonialism as a broader social determinant of health. *International Indigenous Policy Journal, 2*(1).

Davidson-Hunt, I. J. (2003). Indigenous lands management, cultural landscapes, and Anishinaabe people of Shoal Lake, northwestern Ontario, Canada. *Environments, 31,* 21–42.

de Leeuw, S., Cameron, E. S., & Greenwood, M. L. (2012b). Participatory and community-based research, Indigenous geographies, and the spaces of friendship: A critical engagement. *Canadian Geographer, 562,* 180–194.

de Leeuw, S., Maurice, S., Holyk, T., Greenwood, M., & Adam, W. (2012a). With reserves: Colonial geographies and First Nations health. *Annals of the Association of American Geographers, 102,* 904–911.

Deloria, V. (1995). *Red earth, white lies: Native Americans and the myth of scientific fact.* New York, NY: Scribners.

Deloria, V. (2003). *God is red: A native view of religion.* Golden, CO: Fulcrum Publishing.

Durie, M. (2005). *Indigenous health reforms: Best health outcomes for Māori in New Zealand.* Palmerston North: Massey University.

Ermine, W., Nilson, R., Sauchyn, D., et al. (2005). Isi Askiwan—the state of the land: Summary of the Prince Albert Grand Council Elders' forum on climate change. *Journal of Aboriginal Health, 2,* 62–72.

Garnett, S. T., Sithole, B., Whitehead, P. J., Burgess, C. P., Johnston, F. H., & Lea, T. (2009). Healthy country, healthy people: Policy implications of links between Indigenous human health and environmental condition in tropical Australia. *Australian Journal of Public Administration, 68,* 53–66.

Green, D., King, U., & Morrison, J. (2009). Disproportionate burdens: The multidimensional impacts of climate change on the health of Indigenous Australians. *Medical Journal of Australia, 190,* 4–5.

Hunting, G., & Browne, A. J. (2012). Decolonizing policy discourse: Reframing the "problem" of fetal alcohol spectrum disorder. *Women's Health and Urban Life, 11,* 35–53.

Israel, B., Eng, E., Schulz, A., & Parker, E. (2005). *Methods in community-based participatory research for health.* San Francisco, CA: Jossey-Bass.

LaDuke, W. (1999). *All our relations: Native struggle for lands and life.* London, UK: Zed Books.

Luginaah, I., Smith, K., & Lockridge, A. (2010). Surrounded by Chemical Valley and "living in a bubble": The case of the Aamjiwnaang First Nation, Ontario. *Journal of Environmental Planning and Management, 53,* 353–370.

Macaulay, A. C., Delormier, T., McComber, A. M., Cross, E. J., Potvin, L. P., Paradis, G., et al. (1998). Participatory research with Native community of Kahnawake creates innovative code of research ethics. *Canadian Journal of Public Health, 89,* 105–108.

Marmot, M. (2007). Achieving health equity: From root causes to fair outcomes. *Lancet, 370,* 1153–1163.

McGregor, D. (2011). Aboriginal/non-Aboriginal relations and sustainable forest management in Canada: The influence of the Royal Commission on Aboriginal peoples. *Journal of Environmental Management, 92*, 300–310.

Minkler, M. (2005). Community-based research partnerships: Challenges and opportunities. *Journal of Urban Health, 82*, ii3–ii12.

Modeste, D., Elliott, D., Gendron, C., Greenwell, B., Johnny, D., Payne, H., Peekeekoot, G., Peter, R., Rice, R., & Williams, C. (1995). *S'huli'utl Quw'utsun*/the spirit of Cowichan: A journey through the Tsewultun Health Centre/*uytseep Qu Nu Siiye'yu Kwun's 'I M'I Ewu'u Tuna Tsewultun*. In P. H. Stephenson, S. J. Elliott, L. T. Foster, & J. Harris (Eds.), *A persistent spirit: Towards understanding Aboriginal health in British Columbia* (pp. 331–356). Victoria: Western Geographical Press.

Natcher, D. C., Hickey, C. G., Nelson, M., & Davis, S. (2009). Implications of tenure insecurity for Aboriginal land use in Canada. *Human Organization, 68*, 245–257.

O'Bonsawin, C. M. (2010). "No Olympics on stolen Native land": Contesting Olympic narratives and asserting Indigenous rights within the discourse of the 2010 Vancouver Games. *Sport in Society, 13*, 143–156.

O'Neil, J. D. (1995). Issues in health policy for Indigenous peoples in Canada. *Australian Journal of Public Health, 19*, 559–566.

Parlee, B., Berkes, F., & Gwich'in, T. (2005). Health of the land, health of the people: A case study on Gwich'in berry harvesting in northern Canada. *Ecohealth, 2*, 127–137.

Parlee, B., & Furgal, C. (2012). Well-being and environmental change in the Arctic: A synthesis of selected research from Canada's International Polar Year program. *Climatic Change, 115*, 13–34.

Read, S. (1995). Issues in health management promoting First Nations wellness in times of change. In P. H. Stephenson, S. J. Elliott, L. T. Foster, & J. Harris (Eds.), *A persistent spirit: Towards understanding Aboriginal health in British Columbia* (pp. 297–330). Victoria: Western Geographical Press.

Reading, C. L., & Wien, F. (2009). *Health inequalities and the social determinants of Aboriginal peoples' health*. Prince George, BC: National Collaborating Centre for Aboriginal Health.

Richmond, C. A., & Ross, N. A. (2009). The determinants of First Nation and Inuit health: A critical population health approach. *Health & Place, 15*, 403–411.

Richmond, C. A., Ross, N. A., & Egeland, G. M. (2007). Social support and thriving health: A new approach to understanding the health of Indigenous Canadians. *American Journal of Public Health, 97*, 1827–1833.

Rigby, C. W., Rosen, A., Berry, H. L., & Hart, C. R. (2011). If the land's sick, we're sick: The impact of prolonged drought on the social and emotional well-being of Aboriginal communities in rural New South Wales. *Australian Journal of Rural Health, 19*, 249–254.

Takeda, L., & Røpke, I. (2010). Power and contestation in collaborative ecosystem-based management: The case of Haida Gwaii. *Ecological Economics, 70*, 178–188.

Tobias, J., Richmond, C. A. M., & Luginaah, I. (2013). Community-based participatory research (CBPR) with Indigenous communities: Producing respectful and reciprocal research. *Journal of Empirical Research on Human Research Ethics, 8,* 129–140.

Turner, N. J., Plotkin, M., Kuhnlein, H. V., Erasmus, B., Spigelski, D., & Burlingame, B. (2013). Global environmental challenges to the integrity of Indigenous peoples' food systems. In H. V. Kuhnlein, B. Erasmus, D. Spigelski, & B. Burlingame (Eds.), *Indigenous peoples' food systems and well-being: Interventions and policies for healthy communities* (pp. 23–38). Rome: Food and Agriculture Organization of the United Nations.

Wallerstein, N. B., & Duran, B. (2006). Using community-based participatory research to address health disparities. *Health Promotion Practice, 7,* 313–323.

Wilson, K. (2003). Therapeutic landscapes and First Nations peoples: An exploration of culture, health, and place. *Health & Place, 9,* 83–93.

Windsor, J. E., & McVey, J. A. (2006). Annihilation of both place and sense of place: The experience of the Cheslatta T'En Canadian First Nation within the context of large-scale environmental projects. *Geographical Journal, 171,* 146–166.

Wotherspoon, T., & Hansen, J. (2013). The "Idle no more" movement: Paradoxes of First Nations inclusion in the Canadian context. *Social Inclusion, 1,* 21–36.

CHAPTER 7

Being at the Interface

Early Childhood as a Determinant of Health

Margo Greenwood[1] and Elizabeth Jones

The two-rowed wampum belt is a visual representation of the agreement between different peoples. Some say the white-beaded background of the belt represents the "river of life" while the two parallel rows of purple beads represent the two separate peoples travelling the same river. As I listened to the Mohawk woman speaking at a conference about the two-rowed wampum belt, many stories flowed through my mind, especially stories that teach us about our relationships with one another. My *Moshum* (Grandfather) used to say to me, "always do things in a 'good way.'" These two little words hold a world of meaning—they not only speak to my interactions with other individuals, but also guide my behaviours now as an adult and as a member of a collective that is both marginalized and oppressed in our own land. As I contemplated these things, my mind floated back to the old stories and just how it was that I came to understand the lessons in each and how it is that I teach these lessons to my sons. Of one thing I am sure, it will be for our children, and through them, that we will realize not only our individual health and well-being, but ultimately our collective peace.

~

Early childhood is where identity development begins. For Indigenous children, development of cultural identity is a pathway to survival and well-being. In her writing on health inequities and Indigenous peoples, Cree scholar Madeleine Dion Stout (2012; see also Chapter 13 in this book) states that to achieve a paradigm shift, interventions must focus not on equality but on "fairness" or *nahi*. For *nahi* to be realized, values and inequities must be the focus (p. 12). Values of democracy and nationhood, freedom and equality or *nahi* are at the heart of this discussion of early childhood development and Indigenous children.

Dismal health disparities are the reality of marginalized and oppressed Indigenous peoples around the world. The challenge goes beyond ensuring the availability and cultural appropriateness of health services for children to the question of respect for the Indigenous cultures within which these children are growing up. In the world of public health, where social determinants are seen as central to health outcomes, this question points to the need for systemic and structural change in order to realize the optimal health and well-being of Indigenous children. This fundamental need pushes on normative understandings of early childhood development as a determinant of health by focusing on dimensions of well-being not often considered, including children's roles within the collective and their relationships to the collective.

This chapter explores some of those dimensions of well-being, focusing on the development of young Aboriginal children and their role in cultural continuity, both as individuals and members of their collective, as they negotiate multiple realities. The chapter also examines the practical challenges of developing and implementing early childhood programs specifically for Indigenous children.

WHEN TWO WORLDS MEET: PLACES OF INTERFACE

In all of our considerations of the well-being of Indigenous children, we must take into account their experiences both as individuals and as members of collectives; it is not possible to separate the two. Indigenous children hold a unique place in our collective: they embody the past through our teachings, they experience the present, and they hold our dreams for the future. Their individual identities ensure collective cultural continuity. Historical and continuing assaults on Indigenous children's identity development are reflected in Indigenous peoples' health and well-being today; we can envisage even greater loss in the disappearance of distinct cultures and their diverse ways of knowing and being. This loss of cultures and knowledge(s) diminishes the richness of all humanity.

Many times I have been told to look to the past to inform the future. I reach back once again to the old stories and the Elders' teachings so that I can understand the realities I find myself in. These realities are not mine alone, but form part of the context in which our children—my children—grow and learn. In the tradition of our storytellers, I offer these stories and ideas as a catalyst to questions and to your own ideas of how we relate to each other. The following is an old story that varies in its telling, yet in each rendition the importance of relationships and harmony with each other and the environment are fundamental.[2] This is the story as I remember it.

COYOTE'S EYES

A long time ago, when the mountains were the size of salmon eggs, Coyote came upon Rabbit. Rabbit was singing a special song. As he sang, his eyes flew out of his head and landed on the branch of a nearby tree. Then Rabbit would sing the song again and his eyes would fly off the branch and land back in his eye sockets. Now Coyote was really taken with what Rabbit was doing. He began to beg and plead with Rabbit to teach him his song. Coyote really wanted to learn Rabbit's song, so he kept pleading and begging Rabbit. Finally Rabbit said, "All right Coyote, I will teach you my song, but you have to remember to never sing it more than three times in one day." Now Coyote readily agreed; what he did not know was that Rabbit's song was a spiritual song and had a power of its own.

Coyote practised his song and as he sang, his eyes flew out of his head and when he sang the song again, his eyes flew back into his head. Now Coyote was very proud of his accomplishment and wanted to share his success. He walked to a nearby village and called all the humankind to come out and watch him. He sang his song again and again, and each time he did, his eyes flew out of his head and landed on a nearby branch; when he sang the song again, his eyes flew back into his head. Now Coyote lost track and sang his song over and over again until suddenly, when he sang his song, his eyes did not come back; instead, they just sat on the branch looking down at him. Coyote sang the song again and again and still his eyes did not move. Now the people had begun to snicker and whisper and before too long they were laughing right out loud. After a time, Coyote, with his head down, tail between his legs, slunk out of the village sad and crying.

He continued down the road for some time when he heard a tiny little voice say, "Coyote, why are you so sad?" It was the voice of Mouse. Coyote told Mouse what had happened to him. He was so sad. Mouse thought for a moment and then said, "Coyote I have two eyes, I will give you one of my eyes so you can see." So little Mouse took one of his eyes and gave it to Coyote. Now we all know that a mouse's eye is much smaller than a coyote's, so when Coyote put Mouse's eye into his eye socket, it rolled around and offered Coyote glimpses of light, like a prism, just enough so Coyote could make out the trail. Coyote left Mouse and continued on his way.

Now Coyote was still feeling very sorry for himself, crying and seeing tiny glimpses of the world. All of a sudden he heard a deep, booming voice say, "Coyote, why are you crying?" It was the voice of Buffalo. Coyote told Buffalo his story and Buffalo was greatly moved. He thought for a bit and then said, "Coyote, I have two eyes, I will give you one of mine so that you can see where you are going." Now we all know that buffalo eyes are much larger than a coyote's, so when Coyote tried to put Buffalo's eye into his eye socket, he had to really push and shove and even then the eye hung over half of his face. Because the eye was so large, it let in huge amounts of light, almost blinding Coyote, and everything he looked at seemed twice as large. So here was Coyote staggering along the trail with mismatched eyes that forced him to learn to see the world differently.

There are many lessons to be learned from this story about our relationships in the world. One that especially characterizes the theme of this writing is being able to view the world from many places and to use these different perspectives to thrive in the world. We often switch perspectives as we navigate the complexities of our realities. I, like many children, am left wondering what it would be like not to have to switch world views or not to have to even think about doing so.

Mi'kmaw Elders Murdena and Albert Marshall offer us a guiding principle focused on the idea of multiple perspectives coming together for the common good. They call it "Two-Eyed Seeing" (see Chapter 2). Two-Eyed Seeing refers to the ability to see from one eye with the strengths of one way of knowing and to see from the other eye with the strengths of another way of knowing. Most important is using the eyes together, bringing diverse strengths to bear on understanding and making the world a better place today and in the future. Like Coyote's story, this principle acknowledges the diversity of cultures—their richness and their potential in creating a reality that is fit for all.

These stories and words cause me to remember the teachings of my *Moshum* one more time. Once when I asked him how he could be such a devout Catholic after having spent a decade of his life in residential schools, he said to me, "I take what is good and I leave the rest behind." This teaching, along with the others presented here, reminds me to take that which is good from all perspectives and use it for the benefit of all. These teachings are anchored in values of respect, of love, of caring and sharing, of truth and honesty, of humility, and of peace. With this knowledge and understanding comes responsibility—a responsibility to use the knowledge to create the change necessary for the common good. It is from this place that the inequities affecting our children today must be addressed so that in the future they, and those who are yet to come, will not experience such disparities.

WHEN TWO WORLDS MEET: GROWING UP BICULTURAL

> To young people my grandparents always said, "You'll do all right if your hands are both full to overflowing." One hand could be filled with the knowledge of the white man and the other could be filled with the knowledge of your ancestors. You could study the ancestors, but without a deep feeling of communication with them it would be surface learning and surface talking. Once you have gone into yourself and have learnt very deeply, appreciate it, and relate to it very well, everything will come very easily. They always said that if you have the tools of your ancestors and you have the tools of the White man, his speech, his knowledge, his ways, his courts, his government, you'll be able to deal with a lot of things at his level. You'll not be afraid to say anything you want. . . . When your hands are both full with the knowledge of both sides, you'll grow up to be a great speaker, great organizer, great doer, and a helper of your people. (Elder Ellen White, cited in Neel, 1992, p. 108)

Our children live in a complex reality with a myriad of possibilities. They live not in one community, but in two or more. They are challenged to become proficient at code-switching with confidence and understanding depending on what community they find themselves in. This competence begins in early childhood, when it is most easily and deeply acquired. Some term this as being bicultural.

Becoming bicultural is a result of a dual socialization process that requires you to hold multiple ideas in your head at one time and to imagine and experiment with the relationships between them (Jones & Cooper, 2006, p. 39). Growing up bicultural:

1. offers generational continuity, identity, and pride. It develops confident intelligence—the capacity for smart thinking and decision making;

2. teaches the ability to code-switch—to size up the situation, name it, and behave in the cultural mode appropriate to the time and place; and

3. is a disposition essential in the diverse modern world society. It is smarter and more effective than embeddedness in one's own ethnocentric assumptions. It contributes to empathy and the capacity for perspective taking and conflict resolution and peacemaking.

Coming to know and understand more than one culture requires a solid enculturation into one culture—into the security of belonging and knowing and being known. Acculturation—that is, taking on another culture—requires the construction of logical knowledge, of things and events in relationships, beyond simple absorption of social knowledge. The challenge of acculturation is assimilation, the risk of losing one's roots while adapting to others' culture(s). It is both an individual risk and, ultimately, a collective one. If even one generation of children is assimilated, the unique values of the culture and its language can vanish.

In Canada, at least five generations of Indigenous children were taken from their families and communities and sent to residential schools. Reclaiming these cultures is imperative to their survival and continuity, but the process of reclamation is complicated by a colonial legacy.

For colonized Indigenous peoples around the globe, becoming bicultural may not, in fact, be attainable because of deeply embedded racism supported by systemic and structural attributes of society. However, if enculturation is solid—if one's roots are a source of pride—then adult identity has a significant element of choice in a multicultural society. Some people will retain strong identification with their culture of origin; some will not. Yet, for oppressed Indigenous peoples, maintenance of distinct cultures and a collective nationalism is crucial for them to create the transformation and change necessary to combat oppression and the subsequent inequities in health and well-being they experience.

Nobody wants to believe that their culture will not last as they experience it. However, cultures are not static if contact between cultures occurs; the people constituting those cultures adapt, creating new patterns while selectively retaining the old. Some old traditions will die—this is a loss to be mourned, but it cannot be avoided. I recall Mary (a Secwepemc Elder teacher of mine) telling me about the changes that she experienced in her 80-plus years, and how she would not be wearing her buckskins into town like she used to as a child. She also contemplated the future, speculating how the world would change if a "new" ice age were to come and how "new" animals would inhabit the Earth. I am reminded of Grandfather's words again: "take what is good and leave the rest behind." This teaching is meant to guide us in navigating our realities; the "how" is up to us.

Despite the complexity of the realities we find ourselves in, it is the relationships at the interface of cultures that offer possibilities for finding ourselves among competing pressures and potentials. Cree scholar Willie Ermine describes the space between two worlds as a safe place where we can come to understand each other and where we can imagine a world free of oppression and inequity. He says that "it's a gift to walk in two worlds, but also a responsibility. Ethical space does not exist unless you look at it [and] affirm it" (Ford, 2006, n.p.). Rather than ruptures and expressions of "power over," these interfaces can be places of endless potential. The question is: How do we teach these things to our children?

PRACTICAL CHALLENGES: HOW IS IT DONE?

How do we teach our children to make choices that do not compromise their cultural integrity now or in the future and allow them to be successful in diverse communities?

In the Early Childhood Setting

In her observations of language and literacy development in southern American mountain communities, Heath (1983) observed that children of Trackton, a black working-class community, grew up in the midst of adult events in the community. Like many Indigenous children, they were good improvisers of play. In the early 1970s, preschools were introduced into the area to improve school readiness (not unlike the introduction of early childhood programs in the mid-1990s in First Nations communities on-reserve and for Indigenous children residing in urban settings in Canada). Heath (1983) explains how, although teachers in the newly introduced preschools set up areas for various activities (block building, reading, puppets and dolls, etc.), "children from Trackton and similar communities were puzzled by the space-function ties the teachers expected them to recognize and obey" (Heath, 1983, p. 273). Instead, when teachers told them to play, the children "interpreted play as improvisation and creation [which] called for flexibility in the mingling of materials and the mixing of items from different parts of the room" (Heath,

1983, p. 273). Heath describes the frustration experienced by the mismatch between teachers' expectations about structured activities and the children's early experiences at home:

> At school, there was a time to sit down, a time to listen, a time to draw, a time to eat, and a time to nap; once engaged in an activity, one was not bound by the limit of completion of the task, but by the limit of time allotted for that task. Trackton children had, before their entry to school, lived in a flow of time in which their wants had been met in accordance with the accessibility of individuals who could meet their needs and the availability of provisions. Trackton children from a very early age seemed to initiate a play activity purposefully, almost appearing to have a plan for the task mapped out in their minds. . . . In the preschool, they found it frustrating to have the clay or paints taken away from them before they finished their preconceived project; they resisted having toys put away before they had been able to complete a play strategy in progress. At home there had been few constraints on time; children had not been admonished to sleep, eat or play within certain blocks of time. At home, there were no timed tasks or time-task limits. (Heath, 1983, pp. 275–276)

School (including preschools) is the creation of an industrialized society characterized by synchronicity—clock time (Toffler, 1980). Subsistence modes of living, still found in many parts of the world, follow more spontaneous rhythms, and children reared in such communities develop skills of playfulness, collaboration, and persistence that may be at odds with the clock-watching that characterizes factories, offices, and schools.

Do children in the contemporary world need to learn that clocks are important and that puzzle pieces should not be lost? Yes indeed. Can they learn these things in ways that support biculturality—savvy code-switching and help to maintain their Indigeneity? We think so.

In play, children recreate experience by using symbols that reflect the culture or cultures they are living and growing in. Berk and Winsler (1995) point out that imaginary play is the child's growing edge—in play, the child is stretched to behave "a head taller than him or herself" (p. 52). Further, imaginative play is the most effective context for stimulating a young child's cognitive development because he or she uses symbols to communicate meaning to other players.

Play is also socially constructed and dynamic as children negotiate meanings "seamlessly" from within the frame of the play. This becomes particularly interesting when considering whether Indigenous children can learn about their culture through play in formalized early childhood settings. In this regard, play becomes the vehicle for learning to be, to make meaning, to understand; one could call this the "ontology of play."

Can children learn culture through play? What is the role of the teacher? In her writing about the Tungasuvvingat Inuit Head Start in Ottawa, Reynolds (1999) explores these questions. The Head Start site provided a unique setting in which to discover how teachers in a setting for urban Inuit children are using a rich environment, thoughtful teaching interventions, and quality play to cultivate children's knowledge of their Inuit roots. Reynolds (1999) found that children's curiosity is stimulated in an environment containing an array of strange and wonderful objects from the culture and toys suggestive of Inuit lifestyle, and where they have access to people with a history of living with the objects who want to explain and demonstrate their use. She describes this process:

> Ina takes out a big piece of dried caribou sinew. "What's that, Ina?" the ever curious, four year old Christian wants to know. "It's a thread for making clothing," is Ina's reply. Christian watches as Ina breaks off a long, thread-like piece. She continues, "You know what, my dad used this to clean his teeth. He goes like this." Holding the thread close to her mouth, Ina makes exaggerated flossing motions. They giggle. Christian imitates his teacher's flossing gesture and then asks for a try with the real thing. Christian experiments for several minutes to make the hairy, distasteful piece of caribou sinew work in the spaces between his teeth. . . . Ina describes how the opportunity to work with children to learn about Inuit traditions is bringing back many memories: ". . . today, when I am trying to plan, trying to think about our Inuit ways, my grandma is coming back. They [memories] are coming back to me since we started this program, gradually they're coming back." (Reynolds, 1999, pp. 59–60)

Reynolds's (1999) observations point to the necessity of caregivers and teachers being knowledgeable about the community, its ontology and epistemology, especially in early childhood programs in which the focus is on language and culture. In my own research with Elders, parents, and community leaders and members from First Nations in Canada, the desire for caregivers/teachers to be members of their community, as well as "credentialed" workers, was apparent (Greenwood, 2009). Fulfilling this desire demands that caregivers and teachers must have access to knowledge from community, as well as from outside the community—for example, from early childhood programs offered at post-secondary institutions.

However, there is always a risk when different ways of knowing come into contact with one another. Knowledge gained in early childhood training programs may conflict with the ways of the community. So while accessing multiple sources of knowledge may be challenging, the greater challenge will come in negotiating the space between knowledge systems and deciding when to privilege one source of knowledge over another, or when to combine them and create something new. In these instances, I am reminded of Madeleine Dion Stout's words about *nahi* (i.e., fairness).

Early childhood programs situated in urban locations present special challenges to the reclamation and maintenance of Indigenous cultures. Indeed, as Ball (2005) points out, "Models of child and family support and health care that may be acceptable or effective in urban centres in Canada are frequently not acceptable nor effective in rural and remote circumstances, especially when these are compounded with significant cultural and lifestyle differences" (p. 42). It is also likely that many early childhood programs will have children attending from different cultural backgrounds. For these families, dual-language (at the very least), culture-focused, play-based preschools become essential.

While addressing this diversity presents challenges, it also provides us with opportunities by forcing us to think about how to meet the multiple and singular demands for specific languages and cultural expressions. In some settings, this challenge is met by teaching the language of the tribal group in which the early childhood setting is located. In other settings, the language and ways of the majority of children are taught. Still in other settings, the language of the program is determined on the basis of who is teaching the children—for example, the dialect of the *kaiako* in an urban *Te Kohanga Reo* (Maori language nests).

There is no singular response to this challenge of diversity—nor should there be. There are, rather, multiple considerations necessary to determine how to address it. One place to start is through contemplation of Indigeneity, including conditions that enable, foster, and support its development. A concrete step toward realizing Indigeneity is the inclusion of families and communities in program decision making, particularly regarding what is to be taught and how it is to be taught (Greenwood, 2009, p. 243).

Engaging the Collective:
Families, Communities, and Tribes

How do we engage families, communities, and tribes in formalized early childhood settings?

Families and Communities

From a decolonizing and cultural continuity perspective it makes sense to support families and communities in developing early childhood programs that focus on their language and culture. Focused programs provide children with opportunities to learn their specific ways of knowing and being, thereby ensuring cultural continuity along with the health and well-being of individual children and future generations. There are many pathways to realizing these aspirations, and the following pages present some of those ways.

A first step along the path is to support, encourage, and strengthen those who have the knowledge and language ability to pass it on to succeeding generations. Structuring the practice of language teaching, providing opportunities for teaching and learning the language, and connecting speakers with each other in efforts to revitalize language within tribal groupings are ways to support knowledge holders (Greenwood, 2009).

Along with supporting knowledge holders, there is a need to raise the collective consciousness of community members so that early childhood programs are understood as not only supporting individual children's health and well-being, but also as a concrete step toward supporting the collective and realizing nationhood. In part, the opportunity provided by early childhood programs is perceived in the conscious conceptualization of children as entities in and through which to undertake decolonizing processes. This means valuing children and their centrality to Indigenous collectives even more for their role in cultural survival, reinforcing the focus on identity formation. Leadership for this consciousness raising must come from First Nations peoples and their collective communities (Greenwood, 2009).

The construct of family may be drawn upon and supported to develop and implement Indigenous-specific early childhood programs and services. Families are the building blocks of community. They are the cornerstone through which children learn and grow. Recognition of the role of family in First Nations–specific early childhood programs and services is a first step to building early childhood programs that are congruent with family (and thus collective) ways of knowing and being. Including families in decision making and administration of early childhood programs, as well as teaching the children, rejuvenates and places control of programs and services in the hands of families and communities.

Community governance systems—for example, longhouse ceremonies of the coastal peoples and the *bah'lats* of the Carrier peoples—provide another construct upon which to build early childhood programs. They, too, build on family structures and may serve as formal decision-making mechanisms at the community and regional levels. Together, these actions provide necessary opportunities for building on the strengths and ways of the cultural collective—fostering the growth and development of children, supporting the rejuvenation of families, and building collective capacities.

First Nations and Tribal Groupings

Indigenous knowledge(s) and languages are geographically specific, rooted in the land. Cultural expressions are reflections of relationships with specific environments and the actions within them. In considering this context of geographic specificity, it makes sense to build on those structures in developing culturally specific early childhood programs. Tribal groupings of First Nations and the structures (particularly governance structures) embedded in their environments and bounded by specific languages and cultural practice hold the essences of teachings for children. The sharing of language and cultural resources among members of a tribal grouping distributes responsibility for those resources to multiple nations rather than a single nation or group, and through this sharing, opportunities for horizontal learning between First Nations, communities, and among groups within community can be made apparent. For example, where few language speakers or limited cultural resources remain, resources from neighbouring First Nations may support their revitalization and reconstruction. This example of horizontal learning and sharing can also be applied to the training of early childhood caregivers.

Training modules specific to a tribal grouping of First Nations should be tied to the community and tribe by both the content and processes of the curriculum. These portions of early childhood training should belong to the community and would require similar resources and supports as non-Indigenous early childhood curriculum offered by post-secondary institutions. Partnerships with local post-secondary institutions, which also hold knowledge for the care of children, may lead to the credentialing of caregivers and early childhood programs under the auspices of provincial and territorial governments. In this vision, a partnership between the local post-secondary institution and

First Nations tribal grouping would provide culturally meaningful training for caregivers by creating an "ethical space" in which diverse knowledge systems and sharing of specific knowledge are recognized and promoted.

Culturally specific and meaningful programs will also necessitate changes to provincial and territorial early childhood post-secondary program accreditation, as well as to certification of individuals and program licensing. This credentialing of individuals' specific tribal knowledge demands the involvement of Elders and/or knowledgeable community members. In such a context, external credentialing and licensing bodies take a secondary rather than primary oversight role. An example of this is the attestation process used in Aotearoa/New Zealand (where the *Kaumaatua,* or Elders, verify and attest to the teacher's proficiency with the language), which could be a new step to credentialing and licensing. Ultimately, the desire is to have the credentialing of programs and individual practitioners reside with First Nations and/or groupings in their distinct tribal areas (Greenwood, 2009).

CONCLUSION

I go back now to where I began thinking about early childhood, a place of endless possibility where identity development begins. And in this circle are the pathways for living in a world of multiple realities. It is the teachings of our past that guide our footsteps into the future.

I am reminded of Willie Ermine's words once again: "It's a gift to walk in two worlds, but also a responsibility. Ethical space does not exist unless you look at it and affirm it" (Ermine, cited in Ford, 2006). Ermine's teachings, like those in the Coyote story and those of the Marshalls, focus on the interface and possibility offered when two worlds meet. Rather than ruptures and expressions of "power over," these interfaces can be places of endless possibility for making the world a better place for all—and most especially for our children.

We are the teachers. It is our responsibility to ensure that our children's hands are full "with the knowledge of both sides" so that they will grow up to be a "great doer, and a helper of [their] people" (Ellen White, cited in Neel, 1992). In this way our circle is complete: "And, Coyote will continue on his journey, negotiating the world and finding all sorts of possibilities and adventures."

NOTES

1. This chapter offers text from both an individual and collective perspective. Those sections that are written from the individual first-person perspective are

authored by Margo Greenwood, with the remainder of the text developed by both authors.

2. A written version of this story by Terry Tafoya can be found in the August 1989 Special Edition of the *Journal of American Indian Education* at http://jaie.asu.edu/sp/V21S2coy.htm

REFERENCES

Ball, J. (2005). Early childhood care and development programs as hook and hub for inter-sectoral service delivery in First Nations communities. *Journal of Aboriginal Health, 1,* 36–53.

Berk, L., & Winsler, A. (1995). *Scaffolding children's learning: Vygotsky and early childhood education.* Washington, DC: National Association for the Education of Young Children.

Ford, D. (2006, March 17). *The space between two knowledge systems.* Retrieved from http://www.folio.ualberta.ca/43/14/11.html

Greenwood, M. G. (2009). *Places for the good care of children: A discussion of Indigenous cultural considerations and early childhood in Canada and New Zealand* (doctoral dissertation). University of British Columbia, Vancouver.

Heath, S. B. (1983). *Ways with words: Language, life, and work in communities and classrooms.* Cambridge, UK: Cambridge University Press.

Jones, E., & Cooper, R. (2006). *Playing to get smart.* New York: Teachers College Press.

Jones, E., & Nimmo, J. (1994). *Emergent curriculum.* Washington, DC: National Association for the Education of Young Children.

Neel, D. (1992). *Our chiefs and Elders: Words and photographs of Native leaders.* Vancouver: UBC Press.

Reynolds, G. (1999). Understanding culture through play. *Child Care Information Exchange, 1,* 58–60.

Stout, M. D. (2012). Ascribed health and wellness, *Atikowisi miýw-āyāwin,* to achieved health and wellness, *Kaskitamasowin miýw-āyāwin:* Shifting the paradigm. *Canadian Journal of Nursing Research, 44,* 11–14.

Tafoya, T. (1989). Coyote's eyes: Native cognition styles. *Journal of American Indian Education,* Special Issue, 29–42. Retrieved from http://jaie.asu.edu/sp/V21S2coy.htm

Toffler, A. (1980). *The third wave.* New York: Morrow.

CHAPTER 8

Cultural Wounds Demand Cultural Medicines

Michael J. Chandler and William L. Dunlop

Here are the two headline conclusions to which everything in this chapter is meant to inexorably lead—our "take home" messages, if you will. The *first* is that the sum total of malaise and ill health suffered by Canada's (and the world's) Indigenous peoples is best understood not as some simple aggregate or additive sum of the personal woes of separately damaged individuals, but as a culmination of "cultural wounds" inflicted upon whole communities and whole ways of life. Yes, of course, the raw nerve endings of those in distress are naturally wired to pain centres in the brains of individual sufferers, but the various forms of wholesale damage communally inflicted on whole peoples is collective rather than simply personal, and multiplicative rather than simply additive.

The *second* of these conclusions is that rather than dealing with one individual sufferer at a time, such shared cultural wounds require being addressed collectively and treated with "cultural medicines" prescribed and acted upon by whole cultural communities. Taken together, the broad implication of both of these position statements is that most suicide-prevention efforts have been like fishing in the wrong pond.

What hopefully rescues such summary pronouncements from the jaws of mere homily are the conceptual distances that divide them from those other more ruggedly individualistic frameworks of understanding that typically dominate descriptions of the plights of Indigenous groups—standard "medical model" frameworks within which poor health and well-being are routinely interpreted as "one-off" personal matters, best understood and best treated one Indigenous patient at a time.

Think of this chapter, then, as having ophthalmic intent—as part of a vision quest aimed at fitting those of you still in need of different optics with a more refractory and more collectivist set of Indigenous lenses. Not unlike those "too earnest for words" proselytizers always showing up at your door, we are also here, bent upon saving you from your own prior, if inadvertent, adherence to the West's cult-like commitment to "self-contained individualism" (Cushman, 1990, p. 599)—your own "Judeo-Graeco-Roman-Christian-Renaissance-Enlightenment-Romanticist"-inspired conviction (Rorty, 1987, p. 57) that bad things ordinarily happen to bad people, and that those individuals who do "fall by the wayside" are necessarily marked by some self-contained diathesis or weakness (perhaps of the will), requiring that they be individually diagnosed and separately treated.

If (whenever this shoe fits) we are successful in bringing you along to our own different and more collectivist viewpoint, you will of course remain just as free (as always) to go on ministering to individual sufferers, one "at-risk" victim at a time. This is, perhaps, what common humanity demands, and short of a plan that works to re-understand Indigenous suicide as a collective response to ongoing cultural assaults, the only option apparently available. You will, however, also have been brought to share some wider interpretive horizon that includes the prospect that there are also wounds that supersede the boundaries of single individuals, damaging whole cultural communities at once.

What is required, if our conversion tactics are to work, are clear and convincing reasons as to (1) why the lack of well-being characteristic of some (but, importantly, not all) Indigenous individuals can be understood best using explanatory tools capable of taking whole cultural communities as their operative units of analysis, and (2) why such shared woes require intervention strategies aimed at restoring to such wounded groups ownership and control of their own common past and collective futures. The balance of this account is meant to provide a starter kit of such reasons.

On Choosing a Working Case in Point

Because a short chapter such as this does not have enough space for even the simplest enumeration, let alone some attempted explanation, of all of the various woes now facing Indigenous peoples, some picking and choosing is required. Although prepared to argue that our choice has more generic implications, we choose (some may judge unfairly), as our working case in point, the so-called "epidemic" rates of suicide (especially youth suicide) common to many of the world's, or Canada's (and more particularly British Columbia's) Indigenous communities (British Columbia Vital Statistics Agency, 2001). We focus on suicide in British Columbia not only because we know this literature well enough to say something about it, and it is a population on which we have real data, but also because (unlike certain other ills common to many Indigenous groups—diabetes or alcohol excess, for example) suicide does not particularly lend itself to causal explanations rooted in the well-tilled turf of physiological or genetic accounts. It is a widely imagined and publically proclaimed "fact" that Indigenous groups (measured in the aggregate) do suffer unusually high and disproportionate rates of suicide—an assumed truth that has prompted the widespread view that Indigenous individuals are somehow especially suicide-prone, and has led a great many Indigenous groups in Canada to list suicide-prevention programs as priority services required by their communities (see Kirmayer, Fraser, Fauras, & Whitley, 2009).

If you simply lump together the whole of Canada's diverse Indigenous peoples, count all the suicides on record, and divide by the total number of individuals legislated to be Indigenous, then you will necessarily arrive at something like the startling, if largely meaningless, national suicide rates commonly reported. This is what is most commonly done, and the short judgment is that (as a running average) Canada's Indigenous peoples, and more particularly Indigenous youth, commit suicide at rates somewhere between three to 20 times the national average—numbers thought to be so high as to warrant the oft-repeated claim that our nation's overall rate of Indigenous suicide is "one of the highest. . .of any group in the world" (Kirmayer, 1994, p. 3).

Liar, Liar, Pants on Fire

The problem here is not that the actuaries have somehow gotten their sums wrong. Rather, the common practice of summing across all of a province's (or a nation's) culturally diverse Indigenous peoples, and mathematically arriving at some omnibus, catch-all, summary figure is best understood as a form of "voodoo statistics," yielding misleading numbers that prove a colossal disservice to all involved. Whatever their suspect value, such unadorned "actuarial fictions" regularly peg the overall national rate of suicide among Canada's Indigenous population as being somewhere around three or four times that of the general population. Such empty claims have so far provided the occasions for a public outcry, and a stingy commitment of minimal funds to "correct" the "problem."

Here are only some of the reasons that exposure to such artfully crafted, if misleading, numbers are worse than knowing nothing at all. First and foremost, such statistical artifacts reflect and promote racist assumptions by artificially homogenizing otherwise radically diverse Indigenous communities and "press-gang" them all under one common, politically inspired banner. Although all such crude labelling exercises (e.g., talk of the "blacks," the "Jews," the "Gays," etc.) perhaps arise out of the same stigmatizing intent, a case can be made that such loose talk about generic Indigenous or Aboriginal or Native people may actually win the prize for riding most roughshod over the reality of evident diversity. It has been argued, for example (Hodgkinson, 1990), that more than half of the cultural variability to be found across the whole of the Americas is owed to that small 3 or 4 percent of the population that just happens to be Indigenous.

In Canada, where some 500 to 600 distinctive Indigenous communities still exist, hundreds of mutually un-interpretable Indigenous languages continue to be spoken. Some of these speakers live on the seashore, others in the mountains or on the prairies, where they are marked by radically different spiritual beliefs, differing histories of contact with colonial forces, and distinctive forms of self-governance. Still more specifically, in British Columbia—the province from which yet more detailed information has been extracted (Chandler & Lalonde, 1998, 2009; Chandler, Lalonde, Sokol, & Hallett, 2003)—in excess of 200 unique Indigenous "bands" can currently be identified, none of which is, or wishes to be seen as, interchangeable with the others.

More to the present case in point, the suicide rates characteristic of these diverse bands are also known to be radically different (e.g., Chandler & Lalonde, 1998, 2009; Chandler et al., 2003). Almost exactly half of these 200-plus bands in the province of British Columbia have, for example, never experienced a youth suicide, not one—rates obviously well below that of the general population. Elsewhere, often close around the corner, and in communities not otherwise different according to usual demographic markers, other bands suffer youth suicide rates known to be more than 1,000 times the national average (Chandler & Lalonde, 2009). Clearly, any generic talk about some single, omnibus suicide rate for the whole of Canada's or British Columbia's Indigenous citizens is meaningless, representing a number that describes no one in particular and everyone especially badly.

What findings such as our own do, however (in one fell swoop), is to put the lie to any rumour that Indigenous peoples somehow have suicide bred into their bones—that being suicidal is somehow a by-product of Indigeneity itself. Rather, such findings effectively remove the "race card" from the deck, requiring us to find explanations elsewhere. How, we need to ask ourselves, while struggling against mounting odds to maintain some individualized, essentialized, blame-the-victim perspective on suicide, is it still possible to explain away the fact that neighbouring Indigenous communities have either no suicides or a suicide epidemic? Can you imagine, for example, that suicidal individuals living in apparently "suicide-free" zones somehow conveniently succeeded in moving to other communities especially marked by unusually high suicide rates just to make the numbers come out? Can you think of some other potentially plausible, but still individualistic, explanation? We dare you.

A second and perhaps still more far-reaching consequence of attempting to paint the whole of the Indigenous world with the same broad and indiscriminant brush is that doing so promotes the dangerously mistaken assumption that it is reasonable to imagine arriving at some ideal, one-size-fits-all intervention approach; some nation- or province-wide suicide-prevention strategy that lends itself to being universally put in place. No bureaucrat can long tolerate a patchwork, and so something like an omnibus suicide-prevention strategy is naturally the pipe dream of all centralized governments.

The Limits of Intervention and Prevention

As a consequence of the aforementioned, Canada, like many other concerned nations, is currently in the throes of a multi-pronged "natural" experiment, the usual interim protocol for which has been to encourage separate groups, including Indigenous communities, to invent their own "home-grown" suicide-prevention approach. Although in a more perfect world than this, such a free-for-all strategy might well have been (and perhaps sometimes was) motivated by a newfound commitment to eclecticism and a progressive (dare one say "postmodern") belief that any univocal search for some common, wide-spectrum, suicide-prevention elixir—one equally suitable as a purge against suicide in all quarters—is likely to prove a fool's errand. Rather, and more in keeping with Canada's own recurrent national search for the "golden mean" of Indigenous suicide rates (and so otherwise consistent with our common "free enterprise" approach to problem-solving), the overarching plan appears to have been to throw a lot of unlimited money on the floor, all in the hopes that some winning intervention strategy would somehow naturally disclose itself. This, or at least something like it, is what appears to have been done as varied but commonly befuddled interest groups have struggled to mount some sort of made-from-scratch suicide-prevention strategy.

The open question, you might well ask, is: How, most of a decade into this free-for-all experiment, have things been working out? Although it is still early days, and so one might reason it is still too soon to tell, a recent and especially thorough review of the North American literature carried out by Kirmayer and his colleagues (2009) has come to the harsh conclusion that, notwith-standing the untold millions of dollars invested, there is not a single shred of confidence-inspiring evidence that any of these exploratory, publicly funded suicide-prevention projects has actually worked to prevent a single death.

To be fair, more often than not, the hard-to-indemnify business of directly stopping suicide in its tracks has rarely been the expressed intention of most of these efforts. Instead, the majority of these endeavours have settled for more modest goals, such as educating people about suicide, sensitizing gate-keepers and others to possible early warning signs, or otherwise helping to manage the sad consequences of completed suicides. Admirable work, per-haps. Again, and more often than not, a great many of these intervention pro-grams have neglected to reveal how they came to know what is and is not an actual early warning sign of suicide (more on this later), and most have lacked any defensible strategy for evaluating their own success.

Of course, none of the above is meant to say that everyone involved is necessarily wasting one another's precious time. Some generous measure of compassion and human understanding is always morally required of us, espe-cially when the prospect of suicide is in the wind. Similarly, most (but not all) presume that it is better for everyone to know more rather than less about suicide, and to be prepared to do almost anything rather than nothing, when the prospects of self-harm are judged to be eminent. Still, that is presumably not what was originally hoped for when the public purse was initially opened to fund exploratory suicide-prevention research.

In Search of a Better Way

If everyone concerned is to find better ways of stemming the flood of suicides rising in many Indigenous communities and elsewhere, then it will prove necessary, we will argue, to come to some better understanding of a knot of tightly braided problems. The most central of these concerns is the task of determining an optimal level of analysis from which to approach the task of suicide prevention. Our recurrent refrain throughout this chapter has been, and will continue to be, that while suicide can be (and most commonly is) approached as a private problem hidden away in the secret hearts and minds of troubled individuals, it will prove more useful and coherent to re-envision suicide (especially Indigenous suicide) at the level of whole communities or cultural groups. Pursuing such a proposed shift in levels of analysis, as we mean to do here, also sets the shape of the two remaining strands of our knotty problem: anticipating when and where suicides are most likely to occur, and fashioning some explanatory theory that can be used to guide subsequent prevention efforts. Although it will involve working a bit back to front, the plan here is to first spend moments on the second and third of these matters before addressing, head-on, the choice to seek out some more appropriate cultural level of analysis.

On Anticipating When and Where Suicide Is Most Likely to Occur

Historically, and always within usual individualistic accounting systems, the traditional enterprise of suicide prevention has standardly begun by working to somehow divine who is and who is not at serious risk of committing suicide. Obviously, it is thought, we cannot intervene with everyone. It would, therefore, obviously be a good thing if we had demonstrable grounds for being confident in our ability to decide who really does and does not pose some serious risk to taking his or her own life—to actually know how to properly identify the signs of bona fide suicide in waiting. As it is, evidence that such predictive skills are to be had is similarly largely missing, and when present at all, seem to better resemble some form of art than science.

Given our collective commitment to some version of a conventional individualist framework of interpretation, it is hardly surprising that our efforts to witch-out who is and is not suicidal rarely work, and are likely forever doomed to failure. Consequently, and notwithstanding the fact that the chances of our being wrong are generally greater than our chances of being right, we continue to choose to act upon the shaky diagnostic information available, largely because we fear risking the costs and approbations of doing nothing. None of this sad account comes close to mere speculation, but reflects instead a stone-cold matter of brute, unsentimental probabilities. Here is why.

Suicides, whether in Indigenous or non-Indigenous populations, are spectacularly rare events, even when they are counted as occurring in epidemic proportion. Under usual circumstances, the national suicide rate among ordinary North American citizens is something like three or four per 100,000. In certain subpopulations (Indigenous youth, for example) the rates tend to be importantly higher, but almost never, to our knowledge, higher than one in 1,000, and, in the worst imaginable circumstances, one in 100. Given all of the above, if you simply predict that no one in the general population will ever commit suicide, you will be right some 99,996 times in 100,000 tries, and wrong on a paltry three or four occasions. No self-respecting bookmaker would bet against such odds. Rather, each and every attempt to pick out the suicidal from the non-suicidal proves to be like trying to catch lightning in a bottle.

You could, of course, hedge your bets by predicting suicide only when dealing with those who are manifestly depressed or marked by suicidal ideation, but depression is as common as clay, and the rate of suicidal ideation among ordinary adolescents has been shown to be about 50 percent (Meehan, Lamb, Saltzmen, & O'Carroll, 1992). But perhaps you have access to some newfangled psychometric tool that is touted to be a real state-of-the-art measure of suicidality. Using this measure you could conservatively decide to focus attention only on those who score above the ninetieth percentile, perhaps even the ninety-ninth. Still, despite your best and most cautious assessment efforts, your chance of beating the overall odds (again, three or four hits for every 99,000-plus misses) continue to remain vanishing, and you will be right much more frequently than wrong by simply always anticipating that suicide will never occur. Even locking in on groups of those who have already unsuccessfully made serious suicide attempts will not help. The vast majority of such suicide attempters do so only once (Haukka, Suominen, Partonen, & Lonnqvist, 2008).

Here, however, is one of the many rubs. While proceeding as though suicide simply never occurs may be statistically sound, choosing to do nothing at all naturally registers as cold and uncaring, and may not be among your morally acceptable alternatives. More troubling still, and working against most such "do-good" impulses is the contrapuntal injunction to "do no harm." As it is, most of the usual draconian measures that make up standard suicide-precaution protocols (e.g., no belts or shoelaces, no sharps, etc.) obviously rob people of their freedom, and likely do so on what usually turn out to be unsubstantiated whims. There you have it: the paradox that so often keeps those responsible for the safety and well-being of others so often frozen in place.

A Search for Some Theory or Working Model
to Tell Us What to Do Next

Not much needs or can be said here about individualized theories of suicidality other than to keep insisting that before attempting to prevent something bad, it would be good to have a theory about what actually causes the problem in the first place. As it is, and because the cult of the individual is very much with us, we are well awash in various psychodynamic accounts of what might lead particular people to be depressed, or have low self-esteem, or have no hope in the future. Still, the woods are full of individuals who are depressed or have low self-esteem or little in the way of hope, almost none of whom ever makes serious attempts on his or her own life. Many existing individualistic accounts promote a comfortable sense of better understanding, but what none of them do is actually predict who will and who will not commit suicide. Rather, when the improbable happens, our theories always allow us to invent some after-the-fact "just-so" story that makes everything seem copasetic. About what is likely to happen next, however, we all continue collectively flailing around in the dark. What all of this argues for, we insist, is that we have been searching for ways of understanding suicide at the wrong level of analysis. Of course, talk of level this and level that is always slippery at best, but given our wholesale failure to anticipate or prevent suicide, it seems useful to suppose that there is some different way of approaching this problem that is not fully rooted in the West's otherwise unwavering commitment to untrammelled individualism.

Conclusion: On Switching Levels of Analysis

The sobering reality is that we are particularly inept at picking out in advance which particular individuals are and are not likely to commit suicide. This, combined with the fact that we are both bereft of any convincing individual-level theory of suicide and unable to mount persuasive evidence that it can be prevented, should be enough to seriously disabuse anyone of further false hopes about getting the anatomy of individual suicides right and persuade them instead that we need to go shopping for some new levels of analysis from which to approach the problem.

On the working assumption that all of this is right, the final words on offer here are about how to best get such a new cultural-level of analysis off the ground. Here, our working example of doing just that is extracted from the decade and a half of work that we and our colleagues (e.g., Chandler & Lalonde, 1998, 2009; Chandler et al., 2003) have done on the anatomy of Indigenous youth suicide in British Columbia. Although this work has not been explicitly about so-called suicide prevention, it does contain, we will argue, a blueprint for how such preventative work might be undertaken. Here, already signalled earlier, is a quick synopsis of these earlier findings.

First, what this rolling program of ongoing data collection and analysis makes clear is that the problem of youth suicide is not evenly distributed across British Columbia's more than 200 First Nations bands. Rather, more or less half of the Indigenous communities in the province have no (i.e., zero, have never had any) youth suicides—a status that is repeated across 15 years of study and is in large part replicated at the aggregate level of whole "Tribal Councils" (Chandler & Lalonde, 1998, 2009). By sharp contrast, other less fortunate bands within the province suffer youth suicide rates an agonizing 1,000-plus times the national average. What is one to make of such radical differences among communities?

One response to such data is to wonder how, in the face of prevailing evidence, one could go on insisting that simply being Indigenous is, in and of itself, somehow a risk factor for suicide? A second and more interesting question asks what characteristics distinguish communities with low to absent youth suicide rates from other seemingly interchangeable Indigenous communities in which youth suicide is epidemic. It is this second matter that seems to hold out the best promise of fuelling a coherent program of suicide prevention.

The short answer to the question of what differentiates First Nations communities in British Columbia that have remarkably high and remarkably low rates of youth suicide is no longer a matter for mere speculation. The clear answer provided by our program of research is that communities that have low to absent youth suicide rates are different from their opposite numbers in that they are marked by multiple community-level efforts to achieve a high level of ownership of their own cultural past, and an elevated level of success in controlling their own civic futures. In particular, this means that Indigenous communities with low to absent rates of youth suicide tend to be characterized by such things as self-government, active involvement in attempts to restore title to traditional lands, to preserve Indigenous languages and culture, and to restore the historic place of women in tribal governance. In more forward-reaching ways, such communities have also made special strides in regaining control of their own educational practices and child-protection services, their former dominion over judicial and community safety matters, and have reassumed critical responsibility for ensuring the safety of their children and their own health and welfare. Whenever all of these markers of what we have called "cultural continuity" are present, the aggregate level of youth suicide drops to zero. Wherever such ambitions have been frustrated, the youth suicide rate is heartbreakingly high.

This is the evidence in hand. What is one to make of it when attention is turned to the problem of preventing youth suicide in those First Nations communities in which rates are impossibly high? One could, of course, stick with the failed assumption that the proper causes of suicide are still to be found hidden away in the troubled hearts and minds of single individuals. The problem is that all of our best efforts rooted in such individualistic assumptions have largely come to nothing. If youth suicide is the exclusive by-product of individualized hopes and dreams gone wrong, then how are we to understand that in certain otherwise like-minded communities suicide is epidemic and in others effectively absent? Even if it is true (i.e., that the frustrated hopes and dreams of single individuals are recipes for disaster), what does this tell us about what to do next? Intervention programs focused on ministering to such private ambitions regularly fail, not only because we have no skill at picking out who is the more disillusioned, but, more particularly, because such analyses leave us at sea about what we can actually do about such tragedies.

The more collective and culture-based alternative we advocate here (the next best thing, if you will) turns upon setting aside all of our earlier and failed hopes of picking out and somehow patching up all of those forlorn individuals with suicide on their private minds, and to argue that what is needed instead (or at least in addition) are community-level initiatives that have as their purpose both helping to rehabilitate those frayed connections that so many Indigenous communities struggle to maintain with their traditional pasts, and joining them in their ambitions to enjoy a measure of local control over their own uncertain futures. Our reasons for urging that we proceed in this (some would say roundabout) fashion include the plain facts: (1) that every attempt to put the onus of responsibility for suicide exclusively on the psychodynamic shoulders of those fallen individuals who directly manifest the collective wounds visited upon their lives and culture have failed, both conceptually and empirically; (2) that because of the radical variability in suicide rates known to exist across diverse cultural groups, all individualized, person-centred approaches have not only failed in the past, but will continue to fail to yield anything like convincing evidence of success; and (3) that available hard evidence about what separates Indigenous communities with high and low suicide rates makes it plain that our money and our energies would be better spent in joining with Indigenous communities in their quest to preserve their shared past and to militate for their own collective futures. A part of what this means is that if suicide prevention is our serious goal, then the evidence in hand recommends investing new moneys, not in the hiring of still more counsellors, but in organized efforts to preserve Indigenous languages, to promote the resurgence of ritual and cultural practices, and to facilitate communities in recouping some measure of community control over their own lives.

REFERENCES

British Columbia Vital Statistics Agency. (2001). *Analysis of health statistics for Status Indians in British Columbia: 1991–1999*. Vancouver, BC: Author.

Chandler, M. J., & Lalonde, C. E. (1998). Cultural continuity as a hedge against suicide in Canada's First Nations. *Transcultural Psychiatry, 35*, 191–219.

Chandler, M. J., & Lalonde, C. E. (2009). Cultural continuity as a moderator of suicide risk among Canada's First Nations. In L. J. Kirmayer & G. G. Valaskakis (Eds.), *Healing traditions: The mental health of Aboriginal peoples in Canada* (pp. 221–248). Vancouver, BC: UBC Press.

Chandler, M. J., Lalonde, C. E., Sokol, B. W., & Hallett, D. (2003). Personal persistence, identity development, and suicide. *Monographs of the Society for Research in Child Development, 68*.

Cushman, P. (1990). Why the self is empty: Toward a historically situated psychology. *American Psychologist, 45*, 599–611.

Haukka, J., Suominen, K., Partonen, T., & Lonnqvist, J. (2008). Determinants and outcomes of serious attempted suicide: A nationwide study in Finland, 1996–2003. *American Journal of Epidemiology, 167*, 1155–1163.

Hodgkinson, H. L. (1990). *The demographics of American Indians: One percent of the people, fifty percent of the diversity*. Washington, DC: Institute for Educational Leadership and Center for Demographic Policy.

Kirmayer, L. (1994). Suicide among Canadian Aboriginal people. *Transcultural Psychiatric Research Review, 31*, 3–57.

Kirmayer, L., Fraser, S.-L., Fauras V., & Whitley, R. (2009). *Current approaches to Aboriginal youth suicide prevention*. Montreal: Institute of Community & Family Psychiatry Jewish General Hospital, Culture & Mental Health Research Unit.

Meehan, P., Lamb, J., Saltzmen, L., & O'Carroll, P. W. (1992). Attempted suicide among young adults: Progress toward a meaningful estimate of prevalence. *American Journal of Psychiatry, 149*, 41–44.

Rorty, A. O. (1987). Persons as rhetorical categories. *Social Research, 54*, 55–72.

CHAPTER 9

Activating Place

Geography as a Determinant of Indigenous Peoples' Health and Well-being

Sarah de Leeuw

The arguments I make in this chapter are ones that have been known and made by Indigenous peoples since time immemorial. Indeed, it is likely fair to say that, for the most part and especially when made by Indigenous peoples, the arguments have been made in far more erudite ways than I am able to make in this chapter. This is important to say because it repositions expertise about Indigenous peoples' health and well-being back *where* it belongs (and I emphasize the "*whereness*" of this observation)—with the people and communities upon which the discussions focus. With this in mind, the chapter is also designed to be a suggested reading list of work by Indigenous peoples (covering multiple genres, especially ones not always referenced by health researchers) contemplating "the where," or "the geographies," of Indigenous peoples' well-being.

What this chapter attempts to do, then, is to reposition well-evidenced arguments about the importance of place to Indigenous peoples' health in specific reference to what I suggest is an under-scrutinized and increasingly normalized language that is gradually privileging a "social determinants of health" framework as the best way to ameliorate health inequalities between Indigenous and non-Indigenous peoples in Canada. Specifically, in this chapter I suggest that geography as a physical and material entity—place, earth, land, space, ecology, territory, landscape, water, ground, soil, and the like—is a remarkably powerful determinant of Indigenous peoples' health that is not, cannot, and should not be encapsulated within a "social" determinants of health framework. With this in mind, I contemplate what might be lost, or what might be at risk, if questions about primary, public, or population health continue to be thought about through social determinants of health frameworks. I hasten to add here that social determinants of health frameworks are, from my and many other health researchers' perspectives, a vast improvement upon frameworks that focus exclusively on individual, micro-scale, biomedical models of health, which continue to dominate most health discussions, especially in Canada (see, for instance, Gasher et al., 2007).

This chapter, then, considers and advocates for geography as a fundamental and active determinant of Indigenous peoples' health. I promote a shift from languages solely about the "social" determinants of health instead to theories and practices that account for and even privilege "geographic" determinants of health. I begin by defining exactly what I mean by geography, and the closely related concepts of place and space.

Once the concept of geography has been mapped out, I then tackle how it is at risk of being eclipsed by what I chart as an ascendance of languages, frameworks, and methodologies that focus upon—if not favour—"social" determinants of health perspectives. I then explore ways that place, space, territory, and land—all central tenets of geography and geographic theories— have been considered, lived, and embodied by Indigenous peoples as a determinant of health.

Furthermore, and leading from this, I propose that geography cannot and should not be folded or subsumed into the "social," but instead must maintain and be deployed as a distinct and bounded determinant of health unto itself. Finally, I conclude with some thoughts about ways that health research and practice might embrace geography as a unique and powerful framework through which to think about ameliorating the pressing and unacceptable health inequities between Indigenous and non-Indigenous peoples in Canada.

Although I am very sympathetic with critiques about academic research too often having little utility in the "the real world" or being too "of-the-head" and not enough "of-the-body" and "of-the-soul" (Brant-Castellano, 2004; see also Smith, 1999), this chapter is nevertheless principally theoretical in nature, by which I mean that I have not undertaken interviews with community members, nor have I made commitments to groups of people about reporting back on the arguments and conclusions made in this chapter. Further, I am not claiming that this work is designed to change anything in a material or embodied way on the ground in the immediate or foreseeable future. The work in this chapter is also not explicitly designed or written to inform particular policies.

Instead, I draw upon an existing array of published literatures and theo-retical concepts in order to draw inferences about the role that geography plays in the health and well-being of Indigenous peoples and communities and to advocate for a geographic presence when we—as health researchers, educators, practitioners, professionals, policy-makers, or theorists—con-sider the pressing issue of health inequities in Canada. What I hope to do, then, is encourage a critical rethinking of the ways that solutions to health inequalities are currently being discursively produced and circulated. Social determinants of health frameworks are one tool in a health researcher's kit of methods and methodologies, one lens through which to understand and hopefully change the conditions under which some people in Canada and beyond come to be less healthy than others. What if a "geographical" determi-nants of health framework is added to our toolbox? What if "geography" becomes a new lens through which to understand health disparities? These questions are the focus of this chapter.

So What Is *Geography* and Isn't It *Social* Too?

Translated literally from its Greek roots, the word "geography" (*geo* and *graphy*) means "Earth-writing" or "to write the Earth." Etymologically speak-ing, then, the work that geographers do is deeply rooted in and of the world—the physical, spatial, material world. As I explore further below, this is not so different from the rootedness in Earth, in place, that defines so many Indige-nous peoples in Canada and around the world (Basso, 1996; Battiste, 2000; Battiste & Henderson, 2000; Cajete, 1993; Cruikshank, 1996; Deloria, 1999). At its most basic, geography is the study of

> Interactions and social habits of humans *within* and *across* all spaces. . . .
> [G]eographers critically examine how humans organize and identify them-selves in space—how we create "places". Thus, the science of human geography does not look at location per se, as much as it does at the mobility of, access to, and barriers against human processes. (Mayhew, 2009, n.p.)

To offer a simple analogy: in the same way that one might say historians study time as an active force in organizing all aspects of human life, geographers consider space and place as active forces in human existence. Indeed, "[f]or many geographers, place and the differences between places are the very stuff of geography, the raw materials that give the discipline its warrant. . . . [place is] phenomenological ground. . .irreducible from human experience

[but] without which human experience could not be constituted and inter- preted" (Henderson, 2009 p. 539). The concept of space is equally the "stuff" of geographers, impossible to separate from human existence and an active material entity unto itself: geographers have an "unwavering concern with ontology, with grasping the significance of space not for the constitution of [socio-economic systems] alone, but for being-in-the-world" (Gregory, 2009, p. 708).

Thus, while geographers recognize (and theorize) the reciprocity of human relationship with place and space, they fundamentally understand the two concepts as not solely "of the social." This means that geographers hold true both: (1) that spaces and places are not passive neutral entities or blank tab- lets upon which life unfolds, but instead are active forces that bear down on human lives and organize how we behave, feel, live, and structure ourselves and our systems of being; and (2) that humans actively transform and impact the spaces and places—including our natural environments—in which we exist. This is a cyclical and dynamic relationship. Very simply put, to think about something geographically, or to account for geography as a determi- nant of health, is to acknowledge that *where* we are and *how* we are in that space matters: place and space are never static or neutral entities upon or in which we simply exist or that we entirely socially construct, but instead are always active, independent, and determining life forces.

Considering a human condition (in this case "health" or lack thereof) as geographically determined is different than thinking about it as "socially" determined, principally because—with the exception of some post-structural and postmodern geographical theorists who, for a brief period of time and prior to receiving significant push-back, suggested that almost everything was socially constructed (see, for instance, Pain & Bailey, 2004)—geographers understand that human activity is at least to some degree intrinsically linked to things like land, territory, ground, and the Earth—things that are, in turn, something more than human or social. This is in line with an increasing number of twenty-first-century critical theorists who are arguing for a more "ontological" orientation to power discrepancies and inequalities, reminding us that in the rush to understand everything as socially constructed, there is a risk of minimizing the embodied, the organic, or the material (e.g., non- socio-culturally signified) aspects of human existence.[1] I suggest that this "grounding" of discussions about health disparities is slipping when a focus on the "social" ascends, which is what is happening in many inquiries into health inequalities. Indeed, in a recent survey of health reporting in Canada, although mainstream media continues to emphasize individualized aspects of health, when population health is covered, the "social" determinants of health garner almost exclusive focus (Gasher et al., 2007).

INDIGENOUS GEOGRAPHIES: MORE THAN THE SOCIAL

Considered a touchstone document in Canada by many Indigenous peoples and communities, the Royal Commission on Aboriginal Peoples (1996) made clear that land and territory—indeed, the very broad concept of place—were essential to Aboriginal ways of knowing and being: "Land is absolutely fundamental to Aboriginal identity. . . . land is *reflected* in the language, culture and spiritual values of all Aboriginal peoples" (Government of Canada, 1996, n.p.; emphasis added). Land, it is important to note here, is not enfolded into language, culture, or spiritual values, but instead is "reflected" in the sociological traits of being Aboriginal. Importantly, the term "reflected" shows that land retains its autonomous, non-*anthropomorphized* essence and character. It is separate from a social determinant of Indigenous identity and being.

This is consistent with what a growing number of scholars—both Indigenous and non-Indigenous—are documenting. Not only are land, Earth, and territory (or physical and material geographies) inseparable from what it means to embody or to be Indigenous, but disruption of geographic connection with and refusal of Indigenous claims to place and space were principle aspects of colonization in Canada (Battiste, 2000; Battiste & Henderson, 2000; Brealey, 1995; Carlson, 2010; Clayton, 2000; Harris, 2002, 2004; see also Chapter 6). In all cases, physical geography is not a social or socially constructed phenomenon, but instead is an organic material entity unto itself.

Indeed, since it emerged in the closing months of 2012, the Idle No More movement in Canada— and beyond—has explicitly demanded a (re)focusing on relationships between land, treaties, environment, and physical geography as fundamental components of the flawed (if not totally broken) relationship that colonial states and systems of power have with Indigenous peoples. Clearly, geography—and not geography as folded into and enveloped by social or human systems—matters in the lives and being-ness of Indigenous peoples. Geography means something *more than* just human or social constructions. It exists outside of "the social" and cannot be fully or completely understood by *anthropomorphizing* it or enfolding it into concepts of "the social."

This truth—that there is a physical environment and an organic/biological world that is "more than human" and/or "more than social," and that such an entity (or entities) has resounding power, integrity, agency, worth, and material substance unto itself and far outside/beyond anything inscribed upon it by people or the systems and structures of humans—has been under-stood and expressed by many Indigenous peoples for much of knowable his-tory (Black, 1999; Clutesi, 1967, 1969; Hawker, 2003; Sewid-Smith, 1991). In many cases, human beings have sprung from or been given existence by that non-human realm (Bringhurst, 2000). There is something more than just the social—that which is human-centred and human-created— that has eminence in Indigenous ways of knowing and being in the world. Land and physical environments as valuable (and separate!) from human being-ness and ways of being are fully realized in Indigenous ways of orienting to the world, includ-ing claims of unceded self-determination (Nisga'a Tribunal, 1993; Molloy, 2000; Sterritt et al., 1998).

In many Indigenous cosmologies, physical geographies—the soil, earth, mountains, rivers, ecological non-human organic matter—are understood as animate and powerful, constitutive of human life, but certainly not defined by us or behooved to us. Furthermore, the non- or more than human/social (the physical geography of the world and universe) is deeply understood as intrin-sic to human well-being or lack thereof: the earth, the sky, the rivers, and the cosmos have all, since time immemorial, meted out both punishment and reward to humans and our societies based on our behaviours (Cajete, 1993)— not as extensions of us, but as autonomous, powerful extra-human forces.

The vesting of great significance in non-human geographies is the founda-tion for countless explanations of human nature and human activities among Indigenous peoples (Armstrong, 1993). I worry that this is curiously eclipsed when discussing determinants of human health and well-being within "social"-only frameworks. Indeed, it might be said that a fundamental difference be-tween many Euro-Western non-Indigenous and Indigenous peoples (at least in North America, Australia, and New Zealand) is that Indigenous peoples have always understood geography and geographic systems as non-subordinated to humans and human (or social) systems (see Battiste, 2000; Carlson, 2010). There is something fundamentally important about geography and place for many Indigenous peoples, cultures, and communities. This might be missed if these concepts are disciplined within a framework of "social determinants." How, then, might geography not be eclipsed when thinking about determi-nants of health?

ACTIVATING PLACE: A GEOGRAPHICAL DETERMINANTS OF HEALTH FRAMEWORK?

There is something semi-intuitive, something close to "commonsensical" about asserting the importance of place to human well-being. Where we are almost instinctively seems to matter: think about the ways that certain spaces are actively constructed to induce certain kinds of feeling (e.g., walls are painted in "soothing" colours in a hospital); consider how you feel when you enter a place that is familiar to you (e.g., your childhood home or the town you grew up in) versus entering an unfamiliar terrain. You might have negative associations with the former and positive feelings in the latter—or vice versa. But unquestionably, the physical, material geography has an impact on you. These are, of course, very simplistic analogies, but they highlight that geography does indeed impact us or, articulated slightly differently, can "determine" a human sense of well-being, at least to some degree.

The laudable purpose of a social determinants of health framework is to conceptualize human health (or lack thereof) differently than the ways that gained much traction through the advent and rise of modern medicine (see, for instance, Calman, 2006). Social determinants demand that we do not look only at individual health outcomes (e.g., a person's diabetes), but what upstream and contextual factors might have led to the person's illness (e.g., poverty, social exclusion, lack of access to healthy foods or information about diet). In many ways, and again thinking "geographically," social determinants of health frameworks extended the scale of inquiry about health or health inequities: rather than focusing exclusively at the micro or individual scale, a social determinants of health framework insists on far broader, or more expansive, scales of inquiry. This expansion, however, must not be allowed to remain stagnant.

As others have summarized, a social determinants of health framework encourages health researchers, policy-makers, and providers to examine and actively account for the "causes of the causes"—the "proximal, intermediate and distal" contributors to well-being or lack thereof (Loppie Reading & Wien, 2009; see also Chapter 1). While social determinants of health frameworks have been tinkered with, and while especially Indigenous scholars have expanded the framework's aperture even further by rightly observing that colonization/colonialism is a unique and powerful determinant of health disparities lived by Aboriginal peoples, there is little work that offers explicit and critical push-back against the discursive dominance of the term "social" when thinking about the causes of peoples' (or communities') health inequalities. It seems to me that in efforts to (rightly) complexify and expand the ways that health disparities are understood, those employing and promoting a social determinants of health framework may (likely inadvertently) be again narrowing or rigidifying the theoretical tools that help generate what should be ever-deepening understandings about disparities in human well-being.

For scholars of Aboriginal peoples' health, and for Aboriginal peoples and communities, social determinants of health frameworks make a great deal of sense: Indigenous peoples in Canada and beyond have, since well before the advent of contemporary medical and health models, advocated that health is a holistic phenomenon that cannot be adequately addressed though interventions into or focuses upon the body and the body alone (see Government of Canada, 1996). With this in mind, and especially since Indigenous peoples as compared with their non-Indigenous counterparts live with some of the world's greatest health disparities, social determinants of health frameworks are indeed a needed and important step forward from historical frameworks that conceptualize health disparities as anchored principally in the body of the individual. But why stop with "the social"?

For many Indigenous peoples and communities in Canada and around the world, place is fundamental to health, identity, culture, and being, although it is not fully or robustly conceptualized with a focus on the "social" determinants of health. Rectifying this requires adding to languages, policies, theories, frameworks (e.g., discursive structures) currently being deployed about the rights of Indigenous peoples to achieve optimal health: it means not taking for granted that social determinants offer a complete analytic framework, but instead insisting that they require critical push-back and a constant revisioning.

Stating overtly and persistently that geographic tenets are vital parts of Indigenous peoples' and communities' well-being is at the heart of activating place as an important determinant of health. Indeed, because for many Indigenous communities the inalienable connection with and right to specific ecologies, lands, water and soil systems, and other non-human wildlife is inseparable from human health, and yet not simply an extension of "the social," if health researchers do not articulate geography as a distinct determinant of health, we are potentially overlooking a much-needed means of understanding the specificities of Indigenous peoples' health.

CONCLUSION

To activate the concept of place in discussions and theorizations about health inequalities means, then, at every turn, articulating that human health (or lack thereof) unfolds in and is impacted by *where* its existence occurs. The "where" of human health (or lack thereof) is not solely an extension of human or social projects; instead, it is an active agent unto itself. Imagine, then, if when theorizing health inequities we always accounted for "where" (or geographic) concepts like distance, ground, terrain, land claim, site, territory, ecology, or soil? Another aspect of activating place as a determinant of (especially Indigenous peoples') health would be to vigilantly look at where research about health inequalities is originating from or focusing on—where is Indigenous voice in research about health disparities, and where (what regions, communities, countries, or homes) is the research unfolding or focusing in upon? Finally, must we not also always be asking where the research is destined for, where are researchers hoping the work will take root?

In short, there are many concrete ways to activate place, to activate geography, as a determinant of health, and doing so requires some displacement of "the social" as the dominant determinant of health. By doing this, however, it is possible that new terrain will be forged upon which to more fully theorize and thus potentially ameliorate the pressing health inequities lived by far too many Indigenous peoples in Canada and around the world.

NOTE

1. For an excellent example of this scholarship with reference to feminism, see, for instance, Wilson (2004).

REFERENCES

Adelson, N. (2005). The embodiment of inequalities: Health disparities in Aboriginal Canada. *Canadian Journal of Public Health, 96,* S45–S61.

Anderson, I., Baum, F., & Bentley, F. (2007). *Beyond bandaids: Exploring the underlying social determinants of Aboriginal health.* Casuarina, NT: Cooperative Research Centre for Aboriginal Health.

Anderson, L. M., Shinn, C., & St. Charles, J. (2002). Community interventions to promote healthy social environments: Early childhood and family housing—a report on recommendations of the Task Force on Community Prevention Services. *Morbidity and Mortality Weekly Report, 51,* 1–8.

Armstrong, J. (1993). *Looking at the words of our people: First Nations analysis of literature.* Penticton, BC: Theytus Books.

Barlow, K., Loppie, C., Jackson, R., Akan, M., MacLean, L., & Reimer, G. (2008). Culturally competent service provision issues experienced by Aboriginal people living with HIV/AIDS. *Pimatisiwin: A Journal of Aboriginal and Indigenous Community Health, 6,* 155–180.

Barlow, K., & Reading, C. (2010). A qualitative study of the role of sexual violence in the lives of Aboriginal women with HIV/AIDS. Ottawa, ON: Canadian Aboriginal AIDS Network.

Basso, K. (1996). *Wisdom sits in places: Landscape and language among the Western Apache.* Santa Fe: University of New Mexico Press.

Battiste, M. (2000). *Reclaiming Indigenous voice and vision.* Vancouver, BC: UBC Press.

Battiste, M., & Henderson, J. Y. (2000). *Protecting Indigenous knowledge and heritage: A global challenge.* Saskatoon, SK: Purich Press.

Baum, F., & Harris, L. (2006). Equity and the social determinants of health. *Health Promotion Journal of Australia, 17,* 163–165.

Black, M. (1999). *Huupu Kwanum Tupaat: Out of the mist: Treasures of the Nuu-chah-nulth chiefs.* Victoria, BC: Royal British Columbia Museum.

Blas, E., & Kurup, A. S. (Eds.). (2010). *Equity, social determinants, and public health programmes.* Geneva, Switzerland: World Health Organization.

Blas, E., Sommerfeld, J., & Kurup, A. S. (Eds.). (2011). *Social determinants approaches to public health: From concept to practice.* Geneva, Switzerland: World Health Organization.

Boyer, Y. (2006, June 29). *Self-determination as a social determinant of health. Discussion document for the Aboriginal Working Group of the Canadian Reference Group reporting to the WHO Commission on Social Determinants of Health.* Hosted by the National Collaborating Centre for Aboriginal Health and funded by the First Nations and Inuit Health Branch of Health Canada, Vancouver, BC.

Brant-Castellano, M. (2004). Ethics of Aboriginal research. *Journal of Aboriginal Health, 1,* 98–114.

Brealey, K. (1995). Mapping them "out": Euro-Canadian cartography and the appropriation of the Nuxalk and Ts'ilhqot'in First Nations' territories, 1793–1916. *Canadian Geographer, 39,* 140–168.

Bringhurst, R. (2000). *Solitary Raven: The essential writings of Bill Read.* Vancouver, BC: Douglas & McIntyre.

Burbank, V. C. (2011). *An ethnography of stress: The social determinants of health in Aboriginal Australia.* New York, NY: Palgrave Macmillan.

Cajete, G. (1993). *Look to the mountain: An ecology of Indigenous education.* Durango, CO: Kivaki Press.

Calman, K. C. (2006). *Medical education: Past, present and future.* London/Toronto: Elsevier.

Carlson, K. T. (2010). *The power of place, the problem of time: Aboriginal identity and historical consciousness in the cauldron of colonialism.* Toronto, ON: University of Toronto Press.

Carson, B., Dunbar, T., Chenhall, R., & Bailie, R. (Eds.). (2007). *Social determinants of Indigenous health.* Crows Nest, NSW: Allen & Unwin.

Clayton, D. W. (2000). *Islands of truth: The imperial fashioning of Vancouver Island.* Vancouver, BC: UBC Press.

Clutesi, G. (1967). *Son of Raven, son of Deer: Fables of the Tse-Shaht people.* Sidney, BC: Gray's Publishing.

Clutesi, G. (1969). *Potlatch*. Sidney, BC: Gray's Publishing.

Commission on Social Determinants of Health. (2007). *Achieving health equity: From root causes to fair outcomes*. Geneva, Switzerland: World Health Organization.

Commission on Social Determinants of Health. (2008). *Closing the gap in a generation: Health equity through action on the social determinants of health: Commission on Social Determinants of Health final report*. Geneva, Switzerland: World Health Organization.

Corrado, R. R., & Cohen, I. M. (2003). *Mental health profiles for a sample of British Columbia's Aboriginal survivors of the Canadian residential school system*. Ottawa, ON: Aboriginal Healing Foundation.

Cruikshank, J. (1996). *Life lived like a story: Life stories of three Yukon Native Elders*. Vancouver, BC: UBC Press.

Daniel, M., et al. (2004). Cigarette smoking, mental health, and social support: Data from a northwestern First Nation. *Canadian Journal of Public Health, 95*, 45–49.

de Leeuw, S., Greenwood, M., & Cameron, E. (2010). Deviant constructions: How governments preserve colonial narratives of addictions and poor mental health to intervene into the lives of Indigenous children and families in Canada. *International Journal of Mental Health and Addiction, 8*, 282–295. doi: 10.1007/s11469-009-9225-1

Deloria, V. (1999). *Spirit and reason: The Vine Deloria reader*. Golden, CO: Fulcrum Publishing.

Dunn, J. R., Hayes, M. V., Hulchanski, S. J., Hwang, D. W., & Potvin, L. (2006). Housing as a socio-economic determinant of health: Findings of a national needs, gaps, and opportunities assessment. *Canadian Journal of Public Health, 97*, S11–S15.

Edwards, P. (2007). *The social determinants of health: An overview of the implications for policy and the role of the health sector*. Ottawa, ON: Health Canada.

Fernandez, L., MacKinnon, S., & Silver, J. (Eds.). (2010). *The social determinants of health in Manitoba*. Winnipeg, MB: Canadian Centre for Policy Alternatives.

Frohlich, K. L., Ross, N., & Richmond, C. (2006). Health disparities in Canada today: Some evidence and a theoretical framework. *Health Policy, 79*, 132–143.

Gasher, M., Hayes, M., Hackett, R., Gutstein, D., Ross, I., & Dunn, J. (2007). Spreading the news: Social determinants of health reportage in Canadian daily newspapers. *Canadian Journal of Communication, 32*, 557–574.

Gleeson, S., & Alperstein, G. (2006). The NSW Social Determinants of Health Action Group: Influencing the social determinants of health. *Health Promotion Journal of Australia, 17*, 266–268.

Government of Canada. (1996). Royal Commission on Aboriginal Peoples (RCAP). Ottawa, ON: Department of Indian Affairs and Northern Development.

Greenwood, M. (2005). Children as citizens of First Nations: Linking Indigenous health to early childhood development. *Paediatric Child Health, 10*, 553–555.

Gregory, D. (2009). Space. In D. Gregory & G. Pratt (Eds.), *Dictionary of human geography* (5th ed., pp. 707–710). Hoboken, NJ: Wiley-Blackwell.

Harris, C. (2002). *Making Native space: Colonialism, resistance, and reserves in British Columbia*. Vancouver, BC: UBC Press.

Harris, C. (2004, March). How did colonialism dispossess? Comments from an edge of empire. *Annals of the Association of American Geographers, 94*, 165–182.

Hawker, R. W. (2003). *Tales of ghosts: First Nations art in British Columbia, 1922–61*. Vancouver, BC: UBC Press.

Henderson, G. (2009). Place. In D. Gregory & G. Pratt (Eds.), *Dictionary of human geography* (5th ed., pp. 539–541). Hoboken, NJ: Wiley-Blackwell.

Jenkins, A., Gyorkos, T., Culman, K., Ward, B., Pekeles, G., & Mills, E. (2003). An overview of factors influencing the health of Canadian Inuit infants. *International Journal of Circumpolar Health, 62*, 17–39.

Kelly, M. P., et al. (2007). *The social determinants of health: Developing an evidence base for political action.*The World Health Organization and the Measurement and Evidence Knowledge Network. Retrieved from http://www.who.int/social_determinants/resources/mekn_final_report_102007.pdf

Kelm, M. E. (1998). *Colonizing bodies: Aboriginal health and healing in British Columbia, 1900–50*. Vancouver, BC: UBC Press.

Kumas-Tan, Z., Beagan, B., Loppie, C., MacLeod, A., & Frank, B. (2007). Measuring cultural competence: Examining hidden assumptions in instruments. *Academic Medicine, 82*, 548–557.

Lantz, P. M., House, J. S., Lepkowski, J. M., Williams, D. R., Mero, R. P., & Chen, J. J. (1998). Socioeconomic factors, health behaviors, and mortality. *Journal of the American Medical Association, 279*, 1703–1708.

Larson, A., Gillies, M., Howard, P. J., & Coffin, J. (2007). It's enough to make you sick: The impacts of racism on the health of Aboriginal Australians. *Australian and New Zealand Journal of Public Health, 31*, 322–329.

Little, L. (2006). *A discussion of the impacts of non-medical determinants of health for Inuit mental wellness (draft)*. Ottawa, ON: Inuit Tapiriit Kanatami.

Loppie Reading, C., & Wien, F. (2009). *Health inequalities and social determinants of Aboriginal peoples' health*. Prince George, BC: National Collaborating Centre for Aboriginal Peoples' Health.

Malden, A. G. J. (2000). *The Blackwell dictionary of sociology: A user's guide to sociological language* (2nd ed.). Malden, MA: Blackwell Publishers.

Marmot, M. (2005). Social determinants of health inequalities. *Lancet, 365*, 1099–1104.

Marmot, M., Friel, S., Bell, R., Houweling, T. A. J., & Taylor, S. (2008). Closing the gap in a generation: Health equity through action on the social determinants of health. *Lancet, 372*, 1661–1669.

Marmot, M., & Wilkinson, R. (Eds.). (2006). *Social determinants of health* (2nd ed.). Oxford, UK: Oxford University Press.

Mayhew, S. (2009). *Oxford dictionary of human geography* (4th ed.). Oxford, UK: Oxford Publishing. Retrieved from http://www.oxfordreference.com.ezproxy.library.ubc.ca/view/10.1093/acref/9780199231805.001.0001/acref-9780199231805

Métis National Council (MNC). (2006). *Proposals for measuring determinants and population health/well-being status of Métis peoples in Canada.* Ottawa, ON: Métis National Council.

Mignone, J. (2003). *Measuring social capital: A guide for First Nations communities.* Ottawa, ON: Canadian Institute for Health Information.

Mikkonen, J., & Raphael, D. (2010). *Social determinants of health: Canadian facts.* Toronto, ON: York University School of Health Policy and Management.

Molloy, T. (2000). *The world is our witness: The historic journy of the Nisga'a into Canada.* Markham, ON: Fifth House Publishing.

Nettleton, C., Napolitano, D. A., & Stephens, C. (2007). *An overview of current knowledge of the social determinants of Indigenous health.* Adelaide, Australia: Symposium on the Social Determinants of Indigenous Health.

Nisga'a Tribunal. (1993). *Nisga'a: People of the Nass.* Vancouver, BC: Douglas & McIntyre.

Pain, R., & Bailey, C. (2004). British social and cultural geography: Beyond turns and dualisms? *Social and Cultural Geography, 5,* 319–329.

Raphael, D. (2002). *Social justice is good for our hearts: Why societal factors—not lifestyles—are major causes of heart disease in Canada and elsewhere.* Toronto, ON: Centre for Social Justice Foundation for Research and Education.

Raphael, D. (Ed.). (2009). *Social determinants of health: Canadian perspectives* (2nd ed.). Toronto, ON: Canadian Scholars' Press Inc.

Raphael, D. (2010). *About Canada: Health and illness.* Winnipeg, MB: Fernwood Publishing.

Raphael, D. (2012). *Tackling health inequalities: Lessons from international experiences.* Toronto, ON: Canadian Scholars' Press Inc.

Reading, C., & Reading, J. (2012). Promising practices in Aboriginal community health promotion interventions. In I. Rootman, S. Dupéré, A. Pederson, & M. O'Neill (Eds.), *Health promotion in Canada* (3rd ed.). Toronto, ON: Canadian Scholars' Press Inc.

Reading, J. (2009). *The crisis of chronic disease among Aboriginal Peoples: A challenge for public health, population health, and social policy.* Victoria, BC: Centre for Aboriginal Research.

Reading, J., Kmetic, A., & Giddion, V. (2007). *First Nations holistic policy and planning model: Discussion for the World Health Organization Commission on Social Determinants of Health.* Ottawa, ON: Assembly of First Nations.

Richmond, C., Elliott, S. J., Matthews, R., & Elliott, B. (2005). The political ecology of health: Perceptions of environment, economy, health, and well-being among 'Namgis First Nation. *Health and Place, 11,* 349–365.

Richmond, C., Ross, N. A., & Bernier, J. (2007). Exploring Indigenous concepts of health: The dimensions of Métis and Inuit health. In J. White, D. Beavon, S. Wingert, & P. Maxim (Eds.), *Aboriginal policy research: Directions and outcomes,* vol. 4. Toronto, ON: Thompson Educational Publishing.

Richmond, C., Ross, N. A., & Egeland, G. M. (2007, October). Societal resources and thriving health: A new approach for understanding Indigenous Canadian health. *American Journal of Public Health, 97,* 1–7.

Richmond, C. A. M., & Ross, N. A. (2009). The determinants of First Nation and Inuit health: A critical population approach. *Health and Place, 15,* 403–411.

Sewid-Smith, D. (1991). In time immemorial. In D. Jensen & C. Brooks (Eds.), *Celebration of our survival: First Nations of British Columbia* (pp. 16–33). Vancouver, BC: UBC Press.

Smith, L. T. (1999). *Decolonizing methodologies: Research and Indigenous Peoples.* New York, NY: Zed Books.

Smylie, J. (2009). The health of Aboriginal peoples. In D. Raphael (Ed.), *Social determinants of health: Canadian perspectives* (2nd ed., pp. 280–301). Toronto, ON: Canadian Scholars' Press Inc.

Smylie, J., Williams, L., & Cooper, N. (2006). Culture-based literacy and Aboriginal health. *Canadian Journal of Public Health, 97,* S21–S25.

Steenbeck, A., Tyndall, M., Rothenberg, R., & Sheps, S. (2006). Determinants of sexually transmitted infections among Canadian Inuit adolescent populations. *Public Health Nursing, 23,* 531–534.

Sterritt, N. J., Marsden, S., Galois, R., Grant, P., & Overstall, R. (1998). *Tribal boundaries in the Nass watershed.* Vancouver, BC: UBC Press.

Syme, S. (2004). Social determinants of health: The community as an empowered partner. *Preventing Chronic Disease, 1,* 1–5. Retrieved from http://www.cdc.gov/pcd/issues/2004/jan/pdf/03_0001.pdf

Tarantola, D. (2007). The interface of mental health and human rights in Indigenous peoples: Triple jeopardy and triple opportunity. *Australian Psychiatry, 15,* 10–17.

Tolbert Kimbro, R., Bzostek, S., Goldman, N., & Rodríguez, G. (2008). Race, ethnicity, and the education gradient in health. *Health Affairs, 27,* 361–372.

Wilkinson, R. (2006). *The impact of inequality: How to make sick societies healthier.* New York, NY: The New Press.

Wilkinson, R., & Marmot, M. (1998). *Social determinants of health: The solid facts.* Geneva, Switzerland: World Health Organization.

Wilson, E. A. (2004). Gut feminism. *Differences, 15,* 66–94.

Wilson, K., & Rosenberg, M. (2002). Exploring the determinants of health for First Nations peoples in Canada: Can existing frameworks accommodate traditional activities? *Social Science & Medicine, 55,* 2017–2031.

Young, T. K. (1996). Sociocultural and behavioural determinants of obesity among Inuit in the central Canadian Arctic. *Social Science & Medicine, 43,* 1665–1671.

CHAPTER 10

Embodying Self-Determination
Beyond the Gender Binary

Sarah Hunt

For more than 15 years, I have been working on issues of gendered colonial violence in rural, remote, and urban communities across what is now known as British Columbia. As a Kwakwaka'wakw woman with an undergraduate degree in women's studies and many years of hearing stories of violence from Indigenous peoples in diverse situations, you would think that my analysis of gendered violence would leave room for few surprises. But I was recently stopped in my tracks when I learned that I had missed an important fact about the missing and murdered women in Vancouver's Downtown Eastside: at least one of the missing women, Kellie Little, was a trans woman. How is it possible that after talking to many Downtown Eastside advocates, as well as reading the work of Indigenous scholars, researchers, and activists who focus on this issue, that it took so long to find out that one of the missing women was trans?

While intersections of racism, sexism, poverty, and anti–sex work sentiments have been examined in relation to the prevalence of violence against Indigenous women in this community, little has been said by national Indigenous women's organizations, national Indigenous leadership, local community groups, or scholars and activists working to address violence against Indigenous girls and women about the particular factors impacting violence against trans people. More broadly, gendered analyses of power in Indigenous communities tend to focus on men and women, reinforcing the gender binary and thereby erasing the realities of women like Kellie Little. Further, such binary-gendered analyses miss the opportunity to make connections between the erasure of two-spirit traditions and the impact of colonial patriarchy on the position of women in Indigenous communities. Given the centrality of gender as a health determinant that intersects with other determinants in the lives of Indigenous girls and women, trans and two-spirit people, anti-violence movements require the development of an Indigenous gender-based analysis that accounts for experiences of health for all members of our communities within the true meaning of "all our relations."

In this chapter, I examine the erasure of trans and two-spirit people as an ongoing form of colonial violence that is being perpetuated through current conceptualizations of gender as a social determinant of health for Indigenous communities. Given the lack of statistics on health outcomes for trans and two-spirit people, I will focus less on statistical pictures of health for Indigenous women, men, and two-spirit people and will instead attempt to account for the lived realities of trans and two-spirit people, girls, women, boys, and men in diversely situated Indigenous communities. Through the development of an Indigenous gender-based analysis, I hope to demonstrate how gender intersects with other health determinants such as geography, age, and education for all our relations, not only women and men, and to advocate for the use of such an analysis at local, national, and international scales where social inequities among Indigenous communities are being addressed.

RACIALIZED GENDER CATEGORIZATIONS AS CENTRAL TO COLONIALISM

> Much of what I have read has said that we do not exist, that if we do exist it is in terms which I cannot recognize, that we are no good and that what we think is not valid. (Smith, 1999, p. 35)

At the heart of the colonization of Turtle Island lies the settler colonial project of Native disappearance, which is necessary for the development of a prosperous settler society. Colonial laws and ideologies have entailed the imposition of gendered and racialized categories, which have been used to ensure fewer and fewer Natives over time. Legislated in 1876, the Indian Act established "patriliniality as the criterion for determining Indian status, including the rights of Indians to participate in band government, have access to band services and programs, and live on the reserves" (Barker, 2008, p. 259). Thus, status Indian women, as a separate legal and social category from other Canadians, became disenfranchised through marriage to non-status men, impacting their children for generations to come. As a "total institution" (Dickason, 1992, p. 285) touching on all aspects of the lives of status Indians, the Indian Act was designed with explicit intent to assimilate Indians into Canadian society and anticipated the eventual and total dissolution of band governments with the implementation of gendered power relations among men and women at its core. The Act can thus be seen as an instance of the co-constitutive relationship of sovereignty and gender (Barker, 2008).

Indian residential schools were also integral to processes of imposing racialized gender hierarchies among diverse Indigenous communities. As I have written elsewhere (Hunt, 2007), at the same moment as Native children became "Indians" through their institutionalization at residential schools, they were simultaneously gendered as Indian boys and girls as systems of race and gender were mutually articulated, enforcing and creating one another. "Individual accounts of residential school students clearly show the gender uniforms as one colonizing tool—boys had their hair cut short, girls wore bobs and bangs, and they were physically separated from one another in the schools, kept in different dorms in order to ingrain distinct gender roles into them" (Hunt, 2007, p. 44). Residential schools divided sisters and brothers from one another, imposing racialized gender norms onto the young bodies of Native children while denying their traditional gender roles, which differed cross-culturally. After many generations of Native children being indoctrinated in these gendered educational spaces, along with the imposition of Indian Act governance and many other ways of replacing Indigenous cultural practices with colonial ones, the racialized gender binary has become difficult to question. The erasure and invisibility of those we now call two-spirit and transgender people were accomplished through these combined ideological, socio-legal, and spatialized enforcements of colonial gender norms for "Indians."

Categorization has been central to colonialism in Canada as socio-legal means have been used to impose Western paradigms while actively suppressing Indigenous world views and their categorizations of knowledge. We can thus understand categorization as a process through which world views and ontologies come into being (Stoler, 2009). Within the highly regulated lives of status Indians, the erasure of two-spirit and trans people in the Indian Act has a direct impact on access to rights and resources that come with status. Although much work has been done to address structurally enforced inequality for status and non-status Indian women, the same has not been done for trans Indigenous peoples, and without a way to capture their experiences, the consequences of this erasure are difficult to comprehend.

The imposition and institutionalization of racialized gender roles have meant not only the loss of two-spirit traditions, but also the ways that men and women related to one another, and the spiritual, ceremonial, and cultural significance of what it means to be a "man" or a "woman" or a "two-spirit" within broader cultural systems. Gender, then, plays a central role in understanding and defining who we are as Indigenous peoples, and the forced disappearance of locally defined systems of gender is central to the settler project of Native disappearance.

HISTORICAL CONTEXT OF INDIGENOUS SYSTEMS OF GENDER

Despite these efforts of erasure, the cultural practices, names, ceremonies, belief systems, and embodied realities of two-spirit people did not fully disappear. Recalling pre-contact Indigenous systems of gender pushes at the limits of the English language (Driskill, Finley, Gilley, & Morgensen, 2011) and is further challenged due to the biased nature of historical and anthropological accounts, as well as the suppression of this knowledge through colonialism. Broadly speaking, Indigenous categorizations of gender prior to colonialism emerged within other cultural and social practices, and were as diverse as Indigenous cultures themselves. Much knowledge of Indigenous systems of gender can still be found embedded in Indigenous languages, and in the oral histories and ongoing cultural practices of Indigenous peoples. Recounting and reclaiming this history have been central to validating the lives of diversely gendered Indigenous peoples today as integral to the sociocultural and governance practices of Indigenous nations.

A Diversity of Indigenous Gender Roles

According to Tafoya (1997), two-thirds of the 200 native languages spoken in North America contain terms to describe individuals who were neither men nor women. Many of these terms are difficult to translate because they encapsulate identities that are simultaneously about one's role in a spiritual and cultural system, as well as expressive of gender identity and sometimes sexuality. Driskill (2011) defines the Cherokee term *asegi udanto* as "a different way of thinking, feeling and being that is outside of men's and women's traditional roles" (p. 98). This understanding is rooted in the loose translation of the two parts of the term: *asegi* (translated variously as strange, odd, peculiar, and extraordinary) and *udanto* (translated loosely as heart/mind/spirit). The Navajo word *nadleehe* refers to someone in a constant process of change, understood as a matter of occupational preferences and personality traits, not of sexual orientation (Stimson, 2006). Within some communities, the roles of people who were situated outside the categories of men and women carried unique responsibilities that were vital to the nation's well-being and continuation (Driskill, 2011). These included roles as teachers, knowledge keepers, Healers, herbalists, child minders, spiritual leaders, interpreters, mediators, and artists—roles that were vital to collective survival and the continuation of traditional knowledge (Tafoya, 1997).

However, in recounting pre-colonial gender roles, it is important to avoid generalized statements that idealize pre-contact Indigenous societies as uniformly balanced, accepting, and appreciative of non-gender-conforming individuals. Rather, the diversity of these historical gender systems highlight the ontological distinctions between how we now understand gender within the Western gender binary and Indigenous conceptualizations of gender, which fall beyond these categorizations. The diversity of gender roles across Indigenous nations reflects Indigenous histories in which "gender and gender roles were variables based on multiple societal factors such as tribal tradition" (Gilley, 2011, p. 127). These traditions are evidenced in accounts by early European explorers, ethnographic studies, and oral teachings contained in writings by Indigenous scholars.

Anthropologists became interested in what they termed *berdache* traditions—religious and spiritual roles that were said to be revered within Indigenous societies. Best known is Williams's *The Spirit and the Flesh* (1986), which uses oral histories from the late nineteenth and early twentieth centuries to investigate the Lakota *winktes* and Navajo *nadle*, males who took up women's dress and social roles. In a more recent anthropological study, Lang (1998) documented distinct gender and social roles across a diversity of Indigenous societies, which include serving as Healers or medicine people, conveyors of oral tradition and song, potters, regalia makers and artists, matchmakers, and other ceremonial roles. In Roscoe's *Changing Ones* (1998), oral histories are used in recalling the life of Osh-Tisch, a *boté* or male who took up women's roles and clothing, as well as being a warrior and medicine person, described as "a Crow woman" who was "neither a man nor a woman" (p. 31).

However, scholarly analyses of diverse Indigenous gender roles have more recently been read as an attempt to validate contemporary non-Native gay and trans expressions of sexuality and gender, rather than accurate depictions of Indigenous world views and histories. In addition to the work of anthropologists cited above, this is evidenced in queer scholarship such as Feinberg's *Transgender Warriors* (1996), which recalls historic roles, lives, and attitudes toward transgender people across diverse cultural contexts. A methodological shift has occurred in which Indigenous scholars have worked to assert the validity of Indigenous traditions on their own terms within larger assertions of self-determination, rather than in relation to non-Native gay agendas (Driskill et al., 2011; Morgensen, 2011). This is reflected in the move to replace the anthropological term *berdache* with "two-spirit," a decision that was made in 1994 at the Third Annual Native American Gay and Lesbian Gathering in Winnipeg, Manitoba. The term is not intended to mark a new category of gender, but is an indigenously defined pan-Native North American term that refers to a diversity of Indigenous LGBTQ identities, as well as culturally specific non-binary expressions of gender.

Re-storying Two-Spirit History

In 1984, the Gay American Indian History Project began recording Native histories of gender and sexual diversity and members' own lives, resulting in the collection *Living the Spirit: A gay American Indian Anthology* (Gay American Indians & Roscoe, 1988). Here, diverse historical gender roles are recounted in text and imagery across various national contexts, and pan-tribal terms such as "two-spirit" are explored as ways to cross and link these contexts. Others have developed more complex analyses of roles that were not revered but sometimes feared due to their power, such as the Lakota female-bodied *koshkalaka*, which has spiritual power bordering on sorcery (Allen, 1986).

Creating an historical account of pre-colonial Indigenous systems of gender is thus an engagement with the contested processes of knowledge production on the lives and practices of diverse Indigenous peoples. That is to say, there is no simple "truth" about the terms, roles, experiences, or perspectives of Indigenous non-binary gender expressions. Recent scholarship on two-spirit and other Indigenous conceptualizations of gender have based their analyses within Indigenous peoples' own interpretations and experiences in efforts to "interrupt the authority of anthropological knowledge" (Driskill et al., 2011, p. 10) by actively "re-storying Two-Spirit history" (Driskill, 2011, p. 107) both in North America and other colonized lands. Given these diverse histories grounded both in anthropological research and in Indigenous cultural knowledge and practices, "two-spirit" is a term that holds a multiplicity of meanings and has inherent tensions in its use. These tensions might be productive in disrupting normative gender roles and their attendant colonial qualities.

While these culturally specific understandings of gender have been fractured, individuals and communities are involved in revitalizing the spiritual and cultural significance of roles for two-spirits, men, women, and children, though they fail to be accounted for in gendered analyses of health. The consequences of our inability to account for gaps between colonial patriarchal norms of gendered heteronormativity and the lived realities of Indigenous peoples in diverse communities across Turtle Island are apparent in the gendered health disparities among Indigenous girls and boys, women and men, as well as two-spirit, transgender, and other people whose gender identity does not fit within the gender binary. In the next section, I will discuss some of the ways that gendered health inequities have been approached to date.

Current Framings of Gendered Health Disparities

The poor health status of Indigenous women due to inequities in social determinants of health has been shown to include lower life expectancy rates, lower quality of housing, poor physical environment, lower educational levels, lower socio-economic status, poor access to health services, fewer employment opportunities, and weaker community infrastructure (Society of Obstetrics and Gynaecologists of Canada, 2001; National Association of Friendship Centres, n.d.; National Aboriginal Health Organization, 2005). Other documented factors resulting in the gendered health inequities experienced by Indigenous girls and women include frequent experiences of spousal, sexual, and other violence, as well as inability to access safe, secure housing both on- and off-reserve. Aboriginal women continue to endure "the poorest socio-economic and health status of all Canadians due to the lack of action to meaningfully integrate social determinants of health frameworks into government policy and action" (Native Women's Association of Canada, 2007, p. 4). Although it's likely that transsexual, transgender, and other two-spirit people face similar and additional factors, this has yet to be documented in health literature, due in part to the compounding of transphobia with other forms of structural power inequities.

Organizations like the Native Women's Association of Canada (NWAC) and the National Aboriginal Health Organization (NAHO) continue to necessarily advocate for improvements in the social determinants of Aboriginal women's health, attempting to address the entrenched gender imbalances implemented through the Indian Act. This includes a focus on violence as a crucial social determinant of health, since violence against Indigenous women and girls continues to be normalized. Death due to violence is three times higher for Aboriginal women and five times higher for women in the 25–44 age group than for non-Aboriginal women (Amnesty International, 2004).

The National Association of Friendship Centres (n.d.) also examined social determinants of health for Indigenous women, addressing intersecting factors specific to urban areas. They focused on a number of areas where Indigenous women experience barriers: early childhood development and education, housing, employment, justice, poverty, and violence.

The marginalization of Aboriginal women in accessing health care has also been well documented (Benoit, Carroll, & Chaudhry, 2003; Browne & Fiske, 2001; Brunen, 2000; Dion Stout, Kipling, & Stout, 2001). The embodied health outcomes of this marginalization were illuminated in a recent study examining the particular experiences of 13 Indigenous women in accessing health services in the Okanagan Valley, which demonstrated how the gendered silencing of Indigenous women through colonialism created barriers to service provision and could be understood as a form of structural violence (Kurtz et al., 2008). Experiences of racism, being devalued or disbelieved, and general communication barriers led the women to refuse some health services or not access care when they needed it, putting their health at further risk. Local studies like these contribute to the inclusion of community members in decision making to shape policy in particular areas of Canada, ensuring health services are shaped by the realities facing local Indigenous women.

While investigating the systemic, local, and interpersonal dynamics of Indigenous women's health inequities is crucial, the needs of *all* Indigenous peoples cannot be addressed in studies such as this one, which reproduces the gender binary. As seen in the stated goals of the NAHO to be "respectful and inclusive of all First Nations, Inuit and Metis populations including men, women, children, youth and the elderly, living in urban and rural locations" (NAHO website), intersecting dynamics of age, gender, and geography continue to construct the lives of trans and other two-spirit people as an impossibility through their categorical omission. As illustrated in the story that opened this chapter, the embodied realities of trans and other two-spirit people demonstrate the inability of current frameworks for Indigenous health to account for the lives of those who fall beyond the gender binary. When an Indigenous trans woman in Vancouver is looking for support and refuge from violence, where does she go, given that transition houses such as Vancouver Rape Relief have fought and won court battles to keep trans women out of their services? Given the impetus to improve the health of *all* Indigenous peoples, a more nuanced understanding of gender is needed.

THEORY IN THE FLESH: ELEMENTS OF
AN INDIGENOUS GENDER-BASED ANALYSIS

As I have shown, the marginalization of Indigenous women and girls is
integrally linked with that of trans and other two-spirit people through the colonial gender binary of federal policies, which played a pivotal role in eroding the
cultural and political strength of Indigenous communities. I suggest that an
Indigenous gender-based analysis is necessary for understanding and addressing social health determinants for Indigenous peoples across diverse gender
identities and expressions. In this final section, I will explore some elements of
an Indigenous gender-based analysis, including the restoration of gender roles
within Indigenous self-determination, and recognizing the erasure of two-spirit
people through the gender binary as linked to the ontological foundations of
how we understand "gender" under the ongoing violence of colonialism.

Restoration of Gender Roles as Self-Determination

Restoring Indigenous gender roles and accounting for the lived realities of
all Indigenous peoples is central to the project of self-determination, and has
been taken up by those concerned with the marginalization of both Indigenous women and two-spirit people. Within an Indigenous gender-based analysis, I suggest these projects are inherently linked and can be taken up together
through efforts to revitalize the roles of two-spirit people, girls, and women
within diverse Indigenous cultural and ceremonial practices, as well as within
the political leadership in our communities. As Barker (2008) argues, a more
nuanced understanding of the relationship between gender and sovereignty
than currently dominates Native politics is necessary, beginning with the recognition that the structures and impact of patriarchal colonialism are still
being lived daily by people of all genders. While it remains true that defend-
ers of Indigenous self-determination often fail to adequately factor in the specific roles of Indigenous women and children in urban settings where violence
and poverty is widespread (National Association of Friendship Centres, n.d.),
it is also true that self-determination frameworks fail to account for trans and
other two-spirit people at all (not including those asserted by two-spirit advocates themselves, of course).

The Native Women's Association of Canada (n.d.) calls for "a cultural
framing that reflects Aboriginal ways of knowing, Aboriginal histories (both
pre and post contact), and contemporary Aboriginal realities in Canada" (p. 2).
The recognition of two-spirit people, including trans people, in Aboriginal
histories and contemporary society is in line with the vision described here,

yet is not reflected in the way gender is understood in NWAC's policy frameworks. For example, NWAC states that "traditionally, the sexes functions [*sic*] as cooperative halves. Roles were equally valued. Independent yet interdependent, each half worked to create the perfect whole in society" (p. 6). NWAC (2007, p. 10) asserts that equality was integral to Aboriginal gender roles as "a natural, fundamental principle and lived reality in terms of social processes and outcomes," yet equality is considered among men and women only. Calls for comprehensive and far-reaching efforts to address violence could be strengthened if the gender binary itself were seen as a colonial construct as it would allow for women like Kellie Little to be considered within the complexity of her lived experience.

The recognition and celebration of diverse gender roles are essential to creating communities that are less alienating and violent toward two-spirit people. As two-spirit Didikai Métis writer Cortney Dakin (2012, n.p.) writes:

> Decolonization involves reframing our concepts about Indigenous governance and working to build strong Indigenous nations that honor self-determination, gender variance, and the contributions of Indigenous women, two-spirit, and LGBTQ individuals. With the re-creation of two-spirit identities and reclamation of traditional roles within our respective communities, the need to withdraw from them dissolves.

The Assembly of First Nations, NWAC, and local organizations and individuals calling for women and girls to have political, economic, and social power and the restoration of traditional roles must begin to ask themselves how non-binary traditional and contemporary realities are being addressed in these efforts. Without this, the violence of colonial erasure is further advanced.

Erasure and Ontological Foundations of Gender

The erasure of trans people has been described as "a defining condition of how transsexuality is managed in culture and institutions, a condition that ultimately inscribes transsexuality as impossible" (Namaste, 2000, pp. 4–5). Similarly, two-spirit people, both those who are transsexual and others whose gender identity falls beyond the gender binary, continue to be erased in gender-based analyses that account for men and women only. This erasure itself is a determinant of health, shaping the ability to be seen, heard, and accounted for in all aspects of the lives of Indigenous peoples who fall outside the gender binary. While Indigenous women are marginalized and given lower status than men in colonial gender relations, trans people fail to appear at all, remaining beyond the scope of everything from Indian status to taking up roles in ceremony to accessing health services.

In community-based research conducted by the Trans PULSE Project in Ontario, interviews with trans people revealed that erasure of trans people occurred within two sites: informational erasure and institutional erasure (Bauer et al., 2009). Examples of this erasure include the lack of knowledge that individual health practitioners and other front-line workers bring to their work, as well as the role of policies in actively imposing gendered services within a binary model. The embodied outcomes of this erasure can be seen in the case study that opened this chapter. While Indigenous women in the Downtown Eastside are marginalized due to a range of factors such as poverty and sexualized violence, trans women face the additional factor of being excluded from gender-based services to address these factors. As Bauer et al. (2009) have argued, it is "difficult to understand how social determinants of health, such as access to health care, affect the lives of trans people without understanding the process through which trans people are actively and passively erased" (p. 358). For Indigenous trans and other two-spirit people, this erasure is directly linked to colonial policies such as the Indian Act, which are also central to the marginalization of Indigenous girls and women.

On the other hand, making two-spirit and trans people visible within an Indigenous gender-based analysis of health reveals interesting possibilities about the factors impacting HIV and AIDS. A recent study with trans people in Ontario (Bauer et al., 2012) found that only 15 percent of Aboriginal trans people had never been tested for HIV, as opposed to 44 percent of non-Aboriginal white people and 67 percent of non-Aboriginal racialized people. The research suggested that higher testing rates among Aboriginal trans people could be due to campaigns for HIV testing that explicitly target, or make visible, two-spirit people. An additional consideration is that increased awareness of HIV-related issues in Aboriginal communities might lead health care providers to encourage Aboriginal trans people to be tested for HIV. Given that Indigenous peoples represent 3.8 percent of the Canadian population, but account for 12.5 percent of all new HIV infections since 2008 (Public Health Agency of Canada, 2010), this targeted education provides an example of how the health concerns of both two-spirit and trans people can be taken into account.

The complexity of accounting for two-spirit and trans people within a gender-based analysis is made more difficult by the ontological difference between Western and Indigenous understandings of "gender." This is made clear in attempts to define "two-spirit," which is diversely understood as accounting for intersections of gender, sex, and sexuality among Indigenous peoples historically and currently. Two-spirit is defined in one context as "North American Indigenous people who identify with elements of both male and female gender roles found in many traditional cultures; some but not all will identify along a trans spectrum" (Bauer et al., 2012, p. 2). In this definition, two-spirit is inherently about gender, not sexuality. However, the term "two-spirit" is used more broadly by lesbian, gay, bisexual, trans, and queer people to denote diverse gender and sexual identities among Indigenous peoples in North America (Balsam et al., 2004). Further, within an embodied experience of defining two-spirit identity, Wilson (2008) writes that it is "about circling back to where we belong, reclaiming, reinventing, and redefining our beginnings, our roots, our communities, our support systems, and our collective and individual selves" (p. 198). Beyond being about gender *and* sexuality, two-spirit identity is, for Wilson and many others, about the reclamation of an embodied cultural role.

Some organizations have already begun making these linkages, as seen in a joint policy statement on the sexual and reproductive health, rights and realities for Indigenous peoples in Canada, produced by the Society of Obstetricians and Gynaecologists of Canada (SOGC) (Aboriginal Health Initiatives Sub-committee, Society of Obstetricians and Gynaecologists of Canada, 2011). Working in collaboration with the Native Youth Sexual Health Network, the SOGC Joint Policy Statement states that in both rural and urban areas, Indigenous women experience reduced access to health care services, as well as poor access to culturally safe care. Here, culturally safe care means care that recognizes more than two genders. Further, the policy statement asserts the need to advance the cultural competence of health service providers to ensure the delivery of culturally safe services, including "promoting initiatives already underway that work to restore reproductive justice, fight homophobia and transphobia, and support people with disabilities" (Aboriginal Health Initiatives Sub-committee, 2011, p. 634).

This definition of culturally safe services is presented together with a general recommendation to protect and promote the health rights of all Indigenous peoples, and measures specifically targeted at women and girls, such as birthing strategies to address maternal health care, and increasing access to emergency and alternative contraceptives, mental and sexual health counselling, and midwifery, as well as the return of traditional birthing for Indigenous communities. The policy reflects a deep understanding of how gender, sex, and sexuality can be framed together in addressing health for Indigenous communities, taking into account the social determinants of health and clinical, structural, and policy-level barriers to care.

CONCLUSION

The near-total erasure of two-spirit and trans people that was accomplished through the imposition of the gender binary is integrally related with the hierarchy that continues to perpetuate the violent marginalization of Indigenous girls and women. Yet these connections remain largely unnamed and unaccounted for in the gender-based analysis utilized by many Aboriginal organizations, researchers, and communities when talking about health policy, violence, and social determinants of health.

Trying to reconcile the need to name and challenge the stark realities of patriarchal violence facing Indigenous women and girls with the erasure of trans and other two-spirit people has illuminated for me the need for an Indigenous gender analysis that displaces colonial gender norms. The failure to do so has resulted in an inability to make the lives of trans and other two-spirit people visible in conceptualizations of the health and self-determination of Indigenous communities. However, a vibrant resurgence of two-spirit scholarship, community organizing, and artwork demonstrates the potential to reclaim and re-story Indigenous gender roles and identities as part of broader efforts to create healthy, self-determining communities. In order to better account for the gendered gaps in service provision at the community level, policies must implement an Indigenous gender-based analysis that aims to restore the full humanity of all members of our vibrant communities, instituting Indigenous gender categories that reach far beyond the gender binary.

REFERENCES

Aboriginal Health Initiatives Sub-committee, Society of Obstetricians and Gynaecologists of Canada. (2011, June). Sexual and reproductive health, rights, and realities and access to services for First Nations, Inuit, and Métis in Canada. *Journal of Obstetrics and Gynaecologists Canada, 33*, 633–637.

Allen, P. G. (1986). *The sacred hoop: Recovering the feminine in American Indian traditions.* Boston, MA: Beacon Press.

Amnesty International. (2004, October). *Stolen sisters: A human rights response to discrimination and violence against Indigenous women in Canada.* Retrieved from http://www.amnesty.org/en/library/info/AMR20/001/2004

Assembly of First Nations. (n.d.). *Demanding justice and fulfilling rights: A strategy to end violence against Indigenous women and girls*. Draft for full discussion. Ottawa, ON. Retrieved from www.afn.ca/uploads/files/archive/21.pdf

Balsam, K. F., Huang, B., Fieland, K. C., Simoni, J. M., & Walters, K. L. (2004). Culture, trauma, and wellness: A comparison of heterosexual and gay, bisexual, and two-spirit Native Americans. *Cultural Diversity and Ethnic Minority Psychology, 10*, 287–301.

Barker, J. (2008). Gender, sovereignty, rights: Native women's activism against social inequality and violence in Canada. *American Quarterly, 60*, 259–266.

Bauer, G. R., Hammond, R., Travers, R., Kaay, M., Hohanadel, K. M., & Boyce, M. (2009). "I don't think this is theoretical; this is our lives": How erasure impacts health care for transgender people. *Journal of the Association of Nurses in AIDS Care, 20*, 348–361.

Bauer, G. R., Travers, R., Scanlon, K., & Coleman, T. A. (2012). High heterogeneity of HIV-related sexual risk among transgender people in Ontario, Canada: A province-wide response-driven sampling survey. *BMC Public Health, 12*, 292. Retrieved from http://biomedcentral.com/1471-2458/12/292

Benoit, C., Carroll, D., & Chaudhry, M. (2003). In search of a healing place: Aboriginal women in Vancouver's Downtown Eastside. *Social Science & Medicine, 56*, 821–833.

Browne, A. J., & Fiske, J. (2001). First Nations women's encounters with mainstream health care services. *Western Journal of Nursing Research, 23*, 126–147.

Brunen, L. (2000, April). *Aboriginal women with addictions: A discussion paper on triple marginalization in the health care system*. Unpublished report written for the Northern Secretariat of the BC Centre of Excellence for Women's Health.

Dakin, C. (2012, September 1). Hearing two-spirits: Two-spirit voices are integral to cultivating community resistance and decolonization. *Briarpatch Magazine*. Retrieved from http://briarpatchmagazine.com/articles/view/hearing-two-spirits

Dickason, O. P. (1992). *Canada's First Nations: A history of founding peoples from earliest times*. Toronto, ON: McClelland & Stewart.

Dion Stout, M., Kipling, G. D., & Stout, R. (2001). *Aboriginal women's health research: Synthesis project. Final report*. Ottawa, ON: Centres of Excellence for Women's Health, Health Canada.

Driskill, Q.-L. (2011). D4Y DβC (*Asegi Ayetl*): Cherokee Two-Spirit people reimagining nation. In Q.-L. Driskill, C. Finley, B. J. Gilley, & S. L. Morgensen (Eds.), *Queer Indigenous studies: Critical interventions in theory, politics, and literature* (pp. 95–112). Tucson: University of Arizona Press.

Driskill, Q., Finley, C., Gilley, B. J., & Morgensen, S. L. (2011). Introduction. In Q.-L. Driskill, C. Finley, B. J. Gilley, & S. L. Morgensen (Eds.), *Queer Indigenous studies: Critical interventions in theory, politics, and literature* (pp. 1–28). Tucson: University of Arizona Press.

Feinberg, L. (1996). *Transgender warriors: Making history from Joan of Arc to RuPaul.* Boston, MA: Beacon Press.

Gay American Indians, & Roscoe, W. (1988). *Living the spirit: A gay American Indian anthology.* New York: St. Martin's Press.

Gilley, B. (2011). Two-spirit men's sexual survivance against the inequality of desire. In Q.-L. Driskill, C. Finley, B. J. Gilley, & S. L. Morgensen (Eds.), *Queer Indigenous studies: Critical interventions in theory, politics, and literature* (pp. 123–131). Tucson, AZ: University of Arizona Press

Hunt, S. (2007). *Trans/formative identities: Narrations of decolonization in mixed-race and transgender lives* (master's thesis). Victoria, BC: University of Victoria.

Kurtz, D. L. M., Nyberg, J. C., Tillaart, S. V. D, Mills, B., & the Okanagan Urban Aboriginal Health Research Collective. (2008, January). Silencing of voice: An act of structural violence. *Journal of Aboriginal Health, 4,* 53–63.

Lang, S. (1998). *Men as women, women as men: Changing genders in Native American cultures.* Austin: University of Texas Press.

Morgensen, S. L. (2011). *Spaces between us: Queer settler colonialism and Indigenous decolonization.* Minneapolis: University of Minnesota Press.

Namaste, V. (2000). *Invisible lives: The erasure of transsexual and transgendered people.* Chicago, IL: University of Chicago Press.

National Aboriginal Health Organization (NAHO). (2005, August). *Aboriginal women and girls' health roundtable final report.* Ottawa, ON: Author. Retrieved from http://www.naho.ca/publications/topics/womens-health/?submit=view

National Association of Friendship Centres. (n.d.). *Urban Aboriginal women: Social determinants of health and well-being.* Ottawa, ON: Author. Retrieved from http://www.laa.gov.nl.ca/laa/naws/pdf/NAFC-UrbanAboriginalWomen.pdf

Native Women's Association of Canada (NWAC). (2007, June 4). *Social determinants of health and Canada's Aboriginal women.* NWAC's submission to the World Health Organization's Commission on the Social Determinants of Health. Ottawa, ON: Author.

Native Women's Association of Canada (NWAC). (n.d.). *A culturally relevant gender application protocol.* Ottawa, ON: Author. Retrieved from http://www.nwac.ca/programs/culturally-relevant-gender-analysis

Public Health Agency of Canada. (2010). Chapter 8: HIV/AIDS among Aboriginal people in Canada. *HIV/AIDS Epi Updates.* Retrieved from http://www.phac-aspc.gc.ca/aids-sida/publication/epi/2010/index-eng.php

Roscoe, W. (1991). *The Zuni man-woman.* Albuquerque: University of New Mexico Press.

Roscoe, W. (1998). *Changing ones: Third and fourth genders in Native North America.* New York, NY: St. Martin's Press.

Smith, A. (2005). *Conquest: Sexual violence and American Indian genocide.* Cambridge, UK: South End Press.

Smith, L. T. (1999). *Decolonizing methodologies: Research and Indigenous peoples*. London, UK: Zed Books.

Society of Obstetrics and Gynaecologists of Canada. (2001, January). A guide for health professionals working with Aboriginal Peoples: Health issues affecting Aboriginal peoples—Policy statement. *Journal for the Society of Obstetrics and Gynecologists of Canada, 100*, 1–15.

Stimson, A. (2006). Two spirited for you: The absence of "two spirit" people in Western culture and media. *West Coast Line, 41*, 69–79.

Stoler, A. (2009). *Along the archival grain: Epistemic anxieties and colonial common sense*. Princeton, NJ: Princeton University Press.

Tafoya, T. (1997). Native gay and lesbian issues: The two-spirited. In B. Greene (Ed.), *Ethnic and cultural diversity among lesbians and gay men*, vol. 3, (pp. 1–9). Thousand Oaks, CA: Sage.

Thomas, W., & Jacobs, S. E. (1999). ". . . And we are still here": From *berdache* to two-spirit people. *American Indian Culture and Research Journal, 23*, 91–107.

Williams, W. (1986). *The spirit and the flesh: Sexual diversity in Native American culture*. Boston, MA: Beacon Press.

Wilson, A. (2008). *N'tacimowin inna nah'*: Our coming in stories. *Indigenous women in Canada: The voices of First Nations, Inuit and Métis women, 26*, 193–199.

CHAPTER 11

Take Care of the Land and the Land Will Take Care of You

Resources, Development, and Health

Terry Teegee

About this interview: On December 19, 2012, Nicole Marie Lindsay sat down with Terry Teegee, tribal chief of the Carrier Sekani Tribal Council (CSTC), to discuss the impacts of resource extraction on the health and well-being of Indigenous peoples. As a PhD candidate whose research focuses on resource extraction and the idea of responsibility in Latin America, Nicole was interested to hear Chief Teegee's perspectives on the impacts of resource extraction on First Nations peoples in northern British Columbia. As a registered professional forester with a bachelor of science degree from University of Northern BC, as well as a member of the Takla Nation, Chief Teegee provides a nuanced and informed view of how resource extraction and responsibility for the land must be balanced in order to maintain both the health of the land and the people who depend on it not only for their livelihoods, but also for their physical, spiritual, and cultural well-being. This interview took place at the Carrier Sekani Tribal Council office in Prince George, British Columbia, in the months before the landmark Tsilhqot'in decision and the devastating Mount Polley tailings breach—both of which have reconfirmed the powerful responsibility and rights held by First Nations toward the land, and the ways in which modern large-scale industrial resource extraction places the health of both the land and First Nations peoples at risk.

NICOLE MARIE LINDSAY: Hi, and thanks for meeting with me. Maybe we could start the interview with a reflection on the history of the relationship between First Nations and resources and resource extraction to contextualize the current-day struggles of First Nations here in B.C.

TERRY TEEGEE: It's the same formula, whether it's colonization, accessing arable land, or the fur trade. The colonizers from Britain or France came in and wanted to exploit the resources. The best way to do it was to get rid of the Indigenous peoples. We're still seeing that happen today. Back then it was the fur traders, the timber barons, and the mining people. Now it's oil and gas as well. The big impediment for the colonizers and modern-day government is Indigenous peoples.

Out here in British Columbia, at least our territory, we're on unsettled treaty territory. As far as we're concerned, we've never given any of our territory up. So we have a say, and the courts of Canada and British Columbia have stated that Indigenous peoples need to be adequately consulted and accommodated.[1] That's a good thing for us and a good thing for a lot of Indigenous peoples across Canada.

I've seen this in many countries. In 2009 I attended Conference of the Parties (COP15) in Copenhagen, Denmark. During that meeting I had a chance to meet with the Indigenous Caucus, made up of all the Indigenous peoples that were in attendance—from South America, Central America, Africa, and Australia. We talked about the issue of oil and gas and the issue of carbon in the atmosphere, but it was also the bigger issue of development in our territories. People were coming up to me, saying, "You know, Canada is a safe haven for human rights and Indigenous rights." And I said, "No. No, it isn't. The companies that are based here that are going to your countries and developing these mining projects are doing the same things in Canada." Whether it's Goldcorp or Teck or whoever, these big mining companies aren't listening to us in Canada, and nor are the federal or provincial governments listening to our concerns in terms of development.

At least in our country, we do have some sort of say. We do have the legal backing. But in a lot of other countries, the company just has to pay off the government and the people are taken off their lands or in extreme cases killed for mining developments. It's a form of genocide.

Here in Canada, during our history with colonization, there was the mandate for the government and church and state to assimilate our people. So we're taken from our lands, we're converted to different religions, we're taught to speak English and not our mother tongue, we're taught about Western society instead of our own Indigenous culture and heritage.

What happens in the end is that we suffer genocide of our culture and heritage, if you want to call it that way. It used to be church and state—now it's corporation and state—to take our people, Indigenous peoples, off the land in order to access the resources. That's the number-one goal.

NICOLE: It seems that that is key. It's very simple—getting people off the land, moving them out of the way in order to access those resources. How has that happened over time and how are those processes still going on? What is the impact of that on communities that are affected?

TERRY: It's quite simple, right? Our people had traditional territories. We travelled in those areas to access the caribou or to access fish in the waterways. Western society's interpretation was, "Oh, they're nomadic, they had no real home." To us, it was by design. We knew, our ancestors knew, through thousands and thousands of years that this is the cycle of our lives, this is the cycle of Mother Earth and this is how we sustained ourselves.

What the governments and church and state or corporations like the Hudson's Bay Company saw was that our people were in the way of development. They said, "These people are in the way. How are we going to deal with them? Okay, let's throw them on reserves." Give them a piece of land and they're locked into their jurisdiction by the government. Each reserve or area had Indian agents and you needed permission to do stuff. It was only a few hundred years ago. It was less than a hundred years ago in some cases.

So that was one way. The other way was converting our people into different religions and utilizing the church and state to conform us to Western society. Residential school was one of the biggest policies. I believe the last one closed down in 1976, which was not too long ago. It was well over 100 years ago that the policy started.

A lot of other countries and states used Canada as a template. South Africa was a good example in the forties and fifties when they imposed apartheid on the African people. They got some of those ideas from Canada. That's just a fact. We've seen the atrocities of apartheid in South Africa, as well as in Canada.

I should also say that early on, in early colonization, was the use of germs, which killed a lot of people. Western states and governments realized that it was a good way to get rid of the Indigenous issue. They realized that and they spread smallpox willingly in British Columbia. A lot of the people up here in Lheidli were killed by smallpox or by the Spanish flu. We had no defence against it. I heard stories of the Musqueam in Vancouver area, Coast Salish people. They had numbers of well over 9,000 to 10,000 people reduced to less than 500. Right there, that was near complete genocide of the Musqueam. It was in full knowledge by the government. That was one way to get rid of the Indian problem and get rid of the Indigenous peoples who were on the land.

This government has blood on its hands from its history. They have to deal with it. There's a shame there that they don't want to deal with. Although there is some level of accountability, especially with the residential school issue with the prime minister's apology and the compensation, I don't think it goes far enough.

We have the reconciliation meetings that are going on throughout this country talking about the impacts of residential schools. I think that's a good start, but the history is so deep that it keeps carrying on. My older brother and sister went to residential school. I know a lot of people in the Carrier Sekani are living with the legacy. We are the children from residential schooling. A lot of issues that we're dealing with are related to our sense of identity. If you're really worrying about and questioning your identity and your loss of identity, you're not a whole person, and that really affects your health.

There's a lot of abuse, whether it's physical or sexual, and mental health issues, which lead to a history of abuse down the line for generations to come. We see a lot of our people in poverty. A lot of the [Vancouver] Downtown Eastside is Indigenous peoples. We see what happened with the Downtown Eastside women, the majority of them Aboriginal, who were preyed upon by a serial killer. Up here [in northern British Columbia] we see poverty and lack of infrastructure. We see the Highway of Tears issue come up because many women don't have either the funds or a way to travel safely. It leaves a lot of the people vulnerable.

So in many respects, the issue of land and our access to it, and our access to our culture and heritage and language deeply affected how we are today and where we're at today. Our bands, chiefs and council, our organizations are trying to deal with those issues, which is very difficult, to say the least. You're trying to change our whole way of life, our whole society, which isn't the easiest task, especially if you have policies from the provincial and federal government that impede your progress.

NICOLE: What you've just been describing is a situation in which you've got policies of essentially genocide, cultural assimilation, moving people off the land, and really devastating effects on social structures, culture, family structures—everything. And then at the same time there is this new rush on resources through the latter part of the twentieth century and the first part of this century. When I look at the news and I hear the number of proposed projects that are coming forward right now, and the policies of the government that seem to be pushing them through as fast as they can, it seems to me that they [the government] just want the money that these projects represent. So I want to talk a little bit about the resilience in the face of this. It's a really overwhelming situation to be in when you've got your population decimated, your culture decimated, and you're trying to defend what's left. Can you talk a little bit about the resilience and that movement for defence and recovery?

TERRY: Yeah. Right now we're coming to the point in an industrial age where, especially with globalization and the demands of capitalism, the exploding population is straining our resources all over the world. We're no exception, especially in Carrier Sekani territory. We have a lot of resources that the rest of the world wants because they've run out already and their populations are exploding.

This means that a lot of the low-lying fruit, the easy resources, have already been exploited. You're getting to this point where these huge mining megaprojects.... The reason they need them to be so big is that they're so low grade. You're going to have these big huge craters and big huge tailings ponds. Another example is the Alberta tar sands. A lot of the sweet crude has run out in the Middle East and the United States. Now we're going into the unexplored areas of the oceans and the Arctic and the Alberta tar sands because we're running out of oil. Our economy is run on oil, and people want this affluent lifestyle that they see in North America and Western states and Europe. They don't want to be left out. That means a lot of exploitation in our traditional territories. First it was the fur trade and the timber, and now we're looking at pipelines and mining. There are so many [projects].

I think that how we as people are resilient, at least in British Columbia, is that we have a lot of people using their power, their Indigenous rights and title. This is being upheld in the courts. There is the ability to negotiate. But under uncertainty, under the reality that we're an unsettled treaty area, people just go out there and put up roadblocks or protests. The government realizes that you can't, as in years before, just arrest them. You're going to have to do something about it.

More often than not, we come down to negotiation of whatever the development is. But there are some areas that aren't up for negotiation. A good example is when we were fighting for Amazay Lake.[2] We said, "There's no way you are going to dam this lake and throw tons and tons of heavy metals-leaching tailings that will be poisoning our people and our animals and our plants." So we used social media, our own research, our archaeology. We conveyed our message to the governments and the public in general and into the international arena to get people on our side, to realize that, hey, maybe this is a bad idea. Let's take that off the table.

We saw that with the Tahltan saving their sacred headwaters.[3] Shell gave up their tenures and stated that they'll never go back there to explore the area. The Tahltan put it on an international stage and talked about their relationship to the sacred headwaters of the Skeena, Nass, and the Stikine. They got support from other Indigenous communities and then they conveyed that to the governments and did some direct action in their territory and got on an international stage. They talked to Shell. They went to company meetings and stated, "This is a really bad idea. We don't want you here. This development—you can't do it here." I think they pressured the provincial government as well to talk to them and stated that this is a no go. There is no changing their minds.

NICOLE: It seems like they had strong unity and support.

TERRY: Yeah. Another example is our current fight with the Enbridge Northern Gateway pipeline. I think in many respects we're doing the same thing here. We're utilizing the same tactics that the Tahltan used, except this time I think Enbridge is such a national and even international issue. Everybody's really interested.

We've done our own studies, the Aboriginal Interests and Use study that you can find on our website.[4] We've made an informed decision, talking about our watershed of the Fraser [River], and how the risk of an oil spill would affect our people. We looked at a history of oil pipelines in general and did a look at the Enbridge company itself. We presented this to all eight communities and said, "Is this a good idea?" Everybody resoundingly said, "No, this is a bad idea." It was pretty certain that a lot of our people are saying, "No. We don't want this." They gave us [the CSTC] a mandate to stop it.

We took it to a different level. In 2006, we filed litigation. We managed to stall the process. We never followed through with the full court case, and they came back in 2008. That's what we're seeing here in this current proposal. They changed a few things—a little bit of the route and a little bit of their numbers in regards to long-term and short-term employment. But even with those changes and a 10 percent share into the pipeline, our people said, "No, we're not changing our minds. We want to fight this. We're going to stop this."

And so our people started the Yinka Dene Alliance. *Yinka Dene* means *people of the land.* We have well over 136 communities from British Columbia,

Alberta, and Northwest Territories who have signed on and supported us. So right there, there's so much resistance and unity. We're unified with non-Aboriginal communities such as Smithers, the city of Vancouver. We've partnered up with other groups, non-governmental groups, environmental groups, who've supported us and believe in our cause.

On the international stage, we've brought this to the Conference of the Parties. One of our members from the Tl'azt'en area, Grand Chief Ed John, brought it up in the United Nations in New York. We're really putting it out there to everybody. That plays a big influence on a lot of the investors, so not only are you influencing the credibility of the company, but you influence their investors.

Over the last three or four years we've attended the Enbridge annual general shareholders' meeting. In 2011, I presented at the shareholders' meeting and stated how the Enbridge Northern Gateway pipeline would affect our people and how much opposition we had. I presented to the Royal Bank at their annual general meeting. I know some other community members have gone to other banks like the Bank of Montreal and TD. The big influence in terms of financial institutions is that VanCity took all their shares out of Enbridge.

I think a lot of Indigenous peoples, with the help of environmental groups, have become really savvy in terms of influencing the general population and other influential people such as financiers and government. We have government people who agree with us. The NDP is a good example—provincial and federal. There's a wide array of people that we have aligned ourselves with and presented to and received support from.

NICOLE: It seems to be an enormous amount of work to do all the baseline research, reading all the materials that you get sent for environmental impact assessments. What is the impact of that and how have First Nations communities dealt with the onslaught of all this work?

TERRY: In 2010 a group of researchers from the International Human Rights Clinic at the Harvard Law School published a report on this called *Bearing the Burden: The Effects of Mining on First Nations in British Columbia*. It focused on exactly that issue in regards to the burden on First Nations and looked at the Northgate Minerals proposal for the Kemess North mine. Kemess North was actually one of the first proposals that was refused in Canada, so it was a huge victory. The government said, "No, that's bad. They can't proceed," and they gave 30 recommendations. It was just a procedural, you know—go through with this and take care of all these issues and you can proceed with the mine. But there was one [point] in there that stated, "How are you going to mitigate culture and heritage?" and they had no answer. So that was the one that stopped them. They said, "We have no way of mitigating the development and taking care of your culture and heritage and alleviating that." So we were successful in stopping the project.

NICOLE: Can you explain a little bit about the impacts on culture and heritage of that project?

TERRY: Well, we did our own baseline study. We looked at our history. We found a lot of the arrowheads, graves, culturally modified trees, a lot of trails. That history showed that there was a use there, and that there was occupancy there. That's powerful in any court of law.

In terms of how it would affect our culture and our heritage..., it would have not only destroyed a lot of our culture and heritage, but also the land was still being used. So not only did we show a history, we showed that there are still people up there going hunting for groundhog or for caribou. It is an area that was within our traditional government of the clans. There was somebody's name up there representing that area. It really showed that we were still practising our traditional form of governance and still using that land. If you prevent us from doing that, you've killed a part of our culture and heritage, and there's no way that a government or mine can replace that. I think that's clearly what they couldn't mitigate, and that's why they stopped the mine.

NICOLE: There's another proposal, is there not, for a new mine in that area?

TERRY: Yeah. I think it should be stated here that with the Kemess North proposal, they spent well over $40 million, and these big corporations aren't going to walk away easily. They'll never go away. In many respects, that's like the Enbridge Northern Gateway pipeline. At the end of this, I don't know how many millions will be spent on the environmental assessment process. There will be a lot spent on the Northern Gateway Alliance, which was to help the process. They were funded to the tune of $120 million. They won't go away. This oil pipeline—originally it was proposed in the seventies. There's an old proposal there from a different company way back in the seventies and it was abandoned.

But going to back to the Kemess North project, they're looking at a new proposal for an underground mine using the old mine site as a place to put the tailings. It may be a little less environmentally destructive, but it's still a mine. There's infrastructure up there. There's that mill that's still up there.

There's a lot of investment still up there. It's our duty as Indigenous peoples and governments to look at that and say, "Well, is this feasible?" But the reality is that they won't go away. That's always a big concern.

So how do we deal with that? I think it's up to our people, our community, to really look at it. That original fight. . .did we do it for nothing? Should we use that leverage we gained to maybe benefit our people? Maybe economically it can benefit our people and maybe we can use those benefits to reinvigorate our culture and heritage. I don't know. It's up to the communities, really.

NICOLE: Looking at the amount of work that's gone into dealing with these proposals and these projects—just going through the process—how is that changing the communities?

TERRY: Well, during these studies—some of these were funded by either the government or by the proponent itself, but I think our communities, chiefs, and council, our organization here, the CSTC, we have become more proactive in training our own people, basically building up capacity. We have some of these projects that we are considering—not supporting—but they do provide funding. We utilize some of those resources, put them back into the community to get somebody trained. Then we could get that person to look at another project down the road. And here at the [Carrier Sekani] Tribal Council we are active in seeking other types of funds so we could have a mapper or a geographical information person that can assist with any of our communities that have issues—not only monitoring, but looking at specific projects. Even here, we're strained with a limited amount of capacity and funding.

When you talk about capacity, to me it just converts to: Where do you get your money? Because you need the money to get the research done, to train people. You need the money for lawyers and whatnot. That's how a lot of our communities do it is to train our own people, have homegrown people with you ready for not only the project you're looking at but projects in the future.

NICOLE: Some make the argument that industrial development, mines, pipelines, resource extraction are not only necessary but inevitable. There's this way of thinking that, "Oh, it's going to happen." What is the vision of the communities? Do they see this type of development as inevitable? Are there alternative visions?

TERRY: No. If you believe that it's inevitable, then you're defeated. A lot of our people don't think that way, at least from what I've seen. We have a belief that we can stop a lot of these projects. But I understand that it's needed. And if it is needed, let's do it in a really conscious way, really looking at the long-term effects, because once that mine is built and once those tailing ponds are there, they're there forever.

In our mindset, as Indigenous peoples, we're always taught that we're not only speaking for us, we're speaking for seven generations. Is this the legacy that we want to leave the future? Perhaps it is. Perhaps we could partner in some of these projects as a full partner, looking at all our issues, looking at a way to mitigate the environmental effects. Maybe we'd get some sort of benefit in that, but at least from what I hear from my communities here is that it has to be planned very well. It has to be sustainable.

The problem is that today, with commodity prices that are driven by the stock market and capitalism, there's this big rush, a gold rush, if you will. We've seen it happen before. The gold rush came through here before and there were a lot of impacts because of it. But I think our people have the ability to at least put their issues there and at the same time try to alleviate some of those adverse effects, especially on the land because in the end it will affect us health-wise.

NICOLE: So do you see that happening now?

TERRY: No. After looking at the Enbridge Northern Gateway pipeline project and looking at the environmental assessment system, seeing it got gutted in 2003, 2007, and then this past year, we went so far as to say, "Well, what if we had an Indigenous environmental assessment?" What if we were the ones that led the environmental assessment? How would that look? There are a lot of things that we would like to see. We wanted to see the ability of an environmental assessment to say "no" to a project, which the two current assessments, provincial and federal, don't. All they can do is make recommendations.

We would like to see an informed decision. Going back to the seventies and the sixties, when environmental assessments started in Europe, the idea was to get an informed decision and to see if a project was viable. What are the effects of a major industrial project? That's one example we'd like to see in our own assessment process, looking at culture and heritage and having that as a more prominent issue within the process.

NICOLE: What is the relationship between resource extraction and the health of First Nations communities? If we think about resource extraction as a determinant of health, what does that mean to you in the communities that you work with?

TERRY: Well, through history, going back to colonization and what I talked about with the fur trade, the timber barons, the gold rush, and now we're getting back to mining and oil and gas—the more industrial activities you have in your traditional territory, I believe the less healthy your community will be. If you want to go to an extreme example, it would be some of those communities that are in urban centres. For example, in Vancouver, right downtown, the whole area is developed. We've seen čəsnaʔəm, which was a small area that was the Musqueam people's traditional burial grounds. When a developer found it, the people had to go protect it. In terms of health, the Musqueam have a really good healthy idea of their identity, but due to the fact that there's so much industrial and residential development around them, they've lost their access to the land. Their way of life, in a way, has been killed off because of that, because of industrialization and development in general—because of the city. And you could say that for a lot of the First Nations that are within city centres.

But compare that to very isolated areas up here in the North or many other areas of British Columbia. You go there and there's still people trapping, hunting, living off the land. They are really connected, especially in those areas that are undeveloped. You go very far north in British Columbia, and our people have reconnected back to their land because there's that opportunity. I know at least in my territory in Takla, people still just go out and practise what they've been taught. We're still utilizing a lot of the natural resources. On the other hand, that has been lost in many respects in the urban centres. You can't go out and use it because it's not there anymore. If it is, you're going to have to go far away to get it. You're going to have to go outside the urban centres, which is a sad thing. It's sad that some of our people have to live with that reality.

But up here we have an opportunity to go back to the land. If there's no industrial activity or a limited amount of industrial activity out here, we can go back out to the land, build a cabin, do our traditional activities like hunting and gathering. The more connected we are with our traditional diets—the caribou, the groundhog, the moose, the beaver, and all of those things in our territories that were traditionally used—the better off we are, not only mentally with our connection to the land, but physically. That was our traditional diet hundreds of years ago. The reality is that as many Indigenous peoples moved to urban centres and whatnot, our diets have changed. We're seeing a lot of health impacts of Western diet—diabetes, cancer. It's killing our people.

There are also other health impacts related to mining and the oil and gas industry. We're seeing a lot more rare forms of cancer, perhaps because of tailings ponds. A good example is Fort McMurray. Downstream are the Athabascan Fort Chipewyan. They're seeing very rare diseases, high rates of cancer. It's because of those tailings ponds, because of the heavy metals that are leaching into their waterways. So whether it's development in Fort McMurray or Vancouver, I think you're going to have a lot more health problems, whether it's diet or rare forms of cancer or diabetes and whatnot.

It's the government that needs to be held accountable. They make the decisions and they allow corporations to come in and do this. In Takla, where I'm from, my dad's trapline, there was a mercury mine there, so my family and my people from Takla, we weren't allowed to go in that area. They said, "Stay away from there. It has mercury." So we were displaced because of that mine. It was developed in the forties to help during the war effort. Since the war ended, nothing was done with it. It came back into the government's jurisdiction and they didn't do anything. It's been well over 70 years now. It's still not cleaned up. That area was taken out of my family's way of accessing traditional foods, but also taken out of my community in general.

NICOLE: And that's on unceded territory.

TERRY: Yeah, but it's only over the past 30–40 years that things have changed with court cases like *Calder*, *Sparrow*, but more importantly, *Delgamuukw*, which highlighted the duty of the governments to talk to us. That basically empowered us. It wasn't until then that all governments—federal, provincial, and municipal—and companies were put on notice that we were a form of government and jurisdiction that needed to be consulted and give approval.

NICOLE: Is the government responding to that?

TERRY: Oh yeah, they have to. We've seen many developments that are stalled because of that. The Tulsequah Chief [project] up in the Taku Tlingit area hasn't been put through because the First Nations up there have issues with it. It's been in proposal stage since 2003. That's nine years. But we've also seen it in treaty areas too. We've seen it in the Berger Inquiry. We've seen how that gas pipeline up in the Mackenzie Valley would affect the Indigenous peoples. They went to court. Thomas Berger did that inquiry and said, "Well, you know, this is a mega-project that would affect a lot of Indigenous peoples. You need to talk to them. You need their consent." That was in 1970. It's been 42 years and there's still no pipeline. So whether it's treaty, untreaty, I think we still have the power and the ability to dictate what is happening in our territories.

NICOLE: That's a really powerful thing.

TERRY: That is. Going back to the Coast Salish—we had influential people, prominent in Canada. One is Chief Dan George. He had this vision that eventually one day we use the white man's tools to empower ourselves and become productive people—become the best of the society. In his famous speech that he made in 1967, he said, "I shall grab the instruments of the white man's success—his education, his skills, and with these new tools I shall build my race into the proudest segment of your society."[5] It's a very powerful statement.

NICOLE: Can you talk a little bit more about the vision going forward for First Nations communities in regards to resources and health and that relationship?

TERRY: Ideally, in terms of development within our territories, every proposal needs our involvement. Going back to international standards—the United Nations Declaration for the Rights of Indigenous People of free, prior, and informed consent—that's what we believe here at the CSTC and that's what a lot of people internationally believe. We always hold that up in our territory. We want to be involved. We want to know how it's going to affect us. We want to be a part of it. And if a proposal is going ahead, we want to benefit too. It's the new reality, and we should be fully involved and recognized as a government that has jurisdiction. Essentially, we want to take our rightful place in this society—that's our vision.

How that develops. . . ? We need a really good idea of those areas that are off limits and those areas that potentially could be developed. This means that we need a land use plan, which has never been fully or inclusively implemented for our people. That's the start of it and how we move forward in terms of our connection with development.

But in terms of our own people, . . . I have been saying this for a while—go back to the land. One of our Elders, Sophie Thomas from Saik'uz, said, "If you take care of the land, the land will take care of you." That's a very inclusive statement. If you take care of it, you'll reap the benefits of it. I think that's the way forward.

NOTES

1. Landmark court cases include *Delgamuukw v. British Columbia* (1997) and *Haida Nation v. British Columbia (Minister of Forests)* (2004).

2. Amazay Lake, in Tse Key Nay (a coalition of three First Nations with common Sekani heritage: Kwadacha, Takla, and Tsay Key Dene) territory in northern British Columbia, was at risk of being used as a tailings dump by Northgate Minerals' proposed Kemess North mine. In 2007, in the face of significant pressure from Tse Key Nay and a supportive public, a federal joint review panel rejected Northgate's environmental assessment report and recommended the mine not be approved. In 2008, the federal and provincial governments issued a joint decision to respect the panel's recommendation, and the Kemess North proposal was rejected (Laplante, 2009). In 2011, Northgate Minerals was bought out by AuRico Gold Inc., and at the time of this interview in December 2012, AuRico Gold is conducting a feasibility study for a new proposal for an underground mine at Kemess North (AuRico Gold, 2013).

3. See Hume (2012).

4. Carrier Sekani Tribal Council Aboriginal Interests & Use Study on the Enbridge Gateway Pipeline, May 2006. Retrieved from http://www.carriersekani.ca/images/docs/enbridge/AIUS%20COMPLETE%20FINAL%20inc%20maps.pdf

5. See George (1967).

References

AuRico Gold. (2013). Kemess underground. Retrieved from http://www.auricogold.com/exploration/kemess-underground.html

Delgamuukw v. British Columbia [1997] 3 S.C.R. 1010.

George, Chief D. (1967). Lament for Confederation, Empire Stadium, July 1, 1967. Retrieved from http://www.canadahistory.com/sections/documents/Native/docs-chiefdangeorge.htm

Haida Nation v. British Columbia (Minister of Forests) [2004] 3 S.C.R. 511, 2004 SCC 73.

Hume, M. (2012, December 18). B.C.'s Sacred Headwaters to remain protected from drilling. Globe and Mail. Retrieved from http://www.theglobeandmail.com/news/british-columbia/bcs-sacred-headwaters-to-remain-protected-from-drilling/article6504385/

Laplante, J. P. (2009). Kemess North: Insights and lessons. Mining Coordinator's Report. Takla, BC: Takla Lake First Nation. Retrieved from http://www.carriersekani.ca/images/docs/lup/KemessNorthTaklaReportAug2009.pdf

CHAPTER 12

Raven Healing

Roberta Kennedy (Kung Jaadee)

I have been a traditional Haida storyteller for 22 years. I have travelled across the country performing my stories in nearly every province and territory.

These stories are Haida in origin, but I include everyone in my presentations. I have always encouraged others to learn their stories, to share them with one another, and for us to really listen to each other. Though we will always be different, there are some things that will connect us. I share my messages of hope not just with our Indigenous communities, but with all of our communities. It is my hope that through my performances, I am building bridges between our different cultural groups.

I Begin Telling Stories

I started telling stories when my eldest son was five years old. I told my first story to his kindergarten class in Victoria, British Columbia. At the time he was one of two Aboriginal students in the whole school. I did not have a positive experience in my school when I was growing up, despite the fact that it was a Haida community. I wanted to ensure that my son and his younger siblings never felt the shame I felt in my life.

I forced myself to start telling stories so that I would demonstrate pride in myself for my children. I hoped my children might grow up to become proud of themselves. My first story was about my great-grandmother making my button robe for my high school graduation. She was 86 years old when she made it for me. It took her six months to make it, carefully sewing all the sequins onto it. She gave it to me at my graduation ceremony, which was held in front of my community.

When I told this story, I noticed a positive effect on my son's face. Once his classmates commented on how lucky he was, he really lit up! He had the biggest smile. I realized I was telling stories for him, to help him. I only learned a few years ago while telling this story to an audience of storytellers that this really was the beginning of my own healing. Afterwards, the rest of his school invited me to come and to speak in their classes, and before I knew it, I was invited into other schools within and outside the school district. I was invited across the province, and then across the country.

When I shared my stories, I spoke about the history of my Haida Nation. I told about our two main clans: Ravens and Eagles. All Haidas belong to one of them, following our mothers' lines. We are matrilineal in our traditions. Our mothers are our life givers. They're strong enough to carry children and to give birth. And we have always honoured our women by following our mothers' and our grandmothers' family lines. In the beginning I was sharing information to inform audiences of my people's cultural practices. I was also working hard to ensure audiences knew who we were as First Nations peoples.

I listened to my uncle telling stories before and after I became a storyteller. When I first heard him performing, I was a young mother. I was learning about who we are as Haida. Though we rarely saw each other, he taught me how to be a storyteller. He travelled our world, telling our stories. I also learned how to tell stories from one of my cousins. He would invite me to accompany him for presentations in various schools. Together we would wear our regalia, and we would drum and sing traditional songs as well.

During my early storytelling days, my cousin gave me a red cedar bark–woven hat. He called a Cree Elder forward to witness the giving of this gift. He told me I didn't know the impact my stories had on my audiences as he placed the hat on my head. I cried tears of joy.

I learned that stories are healing. I shared my stories of why I became a storyteller in the first place. And in those early days, I cried throughout the telling of them. As time passed, I no longer cried, but I used a strong voice, and I spoke to honour my ancestors. I was striving to make my audiences aware of who I am as an Aboriginal person. I wanted my audiences to know I'm a human being. As the years have passed, I've met people who have taught me important things about living a spiritual life. An Elder has taught me my tears are my strength—that tears indicate one's strength, not one's weakness. She also shared that crying is healing. I now share this teaching with everyone when I perform my stories.

Learning Humility

For many years I was an arrogant storyteller. I believed only people who stood and told stories were real storytellers. A little while into my storytelling career, I had an opportunity to experience two residencies at the Banff Centre for the Arts. During my first residency I noticed the other programs offered at the same time as our Aboriginal storytelling program: music, theatre, Women in the Director's Chair, writing, dance, and visual arts. I became aware of how we are all storytellers. Each of us is telling our stories in our own way in all of these disciplines. These forms of storytelling help all of us to heal. They might be considered frivolous or a waste of time, but in reality, these art forms help to connect us to ourselves, to our spirits.

Today when I perform my stories, I ask my ancestors to support me. I am weak without them. When I get on a stage, I open myself up and let my stories tell themselves. I let my ancestors speak through me. I let go of my own stuff. I let go of my mind, which will stop me from saying anything if I think too much during my presentations. I let go of the tension in my body. It becomes relaxed and I let my breath move deep inside of me. Often I don't remember what I've said when I'm finished.

When I perform my stories, I do my best to share the immense love I have for everyone and for everything. I let go and do my best to help others feel the goodness that exists in all of us. Our Haida creation stories are important because they tell of how our world came to be. They tell of a time when we were humble. These stories are from a time when we recognized the animals as our helpers.

Learning to Love Myself

A few years ago I almost died after contracting a hospital bacterial infection following an emergency hernia surgery repair. I tried to die because I was in immense pain. I am sensitive to all the opiates, and I was allowed only extra-strength Tylenol for pain relief. This didn't even touch the pain I was experiencing. I would leave my body again and again by going into a deep sleep. I went to a place full of light. Each time I thought to myself, *It's so nice here I'm going to stay.* And every time I was finished thinking that, I landed back in my body with a heavy thump! It hurt for a moment.

My first thought was, *Oh good! The pain is gone!* After a few more minutes I realized, *Oh NO! It's NOT gone! OWWWW!* I was moaning all the time I was awake. I recall seeing my daughter, my middle child, and my ex-husband around my bed, in hospital gowns, masks, and gloves. They were seated far away from me. I didn't have the strength to waken enough to visit with them.

One night I was wide awake in the middle of the night. I wasn't vomiting or experiencing other awful symptoms for a short while. I felt rested, though the pain was still there. I was remembering my grandmothers. They loved me unconditionally when I first arrived in our world. They doted on me and held me a lot. I felt their love all around me. I felt safe. I felt warmth and comfort. I took their love and I sent it to the whole world.

I thought of everyone in this world I love. I didn't care if they didn't remember me, or if they hated me. I sent my love to all of them. My body was broken. I was 25 pounds less than I usually am, and I'm already very small and thin as it is. I managed to get all around our world with this love. That's when I realized I had enough love inside of myself that it filled the universe. I started crying at that moment because I realized I loved myself for the first time in my life.

I told myself, *I love me! And I'm going to get well again because I deserve it! It might take a while, but I will be 100 percent one day!*

Once I learned to love myself, I knew I also love everyone in our world. I knew every single human being is beautiful from the inside out, even if they don't know it. I also knew I love those who aren't kind to me, who intentionally try to hurt me. I tell them I love them, regardless of their actions. My dearest friend has taught me there are some in this world who do not understand what love is, and will not learn how to love themselves on their own. He suggested I can encourage others to be kind to themselves as much as they can every day. This is a good start toward accepting and loving oneself. By being kind to ourselves and being kind to others, our world can become a better place.

Sharing Love

I am now travelling in our country and sharing my message with others as much as possible. My friend Denise reminded me: "Storytellers are the ones who speak stories of love." That's what I do. Most recently I was in Burnaby and Vancouver telling students to love themselves as much as they can. Our Creator doesn't make junk. We are perfect as we are. I strongly encourage my audience to look into the mirror every day and tell themselves, "I love you!" And to do this every day for as long as necessary and for the rest of our lives. I told high school students just the other day, "We are meant to love ourselves. Love yourself as much as you possibly can. Love your whole body, how you look, whatever your body is shaped—love yourself now!"

When we love ourselves, we make our world a better place instantly. When we love ourselves, we will see that we automatically love everyone else in our world. We can't help that. We will see that every human being is a beautiful being, too.

What I didn't get to share with them is how we'll put aside the pettiness of gossiping and ugliness that hurts us. We won't need to even consider this as part of our lives because we'll love ourselves enough to make it through the days, even when things get difficult. We will love everyone else more than enough to ignore the terrible darkness some of us bring into our world that hurts others.

One of my main stories I perform for every presentation is about how Raven, our Trickster, and our Creator, made our world.

RAVEN CREATES OUR WORLD

Raven flew in darkness forever and ever. He flew in one direction as eons of ages passed. He hoped and he prayed the darkness would come to an end, but it never did. Soon the blackness slipped under his skin, it surrounded his heart, and started pulling him apart. It would destroy him, but he's the Raven. He knows. He flapped his wings harder and harder. That darkness came out of him, and it gathered around him until it formed into a great ball, our world.

It took his breath away as he shouted, "Haaneeeeeeesgwaaaaaa! That is sooooooo beautiful! I must change myself into a handsome two-legged, into a man. In my new body, I'll go into this new world and I'll fix it. I'll make it a better place than it already is." Raven made the land, the fresh water, the mountains, the hills, the trees, the grass, the swimmers, the crawlers, the four-leggeds, and he made all of us two-leggeds. He set us all on the Earth in one place and we two-leggeds moved to the Four Directions on our own. We were meant to live together—all of us, in all of our differences—but we made the choice to separate, and to move into our own groups.

Raven travelled to our villages. He taught us how to build our homes, how to gather and how to prepare our food, how to look after our children.

Raven helped us in the beginning, in order that we will become the best we can possibly be. He taught us how to be *Haadalaasis*, or Good People. Raven gave each of us a gift, meant to be shared with the world. We are all unique. And at the same time we have many similarities. We are human beings: we get hungry, so we eat; we get thirsty, so we drink; we get tired, so we sleep; we breathe. We all have hearts beating inside of our chests; hopefully, we love more than we hate.

CONCLUDING THOUGHTS: WHEN WE LOVE OURSELVES. . .

When we share our stories with one another, and when we really listen to each other, we will see the similarities between us. We will never be completely the same because we are meant to be different. Every species here in our world is different from one another. There are some things that will bring us together as one: some of us have similar traditional stories; some of us make the same kind of bread; we have similar songs; our beliefs have similarities, too. There will always be something that will draw us together, and it will help us to realize we are not them and us, but that we are all of us.

Stories connect us and confirm us as the human beings we are. We become one through the sharing of our personal tales. These narratives draw us in because we all have similar legends within our nations, within our families, within ourselves. Every nation in our world has endured war, famine, disease, and yet we have survived to the present day. These are the messages I share with my audiences when I perform my stories: we are similar as we are human beings; we are all survivors; we are meant to love ourselves, and we are meant to love one another.

Before I started performing the traditional legends of my Haida Nation, I was extremely shy and awkward. I barely spoke a word to anyone. This stemmed from racism I experienced growing up in a community where the armed forces had moved in. The children of these people were given misinformation about who we were as Haida. They shared what they learned with me in the form of bullying and taunting on a daily basis. I believed their ugly words. I allowed them to sink into my being. Once my children entered the public school system, I could no longer be shy and ashamed. I knew my children would learn to think how I was thinking. I started telling stories of who we are as Haida Aboriginal people.

I have learned that the sharing of my stories is a form of healing for others. After noticing my child was only one of two Aboriginal students in his public school, I forced myself out of my shame and silence. I told stories of our traditions, our beliefs, and our legends. I learned how to accompany myself on my hand drum and I sang our traditional songs, too. As I grew in my story-telling role, I gained strength. Encountering my own death after having emergency surgery allowed me to love myself inside and out. Through this self-love I know I now love everyone else. Sharing this message of self-love is the main message in my performances. We improve our lives and everyone's around us when we decide to love ourselves.

We are all beautiful as the Creator has made us. We are all storytellers, bringing healing to those around us. We can all tell our own stories, in our own way. And we can listen to one another, and see who we really are.

Haw'aa, thank you.

PART 3

WELLNESS IS KNOWING WHO WE ARE

Culture, Language, Identity

atikowisi miýw-āyāwin, Ascribed Health and Wellness, to *kaskitamasowin miýw-āyāwin,* Achieved Health and Wellness

Shifting the Paradigm[1]

Madeleine Dion Stout

My Cree name is *kétéskwēw,* which means ancient woman or child with an ancient spirit. This is the name I was called from the time I was born on the Kehewin Cree Nation in Alberta. My "spice" of four decades and more is Bob Stout. We have two daughters: *osāwiwaskoh- pihēsiwsew iskwēw,* or Yellow Cloud Thunder Spirit Woman, and *okisiko iskwew,* or Angel Woman. We are grandparents to two grandsons: *Xuē,* Sun god in the Muisca language, and *Inti,* Sun god in the Quechua language. Our granddaughter has a Cree name, *Miyawata,* which means celebrate.

I'm a Cree speaker, a survivor of residential schooling, and I became a registered nurse 46 years ago. Over these years I've witnessed, learned, and reflected a lot about the health of Indigenous peoples. I've also come to realize that many people, including health care professionals, want to understand us and our current health realities and conditions.

I use the Cree language to describe our experiences, realities, and aspirations because it provides a ready and relevant window into our society and our health. Cree is very fitting for this because it is verb-based, gender-neutral, collective, and embedded with original instructions. By leaning heavily on my Indigenous language, I hope to open vistas into the Cree culture, *neheýew-isicikewin,* and to provide insights into what shapes our health and wellness. When introduced to some Cree concepts, people can grasp our world views and views of the world in a more meaningful way.

NATURE OF THE PARADIGM SHIFT

This chapter focuses on an important transformation that is taking place in our lives as we move from *atikowisi miýw-āyāwin*, ascribed health and wellness, to *kaskitamasowin miýw-āyāwin*, achieved health and wellness. This is not a linear or a straightforward process, and it is not happening in isolation from our mainstream health systems, which, with the proper understanding of our perspectives and experiences, can help to bring favourable change. More attention has to be paid to the location and flow of significant markers on this journey. If *atikowisi miýw-āyāwin* is at one end of a spectrum (where we are coming from) and *kaskitamasowin miýw-āyāwin* is at the other end of the spectrum (where we are going to), then *nātamakéwin miýw-āyāwin*, or assisted health and wellness, has to be located in the middle, where a supportive system goes hand in hand with a growing sense of the helping "self."

Meanwhile, Indigenous perspectives have to be examined and utilized in order to critically analyze the determinants of Indigenous peoples' health in Canada and to adopt appropriate health determinants for ourselves. When the visions of traditional peoples in Indigenous communities formulate Indigenous concepts of health and wellness and its requisites, outside experts can no longer single-handedly determine the parameters of health practice in our communities. Rather, it is Indigenous peoples who must introduce and think through our own contemporary and timeless interpretations of health determinants.

For us, "keeping systems," or *kanwéyihicikātéki*, are the fundamental practices, beliefs, and values that maintain, reinforce, and uphold our cultures and communities in the long run. Similarly, *nanātawihiwēwin* is the daily ritual of healing and helping ourselves, which enables us to take more responsibility for our own health and wellness. Strengths like this involve a *self*-centred, substantive, and synergistic process, often disciplined within troublesome social, economic, political, and cultural contexts. Health and wellness will be realized among Indigenous individuals, families, and communities when "self," or *niýa*, is liberated and challenged with shifting from a mainstream to a holistic paradigm based locally and experienced organically. Moreover, the struggle toward health, social, and health care equity has to be fought out in the spirit of every individual and must find expression in the living contexts, or *éýihta*, particular to Indigenous peoples.

PACE OF THE PARADIGM SHIFT

The shift from ascribed health and wellness, *atikowisi miýw-āyāwin*, to achieved health and wellness, *kaskitamasowin miýw-āyāwin*, is being accelerated by a number of forces. First, the worldwide economic recession bears down on our health and social supports, such that creativity and innovation become all important in our pursuit of health and wellness. Second, governments are awakening to the need for "close-the-gap" adjustments to address our health inequities. Third, our communities are expressing new socio-economic and political aspirations to move beyond the old paradigm of *atikowisi miýw-āyāwin*, where we internalized colonization through the entrenched domination of governments and our dependency on them.

On the one hand, *atikowisi miýw-āyāwin* is imposed upon us, prescribed by policy and based on the benevolence and largess of a colonizer society that has effectively erased our traditional systems of health and wellness. The internalization of colonization, fatalism, and historical trauma has decimated our internal human reserves, and so ascribed health and wellness, *atikowisi miýw-āyāwin*, being told from the outside how to be healthy and well, no longer sits well with us. We now see that moving away from *atikowisi miýw-āyāwin* is a vital measure for taking back our health and wellness.

On the other hand, *kaskitamasowin miýw-āyāwin*, achieved health and wellness, is poised to fully exploit our human agency and traditions in a good way so that we do not remain complacent, fatalistic, and unwell due to past injustices. *kaskitamasowin miýw-āyāwin* is health and wellness we have conjured up and created for ourselves. *kaskitamasowin miýw-āyāwin* means achieving the health status that we wish upon ourselves and our families, communities, and nations. We achieve *kaskitamasowin miýw-āyāwin* with our own will and abilities and with the resources we have at our immediate disposal. *kaskitamasowin miýw-āyāwin* comes from our inner strength, inner forces, and inner voices. This means we have to affirm ourselves as sacred beings and be treated with love and respect. At the same time, we have to recognize that although the entirety of ourselves often overrides the totality of our environments, both can make or break our health and wellness.

CHALLENGES OF THE PARADIGM SHIFT

Much mainstream reflection, *māmitonēýihcikēwin*, on the devastating health and social consequences of colonization for Indigenous peoples has assumed relative homogeneity in the construction and interpretation of our human condition and realities. Little differentiation has been acknowledged on the basis of Indigenous languages such as Cree, or *nēhiýiwēwin*, despite the salience of this variable in deepening our understanding of risk factors like enslavement, or *awahkānowi*; unhealthy policies and practices, or *māýi-owýasiwēwikimākanā*;

and *kakwātakitā*, or the ensuing imprisonment in pain-wracked minds, bodies, and spirits. Scant acknowledgement is given to whether and how the responses, or *naskomowēnā*, and the human reserves, or *sōhkātisiwinā*, of Indigenous peoples with lived experience might inform new thinking about ancient ideas by drawing on old actions for new interventions.

Shifting from *atikowisi miýw-āyāwin* to *kaskitamasowin miýw-āyāwin* presents other challenges because while ample evidence exists to describe social, health, and health care inequities experienced by Indigenous peoples internationally, information about effective ways of reducing these inequities is very limited. As well, the evidence shows that different populations respond very differently to identical interventions. To be transformative for Indigenous peoples, the paradigm shift under discussion must focus on interventions that draw on fairness, or *nahi*, rather than equality, *tipi*. For *nahi* to be realized, the values that inform fairness have to be made explicit, along with the commitments for mitigating unfair variations in health status.

Uncertainty and potential pitfalls are hallmarks of change; therefore, shifting from dependence to independence can be an arduous journey. Transitioning from *atikowisi miýw-āyāwin* to *kaskitamasowin miýw-āyāwin* will curb expenditures that have not improved the health of Indigenous peoples, but other risks will surface along the way. There will be people who become lost or disoriented when things change, and so if we are not aware, this shift can inadvertently cause a risk pileup of *kitimakisona*, or poverties and pathologies resulting from unmet human needs. Experience tells us that poverties of all kinds have stolen our productive capacity and independence, leaving us confused, traumatized, and unhealthy.

Still, our conception of poverty cannot be limited to just economic deprivation because this interpretation does not consider the social suffering and inequities commonly associated with our *kitimakisona*. The root causes of the health, social, and health care inequities experienced by Indigenous peoples lie in colonization, or *mipahi kayás*—an extreme, toxic, and deadly past that has insidiously disconnected and dislocated individuals, families, and communities. We are now tattooed with *kayás óma ka nóhcikweyā*, the interminable and blunt assault that has inflicted historic trauma on us on a massive scale. Generations of us have been relegated to the margins of mal-development on reserves known as *iskonkana*, leftover plots, or *tipahaskāna*, measured lots. As well, residential schools, which we named *kiskinwahamátowikamokwa* or teaching and learning structures, were unnatural, unhealthy environments that severely damaged our cultures, languages, traditions, and heritage.

The net effect of these historical patterns is *māỳi-mācihowin*—the bad, ugly, nasty, evil, wicked state of physical, mental, emotional, and spiritual unwellness— which causes much suffering for Indigenous peoples in many communities. Meanwhile, *kitimahitowin*, making one another poorer through lateral violence, has us at war against ourselves where the weaponry is *pāstāhowin*, transgression of taboos. Losing personal control over our health and wellness unleashes intense emotions in us like *pakosēỳi-mowin*, a yearning for a better quality of life and happier times. Still we aim for the end point of *wāskāmsiwin*, or recovery—to "come to," to become altered, to pass gradually into the present, to pass from one phase to another—where health, social, and health care equity are found.

Opportunities of the Paradigm Shift

Wholehearted commitment to and personal involvement in constructing solutions has begun the paradigmatic shift, but the process has been burdened by *tāpiscōc kipihkitonēhpitikoweya*, the pain of being strangled by grief and loss. This hurt is eased by spiritual assistance, counselling, or the offering of appropriate gifts to a drum song or ceremony—*tipahikēwin*—since we know that traditional practices bestow a spiritual advantage and a competitive edge culturally, socially, and politically. When traditional ceremonies facilitate a catharsis of emotions and enhance the ability of individuals to cope with cumulative trauma, then *mōcopiyōwin*, the crazed state due to overwhelming experiences and circumstances and corresponding power imbalances, is held in abeyance.

Thus the consciousness and health actions of Indigenous peoples are strengthened when we adopt traditional perspectives, correct power imbalances, and trust ourselves. Through our efforts to advance the shift from *atikowisi miỳw-āyāwin* to *kaskitamasowin miỳw-āyāwin*, we ride new waves such as health, social, and health care equity, and in so doing move the "self" from the margins to the centre of health development.

Holistic and traditional health interventions call for personal involvement and commitment because this resolve is seen as the best antidote to modern diseases, illnesses, and sickness. Diabetes, or *sēwankānāspinēwin*, the inability to process the sweetness of life, has to then be addressed by applying the very principles that are celebrated in feasts and ceremonies: *pimēỳimowin*, thinking well of "self"; *mamāhtāwisiwin*, personal power; and *wāpātikosowin*, manifesting sensorial evidence. Indigenous peoples living with diabetes do justice to *nahi*, or fairness, when we embrace cultural and spiritual teachings as a way of reversing our fortunes and living longer, healthier, happier lives.

The old paradigm of ascribed health and wellness, *atikowisi miýw-āyāwin*, granted by outside sources, has to be replaced by the new paradigm, *kaskitamasowin miýw-āyāwin*, which is earned through individual autonomy, collective interests, and creative genius. However, this shift has to move to the rightful faces, places, and spaces. The leaders, those who are in positions of power and influence, must present with a *mihkwakākan*, a human face rather than a mask, when they create space, a lot of room, or *misi-tawow*, in every place, or *misiwē*. This ethos helps to secure health, social, and health care equity for us, even in complex, hierarchical, and socially and economically fractured health systems.

DIRECTION OF THE PARADIGM SHIFT

Whether we base it on soft logic or hard evidence, *kisēwātisowin*, affection, possessing a great, merciful, kind, and gentle disposition, has to coexist with *itamahcihowin*, feeling healthy. Basic human needs like these remain unmet for Indigenous peoples who are suffering inordinately high rates of physical, emotional, social, and mental health problems. Such situations pose ongoing challenges and opportunities for us, with life and death being our constant polarizing companions.

Even as we throw off the shackles of colonization, both existentially and literally through *nimihitowin*, dancing, moving rhythmically, insidious and threatening structures have to be destroyed to avert our *poni-waskawewin*, immobility in death. Structural violence has to be isolated and treated as a detriment to our health, social, and health care equity. Clear pathways from *atikowisi miýw-āyāwin* toward *kaskitamasowin miýw-āyāwin* have to be established and travelled on with coordinated efforts, pooled resources, and personal responsibility. Essential requirements for this journey or *pimohtewin*, include *āniskētastāwin*, attachment, where all things are connected, and *wāhkōhtowin*, kinship, where everyone is related. For its part, creativity, *ōsihickēwin*, builds on the pragmatism and traditions of individuals in communities who are personally involved and responsible for their own health and wellness. Advancing our innate ability to channel far-back memory, *ochcikiskisiwin*, and its original instructions, will help us translate our visions and dreams into helpful action and policies.

The old paradigm of *atikowisi miýw-āyāwin* will have to give way to *kaskitamasowin miýw-āyāwin* since the latter is more humane, far-reaching, and long lasting for Indigenous peoples. However, until *miýo-paýowin*—good turns from changing fortunes—is given its due, negative sentiments like fear and ambivalence can be expected and must be acknowledged and addressed. To begin, all concerned individuals, families, and communities need to be engaged and supported in negotiating the profound and rapid changes that will be encountered. To support the engagement of helping individuals and communities, *nātamakéwin miýw-āyāwin,* or assisted health and wellness, will have to be integrated into the shifting paradigm. When help is sought out and provided during times of change, it valorizes our will and ability to struggle toward health, social, and health care equity and ultimately to health and wellness.

CONCLUSION

Again, old structures in a new paradigm have to be weighed against their potential to continue exacting harmful effects on Indigenous peoples. As well, our conception of health determinants must account for our languages and histories; imagination, *kosāpahtamowin;* sensorial analysis, *mōsihowin;* evidence, *wāpātikosowin;* and knowledge, *kiskēyihtamohwin,* which are all central to the social and cultural thought leadership of Indigenous peoples. Most importantly, paradigms will change through revolutionary and liberating discourses where we are the true protagonists, *anik katocikēcik,* and purveyors, *anik kaýēýihwēcik,* of our health development. The way forward is to move health determinants from a technocratic and mechanistic conception based solely on rational survival needs to holistic and humanistic views located on *manitowakeýinowin,* a higher or spiritual order. Human agency, pragmatism, personal power, and "self" have to be fully integrated into the fullness of our fourfold conception of the cosmos and our relationships within it, or *nēyowihtā.* This holistic framework is essential if we are to successfully shift from *atikowisi miýw-āyāwin* to *kaskitamasowin miýw-āyāwin,* supported by the mediating force of assisted health and wellness, *nātamakéwin miýw-āyāwin.*

GLOSSARY OF CREE TERMS

anik katocikēcik: true protagonists
anik kaýēýihwēcik: purveyors
āniskētastāwin: attachment, where all things are connected
atikowisi miýw-āyāwin: ascribed health and wellness
awahkānowi: enslavement
éýihta: living context
Inti: Sun god [Quechua language]

iskonkana: reserves, leftover plots

itamahcihowin: feeling healthy

kakwātakitā: imprisonment in pain-wracked minds, bodies, and spirits

kanwéýihicikātéki: "keeping systems"; practices, beliefs, and values that maintain, reinforce, and uphold Indigenous perspectives

kaskitamasowin miýw-āyāwin: achieved health and wellness

kayás óma ka nóhcikweyā: interminable and blunt assault inflicting historic trauma on a massive scale

kétéskwēw: ancient woman or child with an ancient spirit

kisēwātisowin: affection, possessing a great merciful, kind, and gentle disposition

kiskēyihtamohwin: knowledge

kiskinwahamátowikamokwa: teaching and learning structures, residential schools

kitimahitowin: making one another poorer through lateral violence

kitimakisona: poverties and pathologies resulting from unmet human needs

kosāpahtamowin: imagination

mamāhtāwisiwin: personal power

māmitonēýihcikēwin: reflection, thought

manitowakeýinowin: higher or spiritual order

māýi-mācihowin: bad, ugly, nasty, evil, wicked state of physical, mental, emotional, and spiritual unwellness

māýi-owýasiwēwikimākanā: unhealthy policies and practices

mihkwakākan: human face or mask

mipahi kayás: an extreme, toxic, and deadly past (colonization)

misi-tawow: space or room

misiwē: place

miyawata: celebrate

miýo-paýowin: good turns from changing fortunes

mōcopiyōwin: crazed state due to overwhelming experiences and circumstances and corresponding power imbalances

mōsihowin: sensorial analysis

nahi: fairness

nanātawihiwēwin: process of healing, helping and taking responsibility for ourselves

naskomowēnā: responses

nātamakéwin miýw-āyāwin: assisted health and wellness

neheýew-isicikewin: Cree culture

nēhiýiwēwin: Cree language

nēyowihtā: the cosmos and our relationships within it

nimihitowin: dancing, moving rhythmically

niýa: self

ochcikiskisiwin: innate ability to channel far-back memory

okisiko iskwew: Angel Woman

osāwiwaskoh- pihēsiwsew iskwēw: Yellow Cloud Thunder Spirit Woman

ōsihickēwin: creativity

pakosēýi-mowin: yearning for a better quality of life and happier times

pāstāhowin: transgression of taboos

pimēýimowin: thinking well of "self"

pimohtewin: journey

poni-waskawewin: death, stoppage of movement

sēwankānāspinēwin: inability to process the sweetness of life (diabetes)

sōhkātisiwinā: human reserves

tāpiscōc kipihkitonēhpitikoweya: pain of being strangled by grief and loss

tipahaskāna: measured lots

tipahikēwin: drum song or ceremony

tipi: equal, equal portions

wāhkōhtowin: kinship, where everyone is related

wāpātikosowin: evidence; manifesting sensorial evidence

wāskāmsiwin: to "come to," to become altered, to pass gradually into the
present, to pass from one phase to another

Xuē: Sun god [Muisca language]

NOTE

1. The original version of this chapter was published in the *Canadian Journal of Nursing Research (CJNR)*, 44, 11–14. Copyright is owned by McGill University. All requests for reproduction of this article must be sent to *CJNR*, Ingram School of Nursing, McGill University: cjnr.nursing@mcgill.ca.

miyo-pimâtisiwin "A Good Path"

Indigenous Knowledges, Languages, and Traditions in Education and Health

Diana Steinhauer and James Lamouche

Indigenous peoples have explored, researched, refined, and perfected healing traditions for millennia. These traditions continue to provide guidance for the protection and promotion of individual and community health. Elders and Healers continue to carry and develop Indigenous healing traditions to this day, and they continue to make calls for providing support for these traditions as part of any response to the dismal determinants of health and poor health outcomes in many of our communities and nations. The process of colonization has resulted in these traditions being devalued, denigrated, and alienated by mainstream society and specifically by the health system, which has resulted in some of the worst health outcomes in the world found in Indigenous communities in Canada. If government-led health service organizations and training institutions continue to deliver human services and training to Indigenous peoples without a deeper understanding of the Indigenous connections to ceremony, protocols, language, spiritual teachings, community, stories, and the impact of history, they will repeat the cycle of colonization and assimilation.

As a response to these current realities and as an act of sovereignty, resistance, and healing, Blue Quills First Nations College (BQFNC) is developing an Indigenous Health Sciences Program (IHSP), which is based upon *nehiyawak* (Cree people's) concepts, philosophies, and teachings about health and healing. The goal of this program is to create healthy and whole individuals who are able to participate more fully in their academic success—precisely because they have a strong grounding in their cultures, languages, and healing traditions.

Using the development of the IHSP as an example, this chapter argues that the greatest opportunity for the improvement of the health outcomes of Indigenous communities and nations lies in the repositioning, revaluing, and reinvigoration of traditional Indigenous healing practices and concepts, both in the education of health professionals and in the delivery of health and health services. This is in no way a call for combination or integration of "traditional" and "Western" systems. It is a recognition that healthy and strong relationships between individuals, communities, nations, and systems require an understanding of self as well as the other, and as such, professionals with better and deeper understandings of these systems will be best placed to work in, and with, Indigenous communities. This chapter discusses health services and determinants of health in Indigenous contexts; the identification of current gaps and issues in health professional education; as well as the value of Indigenous pedagogy, philosophy, and epistemology in addressing these gaps.

Health Services and Determinants of Health

The history of the provision of human services to Indigenous peoples in Canada leaves much to be desired; a large quantity of research and a vast number of the personal stories of our peoples document the ongoing negative outcomes from these services. While some of these services were delivered with positive intentions, service delivery and training have, for the most part, ignored many essential elements vital to a traditional Indigenous world view. Examples from the early Indian residential schools, to the sixties scoop, to the current data reflecting high numbers of Indigenous children in government care continue to reveal the fact that services that are not sensitive to the history, needs, and perspectives of Indigenous individuals and communities only perpetuate the process of assimilation and colonization. In the view of many, this represents one of the most significant impacts upon the determinants of poor health outcomes of Indigenous peoples in Canada. Loppie Reading and Wien (2009) explain: "The political agenda of the 20th century colonial system was to assimilate and acculturate Indigenous peoples into the dominant culture. This agenda is evident in legislation and social policies that reward assimilation through resources and opportunities, while punishing cultural retention through the creation of inequities" (p. 23).

It is in this context—of colonialism and its effects—that all aspects of community and individual health can be detrimentally affected. Understanding this context may also provide some insight into why poor outcomes stubbornly remain the norm in far too many Indigenous communities, despite all efforts made from within that colonial system. That is, it stretches credulity to expect solutions and improvements in health to come solely from these external systems, which have had a large hand in creating and maintaining those poor outcomes in the first place.

For Indigenous peoples, the relationships between the physical, mental, spiritual, and emotional aspects of being are integral to individual and community health. This holistic view is increasingly being acknowledged and accepted by the mainstream health community, and is often described in relation to non-medical, or social, determinants of health, such as education, housing, economic status, social capital, etc. As stated by Brascoupé and Waters (2009):

> The profound issues that accompany health concerns place additional pressure on government and social services to improve health outcomes for Aboriginal people. The environment in which people live has a profound effect on their health difficulties. These are known as the social determinants of health (SDOH), including poverty, unemployment, poor education, bad nutrition, poor housing, and unclean water. (p. 17)

Through the development and delivery of programming such as the IHSP, BQFNC is attempting to make an impact on as many of these determinants as possible. While the creation of a new generation of Indigenous health service professionals is an admirable goal and will have direct impact on the health and well-being of our communities, we believe that this cadre of professionals will also be instrumental in the amelioration of health inequities across all of these aspects.

ADDRESSING THE GAPS: TRAINING A NEW GENERATION OF INDIGENOUS HEALTH SERVICE PROVIDERS

In 1996, the Royal Commission on Aboriginal Peoples made recommendations for immediate action toward the training of 10,000 health care professionals (Royal Commission on Aboriginal Peoples, 1996). This was in direct response to dire needs within our communities, as well as a burgeoning population. Today, while these needs continue to exist and our population continues to grow, a large number of Aboriginal students continue to face barriers to the successful completion of training in the health sciences.

Human service programs and training that serve Indigenous clients and communities would benefit from having specific competencies, programs, and evaluations to determine and assess effectiveness. Often, however, programs that serve Indigenous clients have been designed from a non-Indigenous perspective, using processes and planning methods more suited to Western or Eurocentric models of training and service delivery. For example, most mainstream programming does not include a spiritual component; often uses a problem-solving or deficit model; frequently ignores traditional kinship mapping and family organization; does not address the trans-generational impacts of history; and does not include the use of Indigenous languages, traditional teachings, and ceremony. With Indigenous program design, delivery, and evaluation, understanding is based in meaning as opposed to measurement and in process as opposed to outcome—and it is in these differences that the expectation of different and better outcomes will result.

Western-based competencies and indicators must be reinterpreted and understood from a community-based Indigenous world view. Concepts such as family, security, child development, parenting, and health can be understood very differently and, in the search for *miyo-pimâtisiwin* (the good path), *iniyiw* (First Peoples') ontology must be at the forefront. Delivery of human services and training to Indigenous peoples without a deeper understanding of the Indigenous connections to ceremony, protocols, language, spiritual teachings, community, ancient teaching stories, and the impact of history is more likely to further promote the process of colonization and assimilation.

It is becoming increasingly clear that culture is vital to healthy individuals and communities, and that recognition and utilization of traditional cultural structures and practices are better determinants of good health than the utilization of external—and in many ways deviant—structures of mainstream society. For example, it has been shown that the more control over, and cultural input into, self-government, health, education, policing, and cultural resources exercised by First Nations communities, the lower the incidence of youth suicide (Chandler & Proulx, 2006; see also Chapter 8). In the process of colonization, all aspects of culture—including social, spiritual, physical, scientific, government, leadership, economy, language, world view, values, sexuality, parenting, and beliefs—are overtaken and replaced by the dominant paradigm. The dominant ideology then labels culture as irrelevant and traditional practices as deviant when in fact the opposite is true.

The current system of education in health careers is foreign to, and alienating of, Indigenous students. This is particularly apparent in the false choice forced upon them wherein they are required to give up or suppress their traditions, languages, and identities in exchange for academic success. This choice may not be explicit or overt but it can be revealed in the simple examination of location. All cultures have links to geography, and this is nowhere more apparent than Indigenous cultures (see, for example, chapters 9 and 11). For Indigenous students to consider further training in the health sciences, they must be willing to endure extended periods of self-imposed exile from their homes, communities, and territories; and, by extension, reduced opportunities to engage in their traditions and languages.

For example, the majority of professional programs in the area of health require three to four years of undergraduate preparation, two to four years of programming, and one to six years of internship and/or practical training. This can result in being absent from their communities for most of the year over the course of an entire decade. This physical disconnection and alienation are also manifested spiritually, culturally, and linguistically, and represent significant disincentives to the pursuit of careers in health. This barrier is unique to Indigenous students, and is in addition to the challenges that all students training in the health sciences will face around costs of education, competitive stresses, time pressures, and balancing family, school, and in many cases employment. When one adds to these challenges the marginalization—and in some cases overt racism—that Indigenous students will face in mainstream institutions and programs, the "puzzle" of why there is currently a paucity of Indigenous health professionals becomes less puzzling.

In this context, and toward the goal of increasing the number of Indigenous health professionals, Blue Quills First Nations College's Indigenous Health Sciences Program significantly reduces the total time away from home, community, and territory, while also providing the skills, strengths, and background to better deal with the challenges of the times spent navigating foreign systems.

THE VALUE OF INDIGENOUS EDUCATION, PHILOSOPHY, AND EPISTEMOLOGY: BLUE QUILLS FIRST NATIONS COLLEGE INDIGENOUS HEALTH SCIENCES PROGRAM

Since 1971, Blue Quills First Nations College (BQFNC) has been a locally controlled Indigenous education centre serving the academic and training needs of people of all cultures, encouraging everyone to experience studying in a unique socio-cultural and academic environment. As an Indigenous non-profit educational institution, a prime objective is to promote a sense of pride in Indigenous heritage and reclaim traditional knowledge and practices (BQFNC, 2012). BQFNC is located on Treaty Six Territory in northeastern

Alberta and is an independent post-secondary institution offering programming from basic adult education through baccalaureate, master's, and doctoral degrees. The board of directors of the college includes representation of seven "Member" First Nations, which includes six distinct Cree Nations and one Dene Nation from the northeastern portion of the province of Alberta.

In undertaking the work of developing an Indigenous Health Science Program (IHSP), a number of goals were identified, including the development of curriculum framework designed for Indigenous students and institutions that fully respects and involves traditional healing practices and philosophies; promotion of health and health sciences as viable and attainable career choices for Indigenous students; creation of a forum for interaction between Indigenous traditional Healers and medically based health practitioners; and promotion of understanding and respect for traditional healing practices and their place in the improvement of the health of Indigenous communities.

The successful development of the curriculum and program framework and their ongoing refinement is due to the support provided by many individuals, especially Elders and Healers, from within our communities, who have graciously agreed to engage with BQFNC on this project. As standard practice of BQFNC when considering new programming or research, the input and guidance of Elders and Healers are actively sought out through traditional protocols and ceremony. The success of the IHSP also depends on their continued participation, which is a requirement for maintaining the relationships necessary to ensure cultural safety in training and education, as well as in maintaining cultural continuity in our communities. The guidance of Elders and Healers has directly influenced the development process, and some examples of their input are included here to provide insight into the richness and depth of their wisdom, caring, and concern for the health of our communities. They also provide some insight into Indigenous, primarily *nehiyaw* (Cree), perspectives on the determinants of health of individuals, communities, and nations.

A number of key points and recommendations were shared by those that participated in the ceremonies and development activities for the IHSP. Broadly, these points can be grouped into three themes. First, health is linked to language, culture, and politics. For instance, Elders noted that "Our languages are where this knowledge lives and it is the best protection of that knowledge. If you are going to teach about it, the students are going to need to commit to learning our language to get to a deeper understanding," and that "Learning and understanding our culture and history is important to understanding health." Elders also pointed out that "You can't really understand health for our communities unless you know the history, especially our treaties. Things like the medicine chest and how we don't have access to our lands and medicines anymore need to be better known." They also pointed to the need for medical professionals to understand our culture: "You should also consider courses for people that are already in professions so that they can also be aware of our traditions and our medicines and our ceremonies."

Secondly, Elders noted the centrality of relationships, and that all ages and genders must be supported. They commented that "You need to make sure to balance men's and women's teachings within the program," and that "We need to prepare our students as best as we can for when they 'go away' to go to school. We are sending them to foreign places and they need to be strong and healthy and resilient to get through." Elders also stated that "*nehiyaw* [Cree] understanding of health is based on relationships. We need to focus on building the students' relationships to our communities, Elders, and programs. This will make them stronger and better prepared when they go away and make it more likely that they will return to serve our communities." Self-care was also an important theme in their comments: "Students need to focus on well-being and health for themselves, especially if they want to help others."

Thirdly, Elders emphasized the interconnections between land, spirituality, and health. They commented that "Our land is linked to our health and it is through our ceremonies that this link is made and strengthened," and that "There needs to be recognition of the role of belief as fundamental to all healing. That includes doctors and their medicine as well." And finally, "We need to look at nutrition and food security and self sustainability as well. Teaching the links between food and health is important" (BQFNC, 2010, pp. 6–8).

This brief summary provides some insight into three of the main areas or themes of the determinants of health from an Indigenous, specifically *nehiyawak* (Cree), perspective. These are land, language, and relationships. It is the ongoing failure of the current system of education of health professionals that none of these are dealt with in any meaningful manner through the preparation, admission, training, apprenticeship, or licensing phases of most health professional programs. For example, knowledge of the chirality in a molecule of glucose is of more importance in the admission of a candidate to medical school than is his or her knowledge of, or vocabulary to describe, sugar in an Indigenous language or even plain English.

The research conducted and the guidance provided also identified some potential challenges that will need to be dealt with in the continued development and delivery of the IHSP. These focused, in large part, on protection and promotion of traditional knowledge, ceremonies, and culture as well as the protection and safety of the individuals involved. For example, Elders and Healers were united in their opinion that it should be very clearly communicated to prospective students and the public that this program is in no way a "how-to" class on traditional medicines or ceremonies. These are sacred gifts from the Creator given to specific individuals or transferred through proper protocols, and a goal of the program should be to prepare and train prospective students in these protocols. "If we don't train young people now in the 'basics' there will be few people to gain the 'deep' knowledge 20 or 30 years down the line" (BQFNC, 2010, p. 9).

It is important to note that while land, language, and relationships were the primary themes in the determinants of health from an Indigenous perspective, the identification of challenges and potential pitfalls focused almost exclusively on relationships. This is an elegant and sophisticated recognition of the fact that the issues that have arisen are not caused by the land, the language, or the culture in question. They are caused by damage to the personal and community relationships to each of these, and the way back to good health is through the restoration of these relationships. The centrality of ceremony and the fundamental aspect of following ceremonial protocols and teachings in guiding the program and in the training and development of the prospective students were repeatedly brought forward in discussions and recommendations. This is further elaborated by Makokis and Bodor (2014) in their discussion of Indigenous concepts important to the delivery of human services.

> Relationships are key in an Indigenous epistemology and ontology. Nothing exists outside of relationship. Knowledge does not and cannot exist without relationship between at least two beings. . . . Without the relationships embedded in the circle, the knowledge cannot and does not exist; consequently attention to the sacredness of the relationships within the circle is tantamount. Creation and transmission of knowledge is a sacred trust. (Makokis & Bodor, 2014, p. 65)

In response to the guidance provided, a number of key components for inclusion in the IHSP were identified. These have been integrated into the delivery of the program and now form part of the curriculum and programming for IHSP students. The foundation of the program is based on ceremony and the establishment and strengthening of relationships between students, instructors, Elders, Healers, community, and the land. Within this framework, the goal of the IHSP is to assist students to become whole, healthy people with the skills, abilities, and strengths to provide health services and healing to our communities and Nations.

Some of these key components in the area of Indigenous conceptions of health and healing include Indigenous philosophy, cosmology, and conceptions of healing; ceremonial protocols; women's health and healing; art, identity, and knowledge; men's health and healing; lands and medicines; and environmental health. In the area of academic preparation, components include literacy and writing skills, numeracy, scientific literacy, and prerequisite preparation. Personal development includes career planning, research, mentorship, shadowing, study skills, adaptation strategies, coping skills, and resiliency.

While some of the programming outlined will be classroom and laboratory based, much of it will also be ceremonial, experiential, and land-based learning. Utilizing a number of different opportunities for getting participants on the land and in ceremony will provide them with the engagement, communication, and adaptive skills necessary to fully engage with Indigenous communities in their future work, whether in their home communities or in other parts of the world. For example, over the course of a recent academic term, students of the IHSP participated in a project that included ceremonial protocols, traditional harvesting activities, environmental sciences, hide and meat processing, comparative anatomy, traditional arts, storytelling, identification and collection of medicines, and traditional tool making.

Food and feasts are a fundamental part of the ongoing activities of the College, and many ceremonies and feasts require the harvest of moose and/or elk, among others. As such, Elders agreed to coordinate the harvest of moose, as well as provide instruction to students on traditional protocols regarding their sacred nature and the intimate relationship between humans and their environment, which can only be expressed through the prayers and protocols associated with the harvesting, processing, and distribution of food. The participation in the harvest was also utilized as an experiential educational opportunity as part of an environmental health course in that term.

Along with the traditional teachings and instruction associated with the harvest itself, portions of the moose were kept as resources for future instructional activities. These included the use of the leg bones for a comparative anatomy laboratory for an introductory biology course and then subsequently using the same bones to make traditional hide-tanning tools. The hide of the moose and the tanning tools were also utilized to provide instruction on traditional hide-tanning techniques as part of an annual Cultural Camp hosted by the College. As part of a separate traditional arts workshop, this hide was then further processed to construct a rawhide box designed to store medicines.

Traditional storytelling was also a part of the workshop, and students were able to actively listen to stories as they shared the work of completing the rawhide box. The completion of the rawhide box then led to the next traditional teaching of the identification and harvesting of medicinal plants, after which the IHSP "medicine chest" was completed and is now used as a ceremonial and teaching tool in its own right. The end result of this process is that the IHSP students attending in that term were given the opportunity to experience and learn from a multiplicity of sources through a diversity of pedagogies, in an engaging and memorable manner. As such, "traditional" and "scientific" pedagogies are treated as distinct but equally valid sources of information and knowledge, which is a lesson that is continually reinforced throughout the course of the IHSP.

CONCLUSION

In contrast to many other preparatory or deficit model programs in the field, the IHSP does not focus on academics and prerequisites exclusively. Many other programs focus on filling in the gaps in students' academic records in the hope of qualifying for a specific level, entrance requirement, or quota. Many participants and contributors to the development of the program believe that programming that utilizes the above components will provide students with a foundation and understanding of traditional health and healing, and help build the skills and abilities necessary to succeed in their ongoing training in the academic, holistic, and medically based health sciences and health care professions.

In essence, students with stronger foundations in their own cultures, languages, and traditions will be better placed and prepared for the demands of future training and education in the health sciences as a by-product of becoming healthy and whole human beings in their own right—*nehiyawak* (people of the four directions: Cree people) who are following *miyo-pimâtisiwin* (the good path) toward *miyo-mahcihowin* (good health), a path that can and must be shared by all.

REFERENCES

BQFNC. (2010). Elder and Healer interviews, community consultations, and personal communications in development of BQFNC Indigenous Health Sciences Program, 2008–2010.

BQFNC. (2012). *Blue Quills First Nations College calendar and handbook, 2012–2013*. St. Paul, AB: Author.

Brascoupé, S., & Waters, C. (2009). Cultural safety: Exploring the applicability of the concept of cultural safety to Aboriginal health and community wellness. *Journal of Aboriginal Health, 5,* 6–40.

Chandler, M. J., & Proulx, T. (2006). Changing selves in changing worlds: Youth suicide on the fault-lines of colliding cultures. *Archives of Suicide Research, 10,* 125–140.

Clement, F., & Kaufmann, L. (2007). Paths towards a naturalistic approach to culture. *Intellectica, 46,* 7–24.

Loppie Reading, C., & Wien, F. (2009). *Health inequalities and social determinants of Aboriginal peoples' health.* Prince George, BC: National Collaborating Centre for Aboriginal Health.

Makokis, L., & Bodor, R. (2014). Indigenous concepts, terms, and frameworks that are important for human service workers. *Journal for Services to Children and Families, 7,* 54–74.

Royal Commission on Aboriginal Peoples. (1996). *Report of the Royal Commission on Aboriginal Peoples.* Ottawa: Author.

CHAPTER 15

Reshaping the Politics of Health

A Personal Perspective

Warner Adam

I was born in Burns Lake, British Columbia, a small town consisting of both First Nations and non-First Nations people. However, I lived on the Woyenne Indian reserve, adjacent to the Village of Burns Lake. I completed high school in Burns Lake. This provided me the opportunity to become grounded in my culture, but also to walk in both worlds.

I had the privilege at an early age to listen to the stories and legends my grandmother told and, more importantly, to listen to the business that my grandmother was responsible for as part of her duties as a hereditary chief in her deliberations with fellow hereditary chiefs. After attending college and university, I made my home base in Prince George, British Columbia, where I had the opportunity to lead the establishment of Carrier Sekani Family Services, an organization providing family and child services, health programs and research to up to 11 First Nations in north-central British Columbia. I have also had the opportunity to work on several councils, boards, and committees representing First Nations issues and concerns, the most recent being the establishment of a B.C. First Nations Health Authority—the first of its kind in Canada. I had the honour of being the deputy chair for this initiative.

I have always had an inquisitive mind about our First Nations culture and how it worked. I was lucky to be around my Elders during some interesting political times. They taught me a lot about health in the broadest sense, and through my years of working and thinking about the health of First Nations communities and people, I have seen that health is more than just people and communities without sickness or disease. It is being in a healthy state of wellness in all that we do and are as First Nations peoples. To be afforded the opportunities that this world has to offer. To be proud, dignified, and independent.

Currently, part of my role is to assist with establishing systems and structures within the health and social services sectors, to work with chiefs and the community, to change policies that have clearly not worked in servicing our communities. When our community members are dying at an earlier age, when our kids are committing suicide, we don't have much time to do this work. Our people keep falling through the cracks despite numerous studies that show the disparity in health, economic, housing, education, and so forth. It's time for measurable action.

~

In reflecting on my upbringing, my grandmother was the one who provided me with lasting impressions on culture, values, and interaction. She was one of many highly respected matriarchs in our clan and nation. My nation, the Lake Babine Nation, operates its political, economic, and social ethos based on the *bah'lats* system. The *bah'lats* is governed by hereditary chiefs from four primary clans: the Beaver, Bear, Frog, and Caribou. Each clan has sub-clans based on family lineages.

My grandmother, Catherine Adam, was born in Moricetown, so she is actually of Wet'suwet'en descent. She married my grandfather, Athanase Adam, from the Lake Babine Nation, and for the most part, both resided in Old Fort, where my mother Mary Ann Adam was born. This village had no hospitals or the conveniences we see today in our communities. The health of the community was dependent on the land and all its offerings and the culture of survival as taught by our ancestors. My grandmother, marrying into the Lake Babine Nation, was relocated from Old Fort to Pendleton Bay, and then to Woyenne. That particular community of the Lake Babine Nation was relocated by Indian Affairs Canada not once but twice.

I believe that disruption was the start of the assimilation of my people. It brought hardship, distrust, poverty, and sickness. Yet our people are adaptable, and my grandmother was no exception. She maintained her strength, and she held her role as a clan leader.

Being raised on-reserve under the guidance of my grandmother, I was always privy to the discussions she had with her fellow hereditary chiefs, discussions about maintaining the social fabric and order of our community and decisions related to strength and challenges of our *bah'lats* system. Issues discussed included celebrating births, rites of passages, inheritance of chief names, and very important land ownership and land use—all having processes, roles, and responsibilities. This allowed me to see how we intersected with each other as chiefs, as hereditary chiefs. With respect. With dignity. With authority.

Incidentally, my grandma was also a medicine woman. She used herbs, plants, and animal parts to mix medicines for varying illnesses. She was also a midwife. Today we have no midwives, but my grandma taught my mother the medicines that she used, and in turn my mom continues to teach the young people how to gather plants and make medicines.

I grew up with medicine men and women, and as such I was taught to be very respectful and careful in terms of how I conducted myself in their presence. To lack respect would have grave consequences. For example, one must not move too swiftly or startle the medicine people or else they might take your spirit! So respect of their space and spiritual powers had to be exercised when in their presence. This demonstrated to me the strong spiritual connection that my people had.

My grandmother taught me the values she grew up with: respect for all living beings, maintaining harmony in your life by balancing your knowledge with spiritual awareness, sharing all wealth and helping those in need, being truthful in all that you do, and maintaining love in all your actions. To do good is to outweigh evil—this was her strongest message. These are the traits, intrinsically connected, that make good leaders. My relationship with my grandmother was based on these teachings, which have always endured.

Prior to being displaced as a people, our community sustained itself by using the land. The men were responsible for hunting and guarding the land and safety of the community, while the women would gather plants and berries and nurture the family or extended family. Each season produced foods that were then preserved. Living off the land included harvesting medicines in order to prevent sickness. But displacement from our homelands and the resulting poverty in our community had a deep impact on us.

∽

I come from a single mother. I have six siblings. We experienced a lot of poverty and racism when we grew up. Our parents didn't allow us to speak our language downtown. When I spoke my language to my mom in a store, she would say, "Don't speak our language!" But finally one day I said to my mother, "No, Mom, I'm going to speak our language because when I bring

Grandma here, we always talk our language, so there's nothing wrong with that. We need to speak our language anywhere we want."

You see? To feel strong I wanted to speak my language. I felt very connected to Carrier, my first language. It provided me with the identity of who I am. I remain very fluent in speaking my language and understanding my traditional government structures.

But I'll give you other examples of the racism we saw growing up. The Catholic church in town, for instance. One side was white people, one side was Indians. In the theatre too: one side white, one side Indian. At the local bar we all witnessed First Nations peoples being literally thrown out, onto the street, hitting their heads on the cement. People were always derogatory toward First Nations. Take their money, get them drunk, and throw them out.

In our high school there were racial slurs and fights. At that point in my life I wondered where all the hatred and negativity came from. When I was in Grade 1, there were 32 First Nations students. At graduation, there were only two of us left. What happened? Many of my fellow students dropped out of school because of the racism they experienced there.

But the move from our homelands to a non-Native village had pros as well as cons. Living next to a white settlement provided us the opportunity to walk in both worlds. Learning the English language and going to a Catholic elementary day school and public high school shaped our ability to survive in mainstream Canadian society. Our experiences of racism made us tolerant and tough enough to protect one another.

But alcoholism has been a big problem in our community. Many of my people fell into this trap and to this day, the dependence on alcohol as a form of escape remains a great challenge. Perhaps this was a result of the fact that Indians were at one time prohibited from purchasing alcohol and entering establishments where alcohol was served. All of a sudden, the prohibition was lifted and alcohol became readily available to our people.

Today, it appears that drug abuse—whether it is prescription drugs or street drugs—is rampant in our communities. Or is it unresolved grief due to attempts of assimilation and impacts of colonization? I say it's both. So many of the Elders I am fond of have a deep concern about drug use in our communities, about the child welfare system, about the number of children being apprehended. We need to ensure that these issues are taken care of by our people with proper resources.

For me, these are the kinds of issues we have to think about when we discuss First Nations health. It is an issue of social justice, of human rights, of people's rights. How can we really advance First Nations rights and issues, and bring them to a level where they are afforded meaningful action? Who makes the rule of law and how can we use that to build healthy communities?

Government turns a blind eye to the struggles faced by our citizens. The impacts of colonization are one explanation for these negative trends. While some would argue that First Nations are provided benefits by government, First Nations are forced to be accountable in every aspect of managing funding—but accountability has always been the centre of our lives. We account for all of our actions. Remaining open, transparent, and honest is nothing new to many First Nations peoples and organizations. These traits are still practised in our *bah'lats*.

Report writing seems to satisfy government process, but government has not done much to address the social injustices born out of assimilationist strategies. At the same time, resources are continually being extracted from our territories, damaging the land that sustains the traditional ways. Despite this, our nations are in the process of rebuilding our governance structures through our culture and traditions.

∿

First Nations peoples know that health is about balance. Interconnectedness of all living matter—the land, animals, the air, the water, our way of being—is what makes us healthy, but our philosophy of health and well-being has been shackled, reshaped by colonialism. The modern mainstream health care system dedicates too much attention to a sickness model and very little to prevention and wellness.

We see that this colonial system of health care is extremely expensive, yet our health remains dismal. Only when First Nations are provided the ability to manage, control, and design their own health programs and services that we will see improvement in the health of our citizens.

In taking on the responsibility for our own lives, we have to recognize the voices of our ancestors and Elders. Their voices echo in my mind: to be respectful of this land, to be mindful of the temptations of the world, to be smart enough to use systems to rebuild our nations with pride and dignity, and to become self-sufficient. We need to change our socio-economic conditions in order to improve health conditions in our communities. We need autonomous First Nations systems and governance. We cannot let ignorance interfere with the health and well-being of present or future generations.

And yet there are always hurdles. I think that's because the colonial government systems of Canada and British Columbia control our First Nations environment and geographies to a point where they suffocate our development and stifle our progress. They still control the policies, the money. It's time that we shape our own destiny and pave the way for a vibrant, healthy road to success for the generations yet to come.

You see, health of First Nations is a financial issue and a political issue. It's an individual responsibility and it's about the well-being of our communities. It's a collective responsibility, a tribal responsibility, and of course all of that comes wrapped up in politics.

While much good work has been done in advancing the health and well-being of our people, much more needs to be done. Health systems alone will not solve poverty. It will take a holistic approach. It takes housing, education, economic development, and rebuilding the foundation of our inherent governance and structures. Anything less will continue the cycles of colonization straddled in poverty.

It is up to us collectively to move forward as First Nations. In walking in both worlds, I recognize we do all have the same goals: to have the healthy, vibrant families and communities that we once had, that we once were. We may have different ways to get to this goal, but at the end of the day it is about rebuilding our nations.

I think the day will come when we take charge of our own policies. We will shape systems and we will close the health gap. We will decolonize our health. Our people will take control of our health and work toward preventative medicine that is rooted in culture. These are always political questions. They are always health questions. Together, we will overcome.

Aboriginal Early Childhood Development Policies and Programs in British Columbia

Beyond the Rhetoric

Karen Isaac and Kathleen Jamieson

Compelling international evidence shows that high-quality early childhood development (ECD) programming can be a catalyst for change in marginalized populations, improving long-term health and social outcomes and contributing to the well-being of families and communities (Britto, Yoshikawa, & Boller, 2011).

Over a combined 40 years of working with the most marginalized people in Canada—Aboriginal children, their families, and caregivers—we have seen first-hand the positive impacts that ECD policy and programming can have on the lives of our children and our communities. We have become convinced that, as imperfect and insufficient and unsung as our current Aboriginal ECD programs are, they have the potential to provide a safe pathway for children, families, and communities to heal from the ravages of the residential school system, colonialism, and the appropriation of Aboriginal lands and resources.

In this chapter, we provide an overview of the policy context for Aboriginal ECD in Canada and British Columbia. We look beyond government rhetoric to explore the ways in which the design and delivery of potentially beneficial multi-sectoral ECD programs are confounded by federal-provincial jurisdictional issues, changing political agendas, inadequate levels of funding, and the diverse rights and needs of the Aboriginal population. We conclude that the current scattergun approach to the provision of Aboriginal ECD programs and projects can negate most efforts to provide the needed high-quality programs, and that such an approach ends up serving a few fairly well and others not at all.

We argue that this picture needs to change. In order to ensure that all Aboriginal ECD programs are of high quality and can provide long-term benefit to young children and their families, we urgently need new, reinvigorated, Aboriginally designed and driven early childhood development policies and programs. However, we maintain that in order to provide space for healing to take place and to close forever the gap in life chances between Aboriginal children and other children in Canada, ECD policies and programs must be part of a comprehensive strategy that recognizes and addresses the political, economic, and social contexts that continue to reproduce the poverty and grim living conditions in many Aboriginal communities, and that high-quality and culturally appropriate ECD programs must be accessible to all Aboriginal children and families, wherever they may live.

ABORIGINAL CHILD AND FAMILY POVERTY

> The face of poverty in Canada is a child's face. . . . This is unacceptable. It is clearly time for Canada to make children a priority when planning budgets and spending our nation's resources, even in tough economic times.
> —David Morley, UNICEF Canada (KidsKan, 2012, n.p.)

If the primary goal of Aboriginal ECD is to eliminate the inequality in life chances between Aboriginal children and other children in Canada, as successive Canadian governments have repeatedly said, a major factor in that inequality in life chances is poverty. The likelihood that a young Aboriginal child will live in and be affected by poverty is high, much higher than that of a non-Aboriginal child in Canada. On-reserve First Nations children are particularly likely to be living in families in poverty. According to the 2009 Report Card of Campaign 2000, one in four children in First Nations communities today likely live in poverty (Campaign 2000, News Releases, 2009).

On family income alone, the differences in life chances between Aboriginal and non-Aboriginal children are significant. In 2005, the median income of First Nations families was $11,224 on-reserve and $17,464 off-reserve—much less than the median income of $25,955 for non-Aboriginal families. The gap in income levels between First Nations and non-Aboriginal families has not decreased in several years (Statistics Canada, 2009, p. 10).

According to the 2006 Census, Aboriginal children were almost nine times more likely to live in families with a crowded home (26 percent) than non-Aboriginal children (3 percent) (Statistics Canada, 2009, p. 10). They also go hungry more often. Indeed, Aboriginal peoples were found to be four times more likely than non-Aboriginal people to experience hunger as a direct result of poverty (Food Banks Canada, 2011, p. 7).

The links between poverty and health have been well established in the social determinants of health (SDoH) literature. As the National Collaborating Centre for Aboriginal Health has recently noted, "poverty has many dimensions—material deprivation (food, shelter, sanitation, and safe drinking water), social exclusion, lack of education, unemployment and low income—each of which diminishes opportunities and limits choices, undermines hope, and threatens health" (National Collaborating Centre for Aboriginal Health, 2009, p. 1).

The need to address poverty in Canada was acknowledged by members of all federal political parties who participated in the two-year study of the House of Commons Standing Committee on Human Resources, Skills and Social Development and the Status of Persons with Disabilities (HUMA). In November 2010, HUMA issued a comprehensive report calling for a federal poverty-reduction plan. On policy and programs for Aboriginal children, HUMA recommended "that the federal government take action to eliminate the gap in well-being between Aboriginal and Non-Aboriginal children by granting as a first step adequate funding to social programs that provide early intervention to First Nations, Inuit and Métis children and their families including the Aboriginal Head Start and the First Nations and Inuit Child Care Initiative" (Canada, 2010, Recommendation 4.3.2). The federal government responded by providing a list of existing programs.

CANADIAN EARLY CHILDHOOD DEVELOPMENT IN AN INTERNATIONAL CONTEXT

> And yet, despite initiatives, programs and projects, Canada's attempts have not been effective in improving Aboriginal children's lives and these children continue to bear the impacts of colonialism, racism and exclusion. (Canadian Council of Child and Youth Advocates, 2011, p. 3)

Despite the recognition that Aboriginal child poverty in Canada is an urgent problem, overwhelming evidence indicates that Canada is falling far behind other developed countries in its support for all young children and families. A 2006 Organisation for Economic Co-operation and Development (OECD) report, for example, shows that Canadian government spending on all early childhood services was extremely low compared with almost all other developed countries, even before the recent recession. Indeed, Canada's spending in 2004 on all early childhood education and care (ECEC) services (for age zero to six) as a percentage of GDP was the lowest of 14 developed countries and the second lowest (after Greece) of an expanded list of 37 countries (OECD, 2006). In 2008, UNICEF published a "league table" that rated ECEC provision in 24 economically advanced countries, again placing Canada at the bottom (Adamson, 2008). More recently, a 2010 UNICEF Report Card on child inequality in 24 developed countries found that Canada was seventeenth out of 24 countries in material well-being, and ninth in health and well-being (Adamson, 2010).

Canadian ECD Policy

Canada's federal ECD initiatives for young Aboriginal children were first established in the mid- to late 1990s as part of a strategy to close the "gap in life chances" between Aboriginal children and other Canadian children (Canada, PCO, 2002, p. 5). Key federally controlled programs that continue to operate today have been expanded somewhat, but remain virtually unchanged in design and content. These include the Canadian Prenatal Nutrition Program, announced in 1994; the First Nation and Inuit Child Care Initiative, established in 1995; the Aboriginal Head Start program for Urban and Northern Communities, started in 1995; and the 1998 Aboriginal Head Start program for First Nations on Reserve (Health Canada, 2010).

Three factors seem to have been important in triggering these initiatives during the 1990s. First, in 1991, Canada ratified the Convention on the Rights of the Child. As a part of its commitment under the convention, Canada is required to report periodically to the United Nations on its compliance. Second, the Royal Commission on Aboriginal Peoples (RCAP), which began in 1991 and culminated in the RCAP report in 1996, brought to light through compelling testimony of Aboriginal peoples before the commission the devastating intergenerational impacts of colonization on First Nations, Inuit, and Métis communities. Third, during the 1990s there was a notable expansion of knowledge about the social determinants of health and the inclusion of inequality, poverty, and early childhood development as determinants of health.

In this context of growing public awareness and concern, in the first part of 2000 the federal Liberal government actively promoted ECD and negotiated early learning and child care (ELCC) agreements with provinces and territories. In 2005, however, with the election of a Conservative government, there was a major retreat from Liberal ECD/ELCC policy. Among the first actions of the new federal government were the cancellation of the still unsigned

ELCC agreements that the previous Liberal government had negotiated with the provinces and Aboriginal peoples and the rejection of the previous government's pre-election promise of a universal child-care program. Another proposed Liberal government initiative, the Kelowna Accord, was also cancelled. The Kelowna Accord was a plan negotiated over an 18-month period among the federal government, first ministers, and Aboriginal leaders that had pledged $5.085 billion to "close the gap" between Aboriginal and non-Aboriginal Canadians (Patterson, 2006, p. 2).

The cancellation of the federal funding for the early childhood programs created immediate uncertainty and confusion; however, the funding for ECD/ELCC was subsequently reinstated. ECD and ELCC agreements have now been extended to 2013–2014. The funds for these programs are transferred to the provinces from the Department of Finance through block funding known as the Canadian Social Transfer (CST). An automatic 3 percent escalator has been applied since 2009–2010 (Department of Finance, 2011). The plan for a universal child-care program floated by the Liberals was quickly discarded by the Conservative government and has never resurfaced.

The diminished level of political support for federal early childhood programs is very clear and acknowledged in a September 2011 federal evaluation of the Understanding the Early Years Initiative, which ended in March 2011. The evaluators concluded that "In terms of current alignment, federal and provincial government representatives noted that current federal priorities have changed, so early childhood development has declined in importance" (HRSDC, 2011, p. 18). It also seems that any hope of comprehensive planning to address the gap in life chances of Aboriginal peoples and their children died with the Kelowna Accord.

Aboriginal ECD in British Columbia: Child Welfare Versus Child Well-being?

Apart from its often unwelcome incursions into reserves and poverty-stricken urban communities as part of its child-protection mandate, the British Columbia government has had little involvement with First Nations children and families on-reserve until the advent of the ECD and ELCC funding of 2000 and 2003. The result of this infusion of funding has been a heady mix of constantly changing early childhood policies and programs, apparently without any cohesive strategy or overall plan that would effectively address the learning and other needs of vulnerable preschool-age children in British Columbia.

It is important to be aware, however, that the broader context for all young families in British Columbia is the continuing waves of cutbacks in provincial support for all children and families (Coalition to Build a Better B.C., 2010). One indication of the effect of the cutbacks is the increase in the use of food banks in British Columbia (34.1 percent between 2001 and 2011). Of those people using food banks in that province, a disproportionate percentage (14.7 percent in urban and 27 percent in rural areas) identify as Aboriginal (Food Banks Canada, 2011). Another indication of the increasing stress on Aboriginal families is that although the number of Aboriginal children taken into care has long been disproportionately high, the proportion of Aboriginal children in care in British Columbia has now reached new heights (or depths), having steadily increased from 4,273 in 2001–2002 to 4,654 children in December 2009. Indeed, the proportion of Aboriginal children in care has increased over most of the last decade from a bad enough 43 percent in 2001–2002 to over 54 percent in 2009–2010 and to 55 percent of all children in care in 2012, when Aboriginal children are about 9 percent of the whole population of B.C. children under 19 years of age (B.C. Ministry of Children and Family Development, 2009; British Columbia, 2012a).

The financial costs for governments of taking children into care are very high—$35,000 for "maintaining" each First Nations child in care in 2008–2009, according to an Indian Affairs and Northern Development report of July 2010 (Indian and Northern Affairs Canada, 2010). Since 4,654 Aboriginal children were in care in British Columbia in 2009, and assuming that the cost for Métis and Inuit children in care is the same as for First Nations children, the cost for the maintenance of Aboriginal children in care in that province in 2009 was about $163 million ($162,890,000) per annum. We do not know what the additional legal or other related costs are. In contrast, the information that we have been able to gather so far on funding for federally administered ECD/ ELCC programs specifically for all young Aboriginal children and pregnant Aboriginal women in British Columbia suggests that it is currently in the range of $28.7 million per annum (BC ACCS, 2012). Where and how it is spent is another matter.

In 2011, at least six B.C. ministries were involved in the planning and delivery of early childhood programs according to the 2011 Early Years Report: (1) the Ministry of Jobs, Tourism and Innovation; (2) the Ministry of Social Development; (3) the Ministry of Aboriginal Affairs and Reconciliation; (4) the Ministry of Education; (5) the Ministry of Health; and (6) the Ministry of Children and Family Development (MCFD). It is not clear which activities are defined as ECD or ELCC by some of these ministries, but the definition appears to be quite elastic. The Ministry of Health, for example, lists tobacco reduction, childhood immunization, and midwifery as ELCC activities in the report, activities that might more usually be considered core functions in public health and budgeted for by public health authorities (Ministry of Children and Family Development [MCFD], 2011).

The British Columbia ministry with primary responsibility for policy and programs for Aboriginal ECD programs is the Ministry of Children and Family Development. The Ministry of Children and Family Development describes its ECD programming as aiming "to assist parents, families, and service providers in providing the best possible start for children from birth to six years of age" (MCFD, 2011, p. 20). MCFD is also responsible for child-care programs, child protection and family development, adoption, foster care, child and youth mental health, youth justice and youth services, and special needs children (MCFD, 2012, p. 1).

Since the mid-2000s, MCFD appears to have made sporadic efforts to move beyond its preoccupation with child welfare to approaches that are more compatible with the development aspirations of Aboriginal children, families, and communities. First Nations and Aboriginal groups were funded to prepare their own ECD frameworks and plans for Aboriginal ECD, and a coalition of First Nations and Métis groups was provided with $5 million to select and fund small Aboriginal ECD projects.

MCFD has had three reorganizations between 2010 and 2012 and put forth different conceptual, strategic, and service plans, each with some corresponding changes in core business areas (MCFD, 2012). It is not clear how much of a priority Aboriginal ECD is in the most recent (2012) plans. Unlike the previous 2011–2012 plans, the 2012/13–2014/15 Service Plan does not include "Aboriginal Approaches" as a service line. The current MCFD budget is "status quo at just over $1.3 billion" and the overall Aboriginal budget is the same as in 2011 at $19.8 million (British Columbia, 2012b, pp. 10933–10934).

Assessing the Impact: What We Do and Do Not Know About Quality Aboriginal ECD

> We cannot simply continue to do the same things in the same way. There needs to be a serious review of programs and services to First Nations. We need to identify what services should be provided and by whom, as well as the funding required and the expected results. (Fraser, 2011, p. 3)

The scientific evidence on the long-term effectiveness of high-quality ECD programs continues to accumulate. For example, the results of the Chicago longitudinal study, published in August 2011 in the journal *Science*, found that "low-income children who had spent two to six years in the [Chicago Child-Parent Center Education] program had higher rates of high school graduation, fewer criminal arrests, reduced instances of substance abuse and earned more money than children of the same age who did not participate in the program" (Reynolds et al., 2011, pp. 1–3). However, as Britto has noted, "Quality is a key feature because when programs of low quality are provided they are unlikely to generate the child and family outcomes intended" (Britto, Yoshikawa, & Boller, 2011, pp. 1–3).

To our knowledge, there is no Canadian research that examines the overall impact or the quality of Aboriginal ECD programs either federally or provincially. We do know from our local knowledge and B.C. Aboriginal Child Care Society's experience of operating and regularly evaluating two inner-city ECD (Head Start) programs, talking to parents, and providing regular training for early childhood educators across the province for many years that Aboriginal children and their families benefit greatly from the existing ECD programs, at least in the short term.

What we do not know, however, is whether or how well the scarce resources invested in the existing miscellany of Aboriginal ECD government programs, which has slowly evolved since 1994, have worked in the long term or are contributing to reducing the gap in the life chances of B.C. Aboriginal children— or if these programs are even meeting their current needs. We are convinced that in order to ensure that all Aboriginal ECD programs are of high quality and of long-term benefit to young children and their families, there is an urgent need for all governments to do the following:

1. assess the impact of current Aboriginal ECD programs;
2. prioritize the creation and strengthening of strategic collaborations around ECD among different levels and agencies of governments and Aboriginal authorities;
3. revitalize ECD policies and make the necessary investments so that all programs are sustainable, accessible, and of high quality to ensure they make a real difference in the lives of Aboriginal children and their families now and in the future; and
4. work in a collaborative partnership with First Nations and Métis communities in the redesign, administration, delivery, evaluation, and impact assessment of ECD programs.

THE FIRST NATIONS HEALTH AUTHORITY:
FINDING A GOOD WAY FORWARD

A recent example of a collaborative partnership that promises a new approach to the design and delivery of Aboriginal ECD in British Columbia that will ensure better outcomes is the transfer of responsibility and funding for the health and well-being of First Nations in that province to the First Nations Health Authority.

The tripartite Framework Agreement on First Nations Health signed by B.C. First Nations, the province of British Columbia, and the federal government on October 13, 2011, reflects the hope of all parties that a more collaborative and Indigenous approach to creating change in health outcomes will lead to greatly increased well-being among B.C. First Nations. The Agreement outlines the new health governance structure for First Nations health services and the funding commitments for the transfer of federal health programs and services to the new B.C. First Nations Health Authority. In December 2014, after a transition period of two years, the transfer was complete. The federal government will provide funding of $380 million per year to start and the province will provide $83.5 million over 10 years (First Nations Health Authority, 2011). Federal ECD programs for B.C. First Nations children and families living on-reserve are among the programs being transferred.

This change in governance provides the opportunity for First Nations in British Columbia to show that they can make a positive and lasting impact on the lives of young First Nations children and their families. The good way to do this is to ensure that the ECD programs that are delivered are of high quality, culturally relevant, and integrated with other programs, and that ECD investments currently in place are not only maintained but enhanced.

CONCLUSION

The poverty and despair in which many young Aboriginal children and their families currently live and the rapid growth in the Aboriginal population are among the reasons why effective ECD government strategies with significantly increased funding continue to be a legal and moral imperative. But beyond these imperatives is the waste of human potential and the high financial and social costs to all citizens of a situation where it seems to be necessary to take so many Aboriginal children into care, and in so doing undermines the hope for the future that children represent to Aboriginal families and their communities.

As we have argued in this chapter, the early childhood policies and programs for Aboriginal children and families that have emerged in Canada over the last two decades, although limited, do have the potential to make a difference in the lives of some Aboriginal children, families, and communities. However, funding for ECD/ELCC programs has and continues to be completely inadequate. As a result, the quality of these programs, and consequently their effectiveness, may be compromised and access to these programs is severely limited for Aboriginal children in urban areas. Fragmented programs and services that are not integrated and do not reflect cultural requirements nor respond realistically to the socio-economic conditions in which so many Aboriginal peoples live will do little to create real change. In addition, though federal administrative evaluations are conducted, the overall impact of these programs in reducing the gap in life chances of Aboriginal children compared with other children in Canada has never been assessed.

Ensuring that ECD programs are expanded and of high quality is crucial, but will not be enough to produce the kind of lasting change that significantly improves the life chances of young Aboriginal children. To be effective in the long term, ECD policies and programs must be part of a comprehensive strategy that recognizes and addresses the political, economic, and social contexts that continue to reproduce the poverty and grim living conditions in many Aboriginal communities. In other words, the real-life circumstances of Aboriginal children and their families need to be factored into the design, implementation, and funding of high-quality, culturally appropriate ECD programs.

References

Adamson, P. (2008). *The child care transition: A league table of early childhood education in economically advanced countries.* Florence, Italy: UNICEF Innocenti Research Centre. Retrieved from http://www.unicef_irc.org/publications/pdf/rc8_eng.pdf

Adamson, P. (2010). *The children left behind: A league table of inequality in child well-being in the world's rich countries.* Florence, Italy: UNICEF Innocenti Research Centre. Retrieved from http://www.unicef_irc.org/publications/pdf/rc9_eng.pdf

Adamson, P. (2012). *Measuring child poverty: New league tables of child poverty in the world's rich countries.* Florence, Italy: UNICEF Innocenti Research Centre. Retrieved from http://www.unicef-irc.org/publications/660/#pdf

B.C. Aboriginal Child Care Society (BC ACCS). (2012). *Finding a good way forward: Early childhood development policies and programs for Aboriginal children in B.C.* West Vancouver, BC: Author.

Blackstock, C. (2008). Reconciliation means not saying sorry twice. In M. Brant Castellano, L. Archibald, & M. Degagne (Eds.), *From truth to reconciliation: Transforming the legacy of residential schools* (pp. 164–178). Ottawa: Aboriginal Healing Foundation Research. Retrieved from http://www.ahf.ca/downloads/from-truth-to-reconciliation-transforming-the-legacy-of-residential-schools.pdf

British Columbia. (2012a). 2012/13 – 2014/15 Service Plan. Ministry of Children and Family Development. Retrieved from http://www.bcbudget.gov.bc.ca/2012/sp/pdf/ministry/cfd.pdf

British Columbia. (2012b). Debates of the Legislative Assembly (Hansard): Committee A Blues, Thursday, April 19, 2012. Retreived from http://www.leg.bc.ca/hansard/39th4th/d20419y.htm

Britto, P. R., Yoshikawa, H., & Boller, K. (2011). Quality of early childhood development programs in global contexts: Rationale for investment, conceptual framework, and implications for equity. *Social Policy Report, 25*. Retrieved from http://www.srcd.org/index.php?option=com_docman&task=doc

Campaign 2000. (2009). *Poverty reduction key to Canada's economic recovery.* News releases. Retrieved from http://www.campaign2000.ca/whatsnew/releases/2009 ReportCardRelease.html

Canada. (2010). *Federal poverty reduction plan: Working in partnership towards reducing poverty in Canada.* Report of the Standing Committee on Human Resources, Skills and Social Development and the Status of Persons with Disabilities. Retrieved from http://www.parl.gc.ca/HousePublications/Publication.aspx?DocId=4770921

Canada. (2012). *Federal activities and expenditures for young children.* Retrieved from http://www.faeyc-adfje.gc.ca/tbl_prcdn-g.jspCTG=2&PRGD=58&DPRT=1& AFY=1

Canada, PCO. (2002). *Speech from the Throne to open the second session of the 37th Parliament of Canada.* Retrieved from http://www.pco-bcp.gc.ca/index.asp?lang =eng&page=information&sub=publications&doc=archives/sft-ddt/2002-eng.htm

Canadian Council of Child and Youth Advocates. (2011). *Special report—Aboriginal children. Canada must do better: Today and tomorrow.* Retrieved from http://www.rcybc.ca/Images/PDFs/Report/CCCYA_UN_Report-Final%20Oct%2027.pdf/

Coalition to Build a Better B.C. (2010). *The cuts.* Retrieved from http://www.betterBC.ca/the-cuts

Cool, J. (2007). *Child care in Canada: The federal role.* Ottawa: Library of Parliament of Canada, Political and Social Affairs Division. Retrieved from http://www.parl.gc.ca/content/LOP/Researchpublications/prb0420-e.pdf

Department of Finance. (2011). *Canada social transfer.* Retrieved from http://www.fin.gc.ca/fedprov/cst-eng.asp

First Nations Health Authority. (2011). *British Columbia Tripartite Framework Agreement on First Nation health governance.* Retrieved from http://www.fnhc.ca/pdf/framework-accord-cadre-eng1.pdf

Food Banks Canada. (2011). *Hungercount 2010.* Retrieved from http://www.foodbanks canada.ca. getmedia/12a3e485-4a4e-47d

Fraser, S. (2011). *Speaking notes for an address by Sheila Fraser, FCA, auditor general of Canada to the Canadian Club of Ottawa, serving Parliament through a decade of change—25 May 2011.* Retrieved from http://www.oag-bvg.gc.ca-internet/English/sp_20110525_e_35353.html

Health Canada, First Nations, and Inuit Health. (2010). *Aboriginal Head Start on reserve.* Retrieved from http://www.hc-sc.gc.ca/finah-spnia/famil/develop/ahsor-papa_intro-eng.php

House of Commons Canada. (2010). *Federal poverty reduction plan: Working in partnership towards reducing poverty in Canada.* Retrieved from http://www.parl.gc.ca/content/hoc/Committee/403/HUMA/Reports/RP4770921/humarp07/humarp 07-e.pdf

Human Resources and Skills Development Canada Strategic Policy and Research Branch (HRSDC). (2011). *Summative evaluation of the Understanding the Early Years Initiative.* Retrieved from http://www.esdc.gc.ca/eng/publications/evaluations/social_development/2011/sp_1019_12_11_eng.pdf

Indian and Northern Affairs Canada. (2010). *Better outcomes for First Nations children: INAC's role as a funder of First Nations child and family services.* Retrieved from http://www.aadnc-aandc.gc.ca/eng/1100100032510/1100100035218

KidsKan. (2012). *UNICEF report shows Canada lagging on child poverty.* Retrieved from http://kidskan.ca/node/632

Ministry of Children and Family Development (MCFD). (2009). *Aboriginal children in care: May 2009 report.* Retrieved from http://epub.sub.uni-hamburg.de/epub/volltexte/2011/11652/pdf/Aboriginal_CIC_Report_may2009.pdf

Ministry of Children and Family Development (MCFD). (2011). *British Columbia's early years: Annual report 2010/2011.* Retrieved from http://www.mcf.gove.bc-ca/earlychildhood/pdf/EarlyYearsAnnualReport2011.pdf

Ministry of Children and Family Development (MCFD). (2012). *Operational and strategic directional plan 2012/13–2014/15.* Retrieved from http://frpbc.ca/media/uploads/files/operational_strategic_plan_2012-2015.pdf

National Collaborating Centre for Aboriginal Health. (2009). *Fact sheet: Poverty as a social determinant of First Nations, Inuit, and Métis health.* Retrieved from http://www.nccah-ccnsa.ca/docs/fact%20sheets/social%20determinates/NCCAH_fs_poverty_EN.pdf

Organisation for Economic Co-operation and Development (OECD). (2006). *Starting strong II: Early childhood education and care.* Retrieved from http://www.oecd/org/edu/preschoolandschool/startingstrongiiearlychildhoodeductionand

Patterson, L. L. (2006). Aboriginal roundtable to Kelowna Accord: Aboriginal policy negotiations, 2004–2005. Library of Parliament, PRC 06-04E. Retrieved from http://www.parl.gc.ca/content/LOP/researchpublications/prb0604-e.pdf

Reynolds, A. J., Temple, J., Ou, S. R., Arteaga, A. I., & White, B. A. (2011). School-based early childhood education and age-28 well-being: Effects by timing, dosage, and subgroups. *Science, 333,* 360–364. Retrieved from http://www.sciencemag.org/content/333/6040/360.abstract?sid=ad7a27d1-b357-4c54-bec

Statistics Canada. (2006). Living arrangements of First Nations and non-Aboriginal children 14 years of age and under. In *2006 Census.* Retrieved from http://www12.statcan.ca/census-recensement/2006/as-sa/97-558/table/t20-eng.cfm

Statistics Canada. (2009). *Canadian social trends, First Nations people: Selected findings of the 2006 Census.* Retrieved from http://www.statcan.gc.ca/pub/11-008-x/2009001/article/10864-eng-htm

CHAPTER 17

Grandma and Grandpa and the Mysterious Case of Wolf Teeth in the House!

Richard Van Camp

This happened on a winter day in Behchoko, the heart of Tlicho territory in the Northwest Territories, in the holiness of my grandparents' love.

What happened was my grandpa got brand new teeth from the dentist. They were false, of course, as he is 90 years old. He was so happy he didn't want to tell my grandma because she would tease him. (She teases him about everything.)

The truth was it was their wedding anniversary coming up and he wanted to give her a proper kiss—the way he used to when he had his own teeth!

So, while she was out visiting (and gossiping), my grandpa went to see the dentist, and he got his false teeth fitted for his mouth. He'd been meeting in secret with the dentist while Grandma was at Bingo (and gossiping). He jigged up a storm he was so happy to even dream he could kiss her like he used to and eat caribou meat once again.

So, once he officially received his false teeth, he hobbled home with his little cane, and he decided to get all spruced up—just like when he was still in his prime. He took his false teeth out and left them on the kitchen counter while he ran his bath. He really wanted to look handsome for when my grandma came home.

Grandpa sat in the tub, poured some of Grandma's bubble bath in the water (even though he always denied he used it), and started to sing a Dogrib love song. It was so lovely, the northern lights danced miles above and lowered their way closer to the Earth to lean in and listen. It was so sweet that every time he hit a high note, a new star was born in the sky. Grandpa was feeling great: no more caribou broth for him! He could chomp down to his heart's delight on his favourite country foods like caribou tongue, moose nose, caribou dry meat, buffalo kidneys, and chew chew chew!

He couldn't wait!

Well, my grandma came home, saw a new pair of teeth on the kitchen counter and said a little Tlicho prayer. She even pulled out her heavy artillery and made the sign of the cross. She saw the garbage truck passing by and ran out of the house with her little kerchief flapping in the wind. With careful aim from her dog-mushing days, she whipped Grandpa's new teeth in the back of the truck!

Meanwhile, back in the tub, my grandpa was singing away with his little purple gums, just crooning away. He couldn't wait to surprise my grandma. My grandma, back in the kitchen, started to make yet another batch of her famous caribou soup.

Well, Grandpa was dressed in his Sunday best when he came out to greet her. He was surprised to see that my grandma had returned home so early. The Behchoko Gossip Train must have been cheap that day, he mused, as he went to grab his teeth so he could smile for her and give her a great big smooch.

But his teeth weren't there.

"Hey," he said in Dogrib. "Where are my teeth?"

"Old man, I knew you were going crazy, but this proves it," Grandma said. "You haven't had teeth in 40 years!"

"I have new teeth," Grandpa insisted. "I put them on the counter."

"Those weren't your teeth," Grandma said. "Those were wolf teeth."

"Wolf teeth?" Grandpa asked. "What do you mean—wolf teeth?"

Grandma shrugged. "One of the hunters in town must have dropped them off as a present. It's bad luck to have wolf teeth in the house, so I threw them away in the dump truck."

"Where?" He asked. "Is it garbage day? I still have time if I run—"

"Too late," Grandma said. "They already took the garbage away. If there's wolf teeth in the house, we'll never catch a moose or caribou again. Bad luck!"

So there was my grandpa as he had been for the past 40 years: no teeth, no moose nose, no caribou tongue. He was left sipping caribou broth on a sad wintry Sunday with my grandma, who insists to this day that she was only doing what any sensible Dogrib woman should.

So what's the lesson here? Take care of your teeth and floss, floss, floss unless you want your fake teeth to end up at the dump!

Ha ha

Ho ho
Mahsi cho
Yo!

CONCLUDING THOUGHTS

Northerners are encouraged to share stories every day because storytelling is good medicine. I think the greatest storytellers learn to listen with their blood and spirit to share the stories that they sense need to be heard and felt by their audience. Storytelling is part of the mind, body, spirit, family, and community connection that we are all craving right now in this time of technology and social isolation. We are all storytellers. The great news about the technology we have right now is that it has never been easier to also record our family members and storytellers we admire to honour them. Storytelling is soul medicine.

It is a joy to share one of our family stories with you. *Mahsi cho!* Thank you very much!

P.S. To be honest, my grandfather did get another pair of false teeth, and he was able to kiss my grandmother properly. And they really did live happily ever after. . . .

CHAPTER 18

Knowing Who You Are

Family History and Aboriginal Determinants of Health

Brenda Macdougall

THE WOMAN WHO MARRIED A BEAVER

Kayâs (long ago), a young woman went out to fast on the land and, after a while, a young man came and spoke to her, asking her to come live with him as his wife. After some persuasion, the young woman eventually went to live with him, leaving her family. Her husband was kind and a good provider, but he was often gone for periods of time. When he returned from his excursions he brought fine cloth, tobacco, silver jewellery, beads, ribbons, metal implements, including knives and pots, and anything else she needed. All the young man asked of his new bride was that she not leave their home and avoid contact with other people. She was content with her husband and her new life and, in time, they had four children together and so she did as he asked.

   As she watched her children grow older, the woman often thought that the behaviour of her husband and children was strange—every so often they would leave their house with other humans who came to visit and, when they returned home to her, they always came with new things such as kettles, knives, cloth, bowls, and tobacco, among other gifts. After many years together, the woman came to realize that she had married a beaver and that her beaver family was going with humans to be killed. In return for the sacrifice of their bodies, their flesh, her beaver husband and children returned home with these gifts people had given them. As a result, her family never really died because the humans who hunted them observed proper hunting protocols of respect and generosity. In turn, the beaver family grew fond of the humans and would visit with them often, forging a strong relationship. One day, after her children had all left home, the woman's husband, now an old man, died and so she was alone in the lodge. She remained there until one day she heard the familiar voices of humans outside her home and so she called out to them. Upon hearing a woman's voice, the hunters broke open the beaver lodge, reached in, and discovered that there was a human living there. As they helped her emerge from her lodge, they saw an old woman with very white hair wearing a beaded skirt, cloak, moccasins, and many silver earrings and necklaces and they were awed by her beauty.

It was on that day that the woman returned to her life with humans, telling the people of her experiences with her beaver family while giving them the protocols they were to follow in order to be successful hunters. She told the people that they should never speak badly of the beaver or behave contemptuously. The people needed to honour the beaver through prayer and gifts or they would no longer be able to kill beavers. Only by feeling love and respect from people would the beaver feel compelled to sacrifice themselves for the well-being of humans. Indeed, the beaver felt as people felt and so people needed to consider how they wanted to be treated in life in order to understand how beavers needed to be treated.

Variations of the above story, known as "the woman who married a beaver," are told by Algonquian language speakers, including the Anishinabe, Cree, Peigan, and Blackfoot. Today, translations and transcriptions of this particular story can be found in published histories and literatures, as well as scholarly articles and books that have used it to illustrate a range of issues related to spirituality and world view, gender and social hierarchy in traditional societies, economic histories based on reciprocity and trade, and environmental ethics.[1] Most recently, Turtle Mountain Ojibway scholar, Heidi Kiiwetineqinesiik Stark, used this story because of its thematic focus on reciprocity to examine Anishinabe treaty-making and diplomacy processes. Regardless of the interpretive apparatus employed, it should be evident that stories such as these provide a multitude of frameworks to understand the lifeways, values, and ethics within Indigenous societies. In my work on family histories, for instance, the story of the woman who married a beaver provides a narrative framework for understanding how relatives are expected and encouraged to behave toward one another; the mechanisms for creating family; and how family could be destroyed. Embedded in the story then is not just a blueprint for a healthy family life but also a warning about the consequences if people failed to meet their familial responsibilities to one another.

In the story of the woman who married a beaver, human hunters left gifts, sacrifices of tobacco, cloth, ribbons, pots and knives, and other items for the beavers, who, in return, allowed themselves to be killed for human subsistence because of such displays of respect. As long as animals such as the beaver were honoured and respected, they permitted themselves to be killed for food. The spirit of the animals survived, so they never really died. Consequently, the relational cycle could continue. There is within the story, however, a warning that if the beaver are not treated with respect and kindness, then they would no longer be bound by the code of reciprocity to sacrifice themselves for their human relatives. The foundation of this story, then, is that humans, Aboriginal peoples, and the beavers are dependent on one another as family via the marriage of the human woman and the beaver man. That beavers are creatures, and being non-human is irrelevant to the broader message that these societies were bound to one another, forging a family circle between humans and beavers. Family, therefore, serves as a blueprint for humanity. The lessons of the story can be applied to relations between humans as much as to relations between people and beavers. In short, this story is an important teaching about how to be a good person, a good family member, because it illustrates the principles of familial relationships, including how they are created, how they are managed and maintained, and how they are destroyed.

It is both the hopefulness and the cautionary note in this story that makes it relevant today as a means to support the health and well-being of our communities. We know that the outcome of the fur trade was the virtual extinction of the beaver from over-hunting for commercial gain. This over-hunting was done in partnership between, on the one hand, fur trade companies and their representatives, who actively sought beaver pelts, fuelling an international market for hats and luxury furs and, on the other hand, Indigenous peoples, who wanted to possess the guns, pots, and other practical trade goods imported for exchange.[2] It has been successfully demonstrated that Indigenous peoples forged new familial relations with the newcomers employed by trade companies. This building of new economic alliances through marriage as a matter of protocol is expressed within the story, but it is also clear that in forging this new familial circle, Native peoples damaged their relationship with the beaver. The over-hunting of beaver for commercial gain rather than subsistence use led to a violation of the principles of reciprocity. The failure to maintain the relationship resulted in the near-extinction of the beaver population (Martin, 1978).[3] Elders have pointed to these types of situations, breaks in cultural norms and values, as potential factors that have contributed to poor health within our communities today. As such, a key to the restoration of health rests with knowing who we are, where we come from, and who our relatives are, as well as with relearning how to make relatives in the absence of family. Part of the solution, then, lies within the story of the woman who married the beaver, with an understanding that the history of our families and our communities are, by extension, the history of our nations. This story then, in its entirety, is a blueprint for healthy communities, healthy families, and healthy people. To be healthy is to know who you are as a human, to know how to live as a human. It is important to understand the role that family has in our individual and collective well-being. Sioux anthropologist, Ella Cara Deloria, in speaking of the Sioux *tiyospaye* (camp circle or family structure), noted that her people defined humanity as being a part of a large family structure; without the struggle to gain and maintain relatives, she commented, one's humanity was lost (Deloria, 1998).

HISTORY: A MODEL FOR CONTEMPORARY WELL-BEING

It may be clear by now that I am not a health researcher. I am, however, aware of the health concerns that our people and communities face daily. I have watched members of my own family suffer from poor health. My scholarly training instead centres on understanding stories such as the woman who married the beaver while also drawing on historical methods (including archival research and genealogical reconstructions) as a means to study how family and familial relationships serve as the cultural and social foundation of Indigenous societies generally and Métis society specifically. It is important to know how a people conceive of themselves—who they are and where they come from—in order to understand how they fashion relationships with the world around them—which is, of course, fundamental to health and well-being (Macdougall, 2014). Aboriginal peoples throughout North America traditionally linked their sense of self with their sense of place—or, to be more precise, with the land that they conceive of as their home or territory. Across central North America, from the Great Lakes westward to the edge of the Rocky Mountains, and from the northern edge of the Subarctic down through the southern expanse of the Northern Plains, the Métis created a way of being that is embodied in the protocols of *wahkootowin*, a Cree term that has been translated as "relationship" or "relation."[4] However, such a translation misses much of the meaning and sentiment that the term and its derivatives actually express. *Wahkootowin* refers to all relationships between people, the spirit world, the land, and nature. Therefore, this is the expression of a world view privileging family—especially interfamily—connectedness. Integral to *wahkootowin* was *miyo-wicetowin* or the principle of having good relations between people whether individually or collectively. *Miyo-wicetowin* embodies the principle of getting along, which is the value by which all relationships are created, nourished, reaffirmed, and recreated in a manner that strengthens both the people and the nation (McLeod, 2007). Together, *wahkootowin* (all relations) and *miyo-wicetowin* (good relations) comprise a core doctrine governing relationships and represents health and well-being of individuals and communities. Although the Cree term is used here, the concept of family as the basis for all relationships and behaviours—economic, social, or political— is understood within other First Nations languages, such as the Sioux conceptualization of the *tiyospaye*. Family is central to Indigenous peoples' conceptualization of society.

The values crucial to successful family relationships, such as reciprocity, mutual support, generosity, decency, and order, in turn influenced individual and community behaviours, actions, and decision making economically and politically. As we shall see, by explaining the role of family in three Métis family histories, complex webs of interfamilial relationships made all relationships workable within this society. The construct of family depended on reciprocity as highlighted in the story of the woman who married the beaver. The story pointed to Beatrice Medicine's conceptualization of the "reciprocity family model," which she argued established familial alliances by providing a broader network for group social and cultural interaction through a web of flexible support systems predicated upon reciprocity and generosity (Medicine, 1981). The expectation of reciprocity is that people will respond to each other in kind, sharing the products of hunting or other wealth and material support with relatives who need such aide. Métis families reciprocally supported one another through intermarriage, group labour (regardless of age or gender), and the sharing of their lives with one another, all of which reinforced a greater sense of family, community, and home within this economy. These frameworks and webs cannot easily be classified simply purely as "social" determinants of well-being but instead must be in part conceptualized as narratives and dynamic relationalities. Family members were bound to one another by ties of loyalty, with obligations to support them materially and emotionally when necessary. Indeed, the relationship between people, the Creator, and the land is understood to be the same as that which existed between living members of a human family. As such, their relationship to the land, the environment, and all living beings are governed by the same principles as family relationships.

STORY OF THE MÉTIS FAMILY

My work with Métis family histories began when I started teaching Métis history for the Saskatchewan Urban Native Teacher Education Program (SUNTEP) at the University of Saskatchewan in the mid-1990s. Annually, students enrolled in this class travelled to Winnipeg to visit the Hudson's Bay Company Archives, St. Boniface Historical Society, and the Métis Family Research Centre. The students did this in order to trace their ancestral family members and learn more about their lives as Métis people. The goal of the field trip was to introduce students to research and, as a learning outcome, they were required to write a small family history essay based on genealogical research from archival records situating their families within the broader context of Métis history. What inevitably occurred during the Winnipeg trip, between new groups of student every year, was that students came home discovering that they were related. By tracing their genealogies, students discovered that they were distantly related to each other and, as a result, their sense of respect and responsibility for one another grew.

Shortly after I began teaching the SUNTEP course, I embarked on my dissertation project on the cultural and social history of northwestern Saskatchewan Métis communities with genealogical research as a primary methodological approach. The genealogies of over 3,000 individuals or 43 families were then triangulated with the narratives and vital statistics about individuals located within church, fur trade, and documents of the Canadian government. I was interested in how family histories reflected the region's broader history economically, politically, and religiously. Those stories exist and, if we listen closely and read carefully, we can locate narratives of Métis families throughout a range of sources. Narrative storytelling remains a fundamental manner in which we can understand our histories as Indigenous peoples and, through the sharing of those stories, we can embark on a process of rebuilding our communities.

Stories and narratives, then, can be understood as a determinant of Indigenous peoples' health and well-being. As such, there are three relevant stories about Métis people that embody expressions of family life across time and space and reflect the principles embodied within the story of the woman who married a beaver. These stories about families can also be conceptualized as relevant to health. The very act of documenting and disseminating these relationship stories is a gesture of renewing health. The three family histories are stories I have researched and studied over a number of years, and details about them can be found in several of my previous publications (Macdougall, 2006, 2010a, 2010b, 2013a, 2013b, 2014). I highlight them again here to demonstrate the centrality of family as a source of well-being historically and to establish a foundation for pursuing and supporting healthy relationships today.

Story 1: The Grants of Rupert's Land and Montana Territories

As my other research has noted, in 1889, Johnny Grant, a man born at Fort Edmonton in 1831 but who lived in the Montana territory most of his life, returned to the site of his birth on the north Saskatchewan River (Macdougall, 2010b). Seeking his mother's grave, he was acutely aware of his connections to the place: "We looked around the country. The weather was fine. I thought I had never saw such a fine country. I wrote to my wife and told her that I had travelled in many places in my time, but I had never seen any country [as] fine as Edmonton, the country of my birth and that we must come to live here" (Ens, 2008, p. 309). A year later, Grant and many of his family relocated to the Edmonton area. Grant had a large extended family that lived throughout western Canada and the northern United States. In many ways, his life story and that of his family were typical of many Métis families in the nineteenth century. Johnny Grant's family originated in the *amiskwâciwaskahikan*, or Beaver Hills House, region around Fort Edmonton, located between the north branch of the Saskatchewan and the Battle rivers, and encompassing places like St. Albert, Lac Ste-Anne, and Rocky Mountain House. *Amiskwâci-waskahikan* is a part of a transitional landscape within the aspen parkland belt (Goyette & Roemmich, 2004).[5]

Johnny Grant was the son of Marie Anne Breland (the daughter of Pierre Breland and Louise Umphreville, who was born in *amiskwâciwaskahikan* in about 1800) and HBC servant Richard Grant. Marie Anne was from one of the original Métis families and oldest Métis communities in Alberta, dating to the 1790s. Grant's grandmother, Louise Umphreville, was likewise also born in *amiskwâciwaskahikan* a generation earlier to Edward Umphreville, a trader with the North West Company, and an unnamed Indian woman, who may have been Gros Ventre or Cree. While Edward Umphreville eventually

returned to Great Britain, his daughter Louise and her brother and sister remained in the land of their birth and are today three of the ancestors to whom
many contemporary Alberta Métis trace their lineage.[6]

Johnny Grant was raised in *amiskwâciwaskahikan* until about 1835, when
his mother died and his father sent him to live with his father's Scottish
mother in Trois Rivière (Macdougall, 2010b). He remained there until he was
about 14. While her grandson was being raised in Quebec, Louise Umphreville remarried, this time to trader John Rowand, a man who would eventually control the trade around *amiskwâciwaskahikan* as chief factor of Fort
Edmonton. Rowand used his influence to have Richard Grant assigned to his
own fort in the Idaho territory. Grant returned to Idaho/Montana after his
fourteenth year, and worked as a rancher and cattle trader until the late 1860s,
when he travelled to Red River.[7]

When he was nearly 60, Johnny Grant returned to the place of his birth. As
he stood on the riverbank, looking for his mother's grave, he was moved by
the beauty of his home. The place where Grant stood, now Rossdale Flats
in Edmonton, was once called *pehonan*, "the gathering or waiting place," in
Cree (Goyette & Roemmich, 2004, pp. 20–24). This place, both ancient
and sacred, served as a gathering place for Cree, Dene, Beaver, Nakoda, Blackfoot, Gros Ventre, and eventually Métis. *Pehonan* was sacred because it was a
space where the protocols of peaceful relations, friendship, and family—*miyo-
wicetowin* or good relations—guided the behaviour of those who gathered
there. By extension, *pehonan* became a place where the fur trade could flour-
ish. Grant's return, then, was to a place well known to the Métis, who raised
their families there and lived for generations. Although Grant left as a child,
others remained and developed large networks of families engaged in the trade
throughout the nineteenth century—many of those families are still there.
My interest in Johnny Grant's history is personal as we share a grandmother,
Louise Umphreville—his maternal grandmother is my great-great-great-great
grandmother. My family line, however, descends from Louise's marriage to
her second husband, John Rowand. I learned about Johnny Grant on a visit to
Montana and a chance conversation, and have since then pursued information about him, the broader family, and the region that we all come from.

Story 2: The Morins of Northwestern Saskatchewan

At about the same time that Grant was finding his place in his ancestral lands,
in 1887, Raphaël Morin was required to identify where he was from as he filed
for scrip at Green Lake.[8] Specifically, the scrip commissioners asked him,

"Where do you live?" and "How long have you lived there and where have you lived previously?" (R. Morin, 1887). Raphaël responded that he was living at Devil's Lake on the Shell River, then added that he "live[d] in the land of my mother who was originally from the lands of [her] parents [because] most of the time [we] were in the. . .lands of her relatives as we had no interest in the lands. . .where my father and myself were born and raised" (R. Morin, 1887). As my previous research demonstrated, this statement is significant because Morin is privileging his mother's family, articulating that this lineage defined both his conception of where he was from, his homeland, and his sense of self (Macdougall, 2010a). Raphaël was a Métis man born around 1830, somewhere along the Athabasca River, to Antoine Morin, a French-Canadian voyageur from Quebec, and Pélagie Boucher, a woman described in Canadian Census records as being Montagnais (Dene) Métis from the La Loche region. Raphaël's assertions of family connections to homeland were echoed two years later by his sister, Marie, in her own scrip application. After her husband's death in 1880, Marie likewise took her three youngest children to the Shell River area to live in the "country of her mother" (M. Morin, 1889).

My earlier research has shown that the Métis families of northwestern Saskatchewan shared with their maternal Cree and Dene relatives a world view privileging family above all other relationships. But they also grew up in an environment framed by the fur trade (Macdougall, 2010a). While the Métis families of this region were grounded in a geographic space infused with the beliefs and behaviours of their maternal relatives, their continued connection to one another was facilitated by their long association with the trade. Métis families coalesced in the region and resided at these particular locations for reasons very much intertwined with the trade. Initially, outsider male employees of various trade companies entered the region for work and, in the process, laid a foundation for the emergence of the Subarctic Métis when they married local Aboriginal women and chose to remain in their adopted homelands. In subsequent generations, this connection between land and economy became entrenched as people continued working in the trade, but doing so while living in a homeland carved out for them by their maternal ancestry.

Raphaël's family and economic background is fairly typical of many first-generation Métis people in the nineteenth century. His father, Antoine Morin, was a trade employee stationed between La Loche and Île à la Crosse, two historic Métis communities located in the Subarctic zone of northwestern Saskatchewan, and it was in this region that Raphaël grew up, worked, married, and eventually left for Devil's Lake, located approximately 200 miles south of La Loche and Île à la Crosse. Devil's Lake was outside the ecological zone of the Subarctic and is actually located in the parkland transition zone between the Subarctic's boreal forest and the Great Plains. This begs an important question: How could Raphaël Morin consider Devil's Lake to be a part of the lands of his maternal ancestors? Clearly, there was a significant connection between the large geographical expanses in which the Métis lived and worked and how they defined their connection to territory and family. For Raphaël and others like him, his sense of self was defined by his connection to the trade, but also, perhaps more importantly, his sense of homeland and personal identity was rooted in his maternal connections.

While the Métis families such as the Grants and Morins were grounded in a geographic space steeped in the beliefs of their ancestors, their ongoing efforts to remain connected to one another was facilitated by their long association with the trade. Métis families gathered at trading zones and resided at these particular locations for reasons very much connected to the trade. Individuals like Raphaël may have conceived of their homeland as a part of a maternal legacy, but moved about the region because of the demands of the trade.

Story 3: John McDonald of Garth and Nancy Small

At the same time, the centrality of mobility within the Métis historical lifestyle necessarily led to the creation of familial structures that supported and sustained relationships over time and place (Macdougall, 2013a). The family of John McDonald of Garth (the latter locational reference distinguished him from a number of other John McDonalds employed in the trade) and Nancy Small reflect the types of patterns found within the stories of the Morins and Grants. Born in Perthshire, Scotland, John McDonald of Garth travelled to North America in 1791 as a 20-year-old to work as a clerk for the North West Company (NWC). In 1799 he married a Cree-Scottish woman, Nancy Small, *à la façon du pays* at Île à la Crosse in present-day northwestern Saskatchewan.[9] I learned about Nancy Small during my research into the families of northwestern Saskatchewan. Nancy was one of three documented children born to NWC wintering partner Patrick Small and his Cree wife (Livermore & Anick, 1976). Nancy had grown up with her sister, Charlotte, and brother, Patrick Jr., at the fur post of Île à la Crosse before marrying McDonald of Garth and leaving the northwest. Charlotte, meanwhile, married trader and cartographer David Thompson and, like Nancy, left her birthplace

to travel with her husband as he mapped the North American fur trade territory. In the meantime, Patrick became a successful trader in the Plains/Park-
lands regions (Glover, 1962; Smith, 1971). It was only when I worked for a
term at Carleton University in Ottawa in 2005 that I discovered that sisters
Charlotte and Nancy had, despite their varied travels with their husbands,
ended up living with their husbands and families at Williamstown, a village
near Cornwall, Ontario (S. Campbell, 2007; Macdougall, 2013b).

As a NWC employee, McDonald of Garth was stationed at a variety of
posts, including Moose Lake, Manitoba, Fort George, Alberta, and Fort
Augustus (later Fort Edmonton), Alberta. The movements of the McDonalds
emphasize the mobility necessary for families relying on the trade for their
livelihood. By the time that John and Nancy's youngest daughter Liza was
born at Fort William (Thunder Bay) in 1804, the family had travelled across
eastern and western North America and back again (Macdougall, 2013b). It
was within this milieu that Liza spent the first few years of life. Her four older
siblings were born in the Qu'Appelle Valley of Saskatchewan and at other
posts where their father worked. And while the family lived at various forts,
this did not necessarily mean that their mobility ceased or even that their
connections to their extended family circles were broken. After McDonald
retired from the NWC in 1814, he and Nancy took their family to Williamstown, a community in which many former fur traders came to reside at the
end of their careers. They were eventually joined there by HBC surveyor and
mapmaker David Thompson and Charlotte Small, Nancy's sister, and their
children. As such, although not in their grandmother's homeland, the grandchildren of these two sisters, nevertheless, spent their youth among maternal
relatives as well as families of other retired NWC traders, so they never really
left a social milieu that did not understand their heritage (S. Campbell, 2007).

What We Can Learn Today
from Families of the Past

The mobility of families such as those headed by McDonald, Grant, and
Morin exemplifies the significant relationship between the large geographical
expanses in which the Métis lived and worked and how they defined their
connection to territory and family. Each of these stories, focused on Métis
families in the eighteenth and nineteenth centuries, provides insight into
aspects of their relationships to one another, to the regions they came from,
and to their maternal relatives as well as the fur trade. Together they create a
window into how this world view based on relatedness existed. When read

together, they reveal the interconnection between individuality, family, spirituality, landscape, history, and tradition. The story of family within Métis
communities is layered and complex. In this way the stories of these types
of relationships provides insight into the health and well-being of not only
individuals but families.

Today we often hear that our families are damaged or even broken. It is
clear we are in crisis—we have more children in care now than we did at the
height of the residential school experience (CTV News, 2011). The reality
of the colonial experience is that people were encouraged and compelled to
disassociate themselves from their cultures, including the tradition of col-
lectivities and extended family structures in favour of assimilating into the
dominant Canadian culture with its emphasis on nuclear families and individuality. As a result, our families and their structure are often described as
the root of our problems (as opposed to our strength) by well-meaning clergy,
scholars, social workers, teachers, and medical practitioners. Funerary practices that require four days and nights of praying and sitting with the body
are regarded as archaic and counterproductive to maintaining employment,
going to school, or otherwise being productive participants in a capitalist
economy. The tradition of grandparents raising grandchildren—a practice
intended to provide children with teachers and an opportunity to learn their
place in this world—is described as a fatal character flaw of parents who
are too lazy or disinterested to take responsibility for their own families.
These traditions, the practice of family life that made us healthy and whole,
were regarded by external agencies as the very thing that held us back from
succeeding in the mainstream. As such, these traditions, much like religious
ceremonies, were a site for our assimilation.

Furthermore, the institutional processes that created categories of Aborig-
inality in Canada has negatively impacted our ability as original people to
accept one another as authentically Aboriginal. The Canadian state institu-
tionalized the category of "Indian," enshrining it in the Indian Act and codify-
ing it within Canadian law. Historically, by Canadian law, an Indian, a person
who held the legal status of Indian, was male; women were granted Indian
status only in relation to their fathers' or husbands' status as Indians. What
happened to women under this system has been well documented and discussed, but what we as Aboriginal peoples have avoided discussing is who
else was disenfranchised by the Indian Act provisions. The reality is that
by virtue of creating Indians, oppositional categories were also created. In
the case of Canada, non-Indians were legally citizens of Canada. Indigenous

non-Indians were labelled as non-status (people who were Mohawk, Cree, Blackfoot, Dene, Saulteaux, etc., culturally, but were not granted status by the state for a variety of historical reasons) or Métis (also a people who are Aboriginal, but culturally not Mohawk, Cree, Blackfoot, Dene, Saulteaux, etc., and a people who also do not hold status as Indians). By virtue of the existence of these legal categories, the bonds of family have been bisected and damaged by colonial laws that determine our authenticity and inauthenticity as original people. Consequently, we have young people who do not know their relatives if they are not in the same legal category as them—the status line is a brick wall that obscures all other permutations of Indigeneity.

CONCLUSION

When I spent time in northern Saskatchewan, my close friend Jeffery Morin drove the hospital taxi. One afternoon we travelled together on one of his trips. We picked up a young girl from the hospital in Île à la Crosse and transported her to her home community of Birch Narrows Dene Nation, located just to the north at Turnor Lake. This young woman was also a Morin and after some questioning, it was clear that she was unaware that she was related to the Métis Morins—Jeffery's family—found in villages across northwestern Saskatchewan. Like Jeffery Morin, though, this young woman was a descendant of Antoine Morin and Pélagie Boucher, who established their family in the region during the late eighteenth and early nineteenth centuries. Through the process of colonial control at the turn of the twentieth century, some Morins legally became Métis while others took treaty in 1910 and therefore became status Indians. These two legal categories have obscured the history of the family(ies) of northwestern Saskatchewan and elsewhere. Her lack of knowledge is understandable—neither our history as Aboriginal peoples nor the history of our families and communities is taught in the K–12 system of the public schools in any province.[10] Furthermore, we as Aboriginal peoples have been trained to think of ourselves according to Canadian legal categories, rather than our own socio-cultural frameworks predicated on relatedness. And so many of our young people grow up not knowing who their families are and even less about their communities and nations. It is precisely through the telling and re-telling of stories to and about each other that this violence against our identities might be remedied. So it is, again, that family stories must be understood as health.

All is not lost, though. Stories that speak to the power of family to nurture and shape us exist. We simply have to open ourselves to them and allow the makers of those stories to share with us the narratives of their lives they left for us in a variety of types of documents. We have been told as Native peoples that we do not have written histories, but that is not correct. We had scholars who wrote the histories of our nations, such as William W. Warren, Norbert Welsh, Louis Riel, Victoria Belcourt Callihou, John Tanner, Johnny Grant, and Ella Cara Deloria, who all wrote the histories of their nations and, as a result, of their families. We also have the imprint of individuals, members of families, embedded in scrip applications, Census documents, fur trade records, historical maps, and church records. Inside these official state-created documents, business records, or religious papers the lives of our families exist— they left us information about their experiences and it is up to us to find them and restore them for ourselves, our communities, our children. Narratives such as the story of the woman who married a beaver provide us with interpretive frameworks to understand the meaning of family, the roles of family members to one another, and the power of self in maintaining relationships across time and space. Our old people tell us that knowing who you are is the key to healthy citizens and healthy nations and fundamentally, when we repair the circle of family, we will restore ourselves; the responsibility (as well as the ability) rests with us alone. We need to make this happen.

Notes

1. While necessarily abbreviated here, this story has been recounted in a variety of written sources, including: White (1999), Martin (1999), Skinner (1911), and Stark (2010). In some versions of the story, such as Skinner's, it is a man who marries a female beaver. There are also similar stories that tell about humans marrying bears, another animal that humans have a close kinship connection with.

2. The role of the fur trade exchange economy is well analyzed and described by Ray (1974).

3. Martin's work is not without controversy because he describes Indians as voracious consumers, but he does point to an important issue—that Indians were consumers and their need to obtain trade goods led to environmental concerns. There have been similar charges levelled against the Métis and their overproduction of buffalo hides and pemmican as a factor in the near-extinction of the buffalo by the end of the nineteenth century. The contradictory nature of emphasizing the spiritual element of human-animal relations and the near-extinction of specific species by Aboriginal peoples who were active participants in commercial trade economies deserves more attention by scholars. Perhaps, though, these two issues are irreconcilable.

4. Elders such as Maria Campbell carry and share the teachings specific to *wahkootowin*, today as a part of their responsibilities as teachers within the Métis

community writ large. Specifically, Campbell, in her role as an instructor at various universities across Canada, has brought the teachings about *wahkootowin* into the classroom to further understandings of Indigenous literature, knowledge and methods, and history. Some of these teachings have been published and are available in texts designed to promote cultural teachings such as *Kisewatotatowin: Loving, Caring, Sharing, Respect* (Jolly, Aby, & Cuthand, 1998), a parenting handbook published to assist in strengthening young families. Campbell has further written about *wahkootowin* in her bimonthly newspaper column with *Eagle Feather News*. See, for instance, M. Campbell (2007). Her teachings have influenced and shaped my work. See Macdougall (2006, 2010a, 2014). For specific translations, see Faries (1938), Beaudet (1995), Wolfart & Ahenakew (1998), and Anderson (1975).

The spelling of *wahkootowin* was provided to me for my initial study of Métis society and culture by Maria Campbell, who taught me about this central philosophical construct. While linguists have tried in recent years to establish a standardized spelling of Cree words, I prefer to use the phonetic spelling variation that is commonly found throughout my published works.

5. For an ecological and environmental examination of the Beaver Hills region, see MacDonald (2009).

6. The preface to Ens's *A Son of the Fur Trade* was written in the early twentieth century by Grant's last wife, Clotilde (née Bruneau) Grant, and should be read in its entirety. In it she explains how she came to record her husband's memoir and explain the history of his family as he understood it in his lifetime. See also MacGregor (1978).

7. Ens (2008) and Meikle (1996) are the two most comprehensive biographies of Grant's life. See also MacGregor (1978) for the history of Grant's grandmother, Louise (née Belly/Umphreville) Breland Rowand.

8. Scrip was offered to Métis families as compensation for the loss of their Aboriginal title and for grievances that led to the 1885 Resistance. Scrip came in the form of either land or money. To qualify for scrip offered in 1885, applicants had to prove that they were living in the Northwest Territories prior to July 15, 1870. Those who applied for scrip from 1886 to 1902 or 1906 had to prove that they were living in the Northwest Territories prior to December 31, 1885. The land scrip entitlement was for 240 acres and had to be selected from land that had been allocated as homestead land. Frequently, this land was a long distance from where the grantees were living, so they sold their scrip to land speculators, often for less money than it was worth.

9. *À la façon du pays* literally translates as after the manner (custom) of the country and is a phrase commonly used to describe unions of fur traders and Aboriginal women that were not formalized by Christian rite or European law. This is a practice that comes to characterize the custom of marriage in Métis communities. After the arrival of missionaries in the mid-nineteenth century, marriages were often solemnized in churches, although customary marriages remained possible and acceptable.

10. In some jurisdictions it's possible to take Native Studies at various levels of the K–12 system, but these courses look at Aboriginal-state relations. They do not address local or regional community histories and experiences.

References

Anderson, A. (Ed.). (1975). *Plains Cree dictionary in the "Y" dialect*. Revised edition. Edmonton: s.n.

Beaudet, G. (Ed.). (1995). *Cree-English English-Cree Dictionary = Nehiyawe mina Akayasimo, Akayasimo mina Nehiyawe ayamiwini-masinahigan*. Winnipeg, MB: Wuerz Pub. Ltd.

Campbell, M. (2007, November). We need to return to the principles of *Wahkotowin*. *Eagle Feather News*, p. 5.

Campbell, S. (2007). "I shall settle, marry, and trade here": British military personnel and their mixed-blood descendants. In Ute Lischke & David T. McNab (Eds.), *The long journey of a forgotten people: Métis identities and family histories* (pp. 81–108). Waterloo: Wilfred Laurier University Press.

CTV News. (2011, July 31). Native children in care surpass residential school era. Canadian Press. Retrieved from http://www.ctvnews.ca/native-children-in-care -surpass-residential-school-era-1.677743

Deloria, E. C. (1998). *Speaking of Indians*. Lincoln: University of Nebraska Press.

Ens, G. J. (Ed.). (2008). *A son of the fur trade: The memoirs of Johnny Grant*. Edmonton: University of Alberta Press.

Faries, R. (Ed.). (1938). *A dictionary of the Cree language, as spoken by the Indians in the provinces of Quebec, Ontario, Manitoba, Saskatchewan, and Alberta* (rev. ed.). Based upon the foundation laid by E. A. Watkins, 1865. Toronto, ON: General synod of the Church of England in Canada.

Glover, R. (Ed.). (1962). *David Thompson's narrative, 1784–1812*. Toronto, ON: Champlain Society.

Goyette, L., & Roemmich, C. J. (2004). *Edmonton in our own words*. Edmonton: University of Alberta Press.

Jolly, G. M., Aby, A., & Cuthand, S. (1998). *Kisewatotatowin: Loving, caring, sharing, respect*. Saskatoon, SK: Aboriginal Parent Program, Inc.

Livermore, C. M., & Anick, N. (Eds.). (1976). John McDonald (known as John McDonald of Garth). *Dictionary of Canadian biography online*, vol. 9. Toronto, ON: University of Toronto/Université Laval. Retrieved from http://www.biogra phi.ca/en/bio/mcdonald_john_1866_9E.html

MacDonald, G. A. (2009). *The Beaver Hills country: A history of the land and life*. Edmonton, AB: Athabasca University Press.

Macdougall, B. (2006). *Wahkootowin*: Family and cultural identity in northwestern Saskatchewan Metis communities. *Canadian Historical Review, 87*, 431–462.

Macdougall, B. (2008). "The comforts of married life": Metis family life, labour, and the Hudson's Bay Company. *Labour/Le Travail, 61*, 9–40.

Macdougall, B. (2010a). *One of the family: Metis culture in the nineteenth century north-western Saskatchewan.* Vancouver: UBC Press.

Macdougall, B. (2010b). *Course guide and study manual design and content development, unit 5: The Metis, Indigenous Studies 5XX, learning in Indigenous communities.* Unpublished course guide.

Macdougall, B., with N. St-Onge. (2013a). Rooted in mobility: Metis buffalo hunting brigades. *Manitoba History Special Edition: Red River Revisited, 71,* 21–32.

Macdougall, B. (2013b). *Schedule C: Teaching First Nations, Metis, and Inuit children and traditional teachings modules specific to the Metis.* Framework for Teaching Teachers, Additional Qualification Courses, Ontario College of Teachers.

Macdougall, B. (2014). Speaking of Metis: Reading family life into colonial records. *Ethnohistory, 61,* 27–56.

MacGregor, J. G. (1978). *John Rowand: Czar of the Prairies.* Saskatoon, SK: Prairie Books.

Martin, C. (1978). *Keepers of the game: Indian-animal relationships and the fur trade.* Berkeley: University of California Press.

Martin, C. L. (1999). *The way of the human being.* Princeton, NJ: Yale University Press.

McLeod, N. (2007). *Cree narrative memory: From treaties to contemporary times.* Saskatoon, SK: Purich Publishing.

Medicine, B. (1981). American Indian family. *Journal of Ethnic Studies, 18,* 17–19.

Meikle, L. (Ed.). (1996). *Very close to trouble: The Johnny Grant memoir.* Pullman: Washington State University Press.

Morin, M. (1889, March 8). *Marie Morin.* Library and Archives of Canada, RG 15, vol. 682, file 320835.

Morin, R. (1887, March 1/October 17). *Raphaël Morin.* Library and Archives of Canada, RG 15, vol. 557, file 167727.

Ray, A. J. (1974). *Indians in the fur trade: Their role as trappers, hunters, and middlemen in the lands southwest of Hudson Bay, 1660–1870.* Toronto, ON: University of Toronto Press.

Skinner, A. (1911). *Notes on the Eastern Cree and northern Saulteaux* (pp. 105–107). New York: The Trustee.

Smith, J. K. (1971). *David Thompson: Fur trader, explorer, geographer.* Toronto, ON: Oxford University Press.

Stark, H. K. (2010). Respect, responsibility, and renewal: The foundations of Anishinaabe treaty making with the United States and Canada. *American Indian Culture and Research Journal, 34,* 145–164.

White, B. M. (1999). The woman who married a beaver: Trade patterns and gender roles in the Ojibwa fur trade. *Ethnohistory, 46,* 109–147.

Wolfart, H. C., & Ahenakew, F. (Eds.). (1998). *The student's dictionary of literary Plains Cree: Based on contemporary texts.* Winnipeg, MB: Algonquian and Iroquoian Linguistics.

PART 4

REVISIONING MEDICINE

Toward Indigenization

miyo-pimâtisiwin

Practising "the Good Way of Life" from the Hospital Bed to Mother Earth

Patricia Makokis and James Makokis

This is the story of a mother, Pat Makokis, and her son, Dr. James Makokis. Together, we share our family story of Pat's hysterectomy and James's experience in becoming a doctor trained in Western medicine. This is not an academic paper with citations and statistics, but rather simply a sharing with other women, medical doctors, and anyone looking to understand an alternative way of practising holistic wellness related to female-specific surgery.

We Cree people understand ourselves to be made up of our mental, emotional, spiritual, and physical aspects. We call ourselves *nehiwayak*, four-part persons. Like the four parts of the medicine circle, we believe we are equal parts mental, emotional, spiritual, and physical, so we constantly seek to balance these four aspects of our being.

The following story portrays what we, the Makokis family (Patricia, Eugene, Janice, and James) did to honour women as the givers of life, and the importance of family in the overall wellness and survival of the Nation. With the deepest of respect to all who choose to read this, we share our story from the perspective of a mom in need of a medical procedure, and as a son in his journey to becoming a Western-trained medical physician.

PATRICIA: FEMALE CREE WAYS IN CONTEMPORARY TIMES

I lay down this afternoon, and before I lay down, I smudged and I prayed that I would find the "right" way to introduce this story. I was quickly blessed with one of the gifts of spring, the songs of the frogs. I love spring. As I lay in my bedroom with my window open, the frogs sang to me. I remembered how each year they go to sleep, only to awake and remind the rest of us on Mother

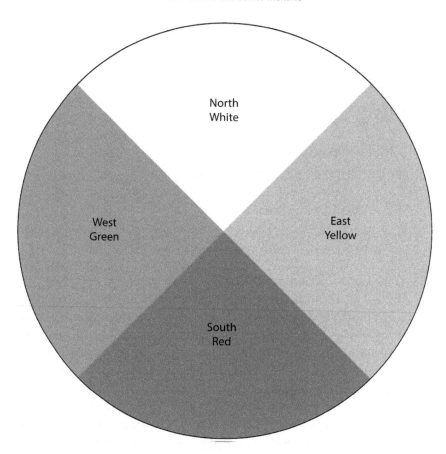

Medicine Circle

Earth of their presence. As I lay there, I thought about their life cycle, and reflected (through them teaching and reminding me) that we are spiritual beings on a human journey. The frogs are awake now, and they let us know of their presence through their beautiful songs. Then come fall, they will go back to sleep, and soon our Mother Earth will have her snow blanket on. In some respects, that little nap lays the foundation for my hysterectomy story; the frogs (the swimmers), like us two-leggeds, are spiritually connected to our Mother, the Earth. We are all born, we come to spend some time on this planet, then we will return to our Mother, the Earth, and so it is with this story.

As a Cree woman, I have much to learn about Cree ways. Part of my lifelong learning journey had to do with my hospital stay in June 2006, during which I underwent major surgery in the form of a full hysterectomy. For approximately two years prior to my hysterectomy, I was challenged with medical conditions related to menopause. I struggled with low iron, low hemoglobin, low energy, severe monthly labour-like pain, and all round unpleasant physical wellness. In fact, at my worst point, I felt like I was going to have a heart attack because I was experiencing a shortness of breath and pain in my chest. I was at the point of not wanting to leave my own home every month for fear of "accidents" that would cause discomfort physically and emotionally.

At the age of 51, I faced the fact that despite my best abilities to help myself holistically, I required surgery to regain my own health. Many questions came up as I prepared myself for surgery. I thought about what I needed to do mentally, emotionally, spiritually, and physically to avoid falling into depression or suffering other possible ailments relating to the loss of very important body parts. My uterus and ovaries privileged me the gift of giving life to my two children, Janice and James.

Having heard that some women suffer emotional turmoil and depression after having a hysterectomy, I wanted to prepare myself in ways that honoured my identity as a Cree woman. Clearly, I knew that I had responsibilities to my own body. I fully understood that I had an obligation to respect and give thanks to my body parts, for without them I would not have had the honour of giving birth. The Creator had lent me my children, so I in turn had to do the right thing. What was the right thing?

James: Preparing for Medical Training as a Cree Physician

Since at least the age of four, I dreamed of becoming a medical doctor. In *nehiyaw opikihawasiwin* (child rearing, the raising of children) it is believed that children will announce to their family and caregivers on a few separate occasions before the age of five what their purpose is in being sent to this *askiy tipimatisiwin* (Earth life) from the spiritual plane. It is the responsibility of the family to be receptive and attentive in listening to their children, and when their purpose is identified, to help guide them on this path to complete their life's work. So finally at the age of 24—after completing an undergraduate degree, a graduate degree in public health, and a great deal of volunteering, all with the goal of getting into medical school—I began my training as a medical doctor at the University of Ottawa in 2006.

In retrospect, I realize now that I had spent so much of my time working on the journey to get to medical school that I forgot to anticipate the many issues I might be faced with once I got there. I wish there was a course I could have taken from the perspective of another Indigenous physician who shared the process of coping with the life, training, and learning scenarios that would challenge my own *nehiyaw* world view in a medical program.

I knew that for each person I encountered, I would be seeing only a small snapshot of his or her overall life. If I was working in my own community, I would have known a large part of people's backgrounds and stories to help me fill in the gaps and missing pieces of why they may be ill. I would have developed a relationship with them, which would change the dynamics of our interaction in a positive way compared to current medical practice, where a quick assessment is completed, followed by an opinion and imposed treatment plan, for a person whose full narrative I do not know.

I would also value the wisdom and teachings that our *kihtehyak* (humble kind ones, Elders) carried, sometimes in the form of plant medicines or ceremonies that could be utilized to help people through their illness, while recognizing this was just as valuable as any pharmaceutical drug or medical treatment of Western medicine. In fact, these medicines and ways kept our people strong, healthy, and surviving well beyond the current shortened life expectancies we have in spite of all the advents of Western medicine. Although some medical institutions recognize the importance of incorporating Indigenous culture and traditions into patient care, I have found that at a fundamental level, the reasons for doing so are not well understood.

I prepared myself spiritually and mentally for medical school by attending and participating in *nehiyaw* ceremonies like our fast, sweat lodges, and others, and by asking for help from our *nokomtak* (Grandmothers) and *nimosomtak* (Grandfathers)—our Ancestors. So the summer before entering medical school, I completed a spiritual fasting ceremony led by Elders in our community and I prayed for *sohkeyitamowin* (Spiritual Law, Natural Law teaching, strength/determination) to complete this journey I would be embarking upon. This was important because it would provide me with the spiritual strength and support from our Ancestors and helpers in the spiritual realm. I would need their help because I was not only engaging in this journey for my own personal reasons, but also in an attempt to help the people and relatives within my Nation. I knew there would be many obstacles to overcome in this process.

PATRICIA: WHY I CHOSE TO PREPARE EMOTIONALLY AND SPIRITUALLY FOR SURGERY

Prior to my surgery, I met with several Cree female friends. We did a women's pipe and feasted together. Collectively the women provided emotional and spiritual support, praying that everything would go well. Surrounded by love and spiritual preparedness, I had much time to reflect upon how I felt about undergoing surgery. Having never been in a hospital other than to have my children, I was a little apprehensive about going into the hospital.

As I prepared spiritually, physically, and mentally for my surgery, one question dominated my thoughts: What should I do with my surgical remains? I knew that I had to do something to honour my own body as a Cree woman, for without my uterus and ovaries I would not have my children as lent to me by the Creator.

I felt that what I should do was bring these body parts home and provide ceremony for them, and I gave this much serious thought. I prayed about it and spoke with other Cree women in my community. In the end, I was advised that what I thought I should do was "what I needed to do." I decided to honour my life-giving uterus and ovaries by wrapping them in sage and broadcloth. Sage is a plant considered by many Indigenous Nations to be a female spiritual smudge (a plant we smudge our body with as we prepare to be in prayer to our Creator). In current times, broadcloth replaces traditional spiritual offerings to represent certain grandfathers and grandmothers (spirit helpers) who reside in the various cardinal directions. In the past, prior to European contact, coloured sticks and willows would have been utilized for the same purpose.

Part of my preparedness meant I spent time talking to my female specialist (gynecologist) about my wishes to bring my surgical remains home. She was very responsive. She listened to me without judgment, and advised me to put my wishes into writing. Once I wrote my letter, I called the hospital Aboriginal liaison worker to discuss my wishes with her too. I faxed the letter to my doctor's office and to the Aboriginal liaison worker's office.

Part of helping myself involved mentally preparing to get up and walk soon after my surgery. This is connected to similar beliefs around giving birth after which our female Elders advise us to "get up and walk"—that we must help ourselves physically. This is part of our own beliefs about taking personal control of our own health, which has now been removed as a result of the colonial experience. I knew that a significant part of my recovery depended on me helping myself mentally, emotionally, spiritually, and physically.

I remember a woman from home telling me about her mother. She said, "My mother almost went crazy after she had that surgery, but I know you have been preparing yourself, Pat." When this woman told me about her mother "almost going crazy" after having her hysterectomy, I thought about the importance of Indigenous women reclaiming cultural teachings about woman-hood. Traditional Cree society honoured the tribe's women, recognizing that women bring life into this world, so women are to be held in high esteem within the tribe. If this is the case, then what responsibilities do we as women have to our bodies in contemporary times, and more particularly in hospital surgeries? How do we ensure that we honour our bodies when we go to hospitals? How do we ensure that we follow our Cree ways so that we don't go "crazy"?

James: Making Those First Steps into Medical School

I clearly remember my first week of medical school was filled with a flurry of activities that included an orientation, signing up for special medical interest groups, trying to get the "best" textbooks for courses I had never taken, navigating a new university in a new city and province, and meeting my classmates, who would be with me exclusively for the next four years of my life. Part of this orientation was a tour of the anatomy lab, where we would study the physical structure of the body for the next two years during our preclinical (years one and two) training and also into our clinical clerkship (years three and four).

The anatomy lab was a space unlike any I had ever seen. There had been some preparation by the faculty about what to expect in working with cadavers (bodies donated to science), including the usual suggestions like "sit down if you feel faint" or "leave the lab if you need to." I remember one of my classmates wearing a bike helmet in case he fainted, but he was not the one who needed it, as it was another student who collapsed and fell on that cold cement floor. Aside from getting used to the smell of the formaldehyde, which clung to your clothes, hair, and skin, the sight of all those bodies of various shapes, sizes, and in different states of dissection was like nothing I'd seen before. The lab instructors encouraged people to partake in the learning journey, discovering the body in all of its wonder. Some took the initiative with eager enthusiasm, others with a bit more reticence and careful calculation, and yet others such as myself did not handle any body part for at least two weeks after we started.

As a *nehiyaw*, I knew that there were particular protocols (cultural/spiritual rules) for working with and being around the deceased. I knew that I had to be respectful, but also to protect myself in such a way that the energy of the deceased person I was working with would not affect me or be brought back to my home and to the people I lived with. For this, I asked for guidance from my relations back home in my community. I was advised to smudge before and after working with the bodies, and also to thank the people (i.e., the bodies) for allowing me to learn from them. This felt like a good way to help ease those worries, and so with that advice, I started my learning from these people.

Later on we were introduced to the morgue area of the anatomy lab, where more donated bodies lay waiting to be dissected by medical students. I was not sure how long they had been there, what their stories were, or which communities they came from. In addition to the cadavers on stretchers, there were various organs and limbs in multiple stages of dissection. Being exposed to this made me think of some of our *nehiyawak* teachings about handling human remains, and I realized that I should probably learn more about the process of death as it would be a natural part of being a physician and of the human life cycle. Although it is not within the scope of this chapter to discuss the entire *nehiyaw* beliefs on death, when someone dies there are certain steps that need to be undertaken rather quickly to ensure that the person's transition back to spirit is not difficult or interrupted. They need to be returned back to *kikawinaw askiy* (Mother Earth) within a certain period of time and with the proper spiritual burial, including having a feast so they will have the food and tools to carry on in the next stage of their journey.

PATRICIA: GRATITUDE AND GIVING THANKS BEFORE THE SURGERY

Recognizing that some women have a hard time mentally, emotionally, spiritually, and physically with this surgery, I wanted to help myself in every way possible. This preparation was very important for me—I wanted to be psychologically "up" as I went into the hospital setting, where there is much mental, emotional, spiritual, and physical illness. So in preparing for my departure for the hospital, I took very specific clothing. I wanted to wear a dress going into and coming out of the hospital. I wore a blue denim dress and a bright yellow T-shirt (symbolic of the East and new Life) that had "life is good" written on it.

When I arrived at the hospital, I reported to the main desk and was met by pleasant nurses who already knew about my request to take home my surgical remains. As I introduced myself, I could see that they had a copy of my letter in their files. After answering questions for them, I was directed to my room, where my new roommate was waiting to be discharged from the hospital. She was very pleasant, and offered some suggestions on how to speed recovery. She was visiting with another lady, who also had the same surgery. Both women were pleasant and appeared to have recovered quite well, apart from gently waddling around.

In the hours before the surgery, as I undressed and put on the hospital gown, I thought again about what I was about to embark on. I tied the four direction colours (yellow, red, green, and white) and grandmother colour (purple) in my hair to invite the spirit world to be with me during this undertaking and so that they would recognize me in this foreign environment. Doing this assured me that I would be okay because I was connected to our ancestral world. I prayed to the Creator, asking the Grandmothers and Grandfathers to be with me in this time of "aloneness." I quickly realized that for the first time in my life, I had to deal emotionally and spiritually with the possibility of my own mortality. My life was in the hands of total strangers.

As I was wheeled into the cold and sterile operating room, I remember thanking all the strangers in that room. I prayed for them as my life was in their hands. I was indebted to all of them and I let them know how grateful I was before the "lights" went out. I was asked to remove these ribbons as part of the operating room procedure, but I requested they be left on. I was grateful that the operating room staff was respectful of my wishes and allowed me to keep them on.

James: In the Operating Room

Transitioning to working in the hospital and applying the first two years of academic knowledge to real people came rather quickly. Without having many, if any, personal experiences in such settings, it was all very foreign. One of these foreign experiences was being in the operating room (OR). I remember trying to grasp what this may be like and prepared by asking the director of our Indigenous Health Program, himself an Indigenous surgeon, what to expect.

It was a bit of an internal struggle to know that my hands would actually be physically touching another person's internal space and organs, and that I would be working inside his or her body. Again I wondered what the *nehiyaw* teachings on sacredness would be with respect to handling another person's body in surgery. All that I could do was smudge daily, and while in the OR pray silently to myself that the surgeon would work diligently, carefully, and meticulously; the anesthesiologist would take care of the person while his or her body was paralyzed; the nurses would ensure the procedure ran efficiently; and the patient would be fine. I remember one time a male Elder shared the process of his prayers when his loved ones were going for surgery. In addition to praying for the safety of the loved one, he prayed that the surgeon and doctors would be alert and loving so that they could do a "good job."

I remembered listening to one female Indigenous doctor describe her experience in the OR and compared the methodical rituals that a surgeon goes through, particularly the scrubbing-in process, to smudging. Scrubbing involves cleaning your hands in a very prescribed manner to avoid bringing any germs or bacteria into the OR. The Indigenous doctor chose to view this as similar to cleansing oneself in smudging, removing any negative energy and inviting more healthy, positive energy into the immediate space. While you are scrubbing, you mentally prepare yourself for the procedure at hand, reviewing in your mind what will take place during the surgery. Similarly, when you smudge, you focus your energies on clarifying your mind and setting your intentions for the day. I would choose to look at this artificial world of the OR in the way that she did, Indigenizing the space and process, even if no one else was aware that I was doing so. In fact, one Elder back home always taught the importance of starting the smudge ceremony by smudging the hands, keeping in mind that we smudge our hands so we will do good with our hands—that everything we touch will be with goodness.

Praying was something that we as medical students were warned not to do publicly. At one point in our lectures, an obstetrician lecturing to us shared a story of an unfortunate case in which a neonate was born prematurely and passed away suddenly thereafter. The resident physician, who was training on that rotation and had worked on the case, shared with the family, who was of a different spiritual faith, that he had prayed for the neonate during birth. This was done in an effort to soothe and ease the parents' fears soon after the death occurred, or so the resident thought. The parents were shocked and they accused the resident of trying to convert their child to a faith other than their own. The ultimate message of this lecture was to hide your spirituality in your back pocket, tuck it away while you are working, and go back to it when your shift is finished.

In the operating room, particularly during the gynecology rotation, I came to realize there were alternate views of the female body that were quite different from those I had learned in our community. Being on a surgery rotation means getting up and being at the hospital by six a.m. so you can do rounds of all the surgical patients your attending physician has admitted or is currently caring for. By the time this whirlwind way of seeing all the patients is finished, there is a rush to get to the OR by around eight a.m. The time pressure is high: surgeons are given an allotted amount of OR time, and if there are any delays, there is the risk that patients may get bumped and the surgeon will not be able to operate until their next OR time slot, which could be days away. All the while the patients would have been prepped, which includes having them fast and not drink any liquids, not to mention the worry and emotional turmoil that the patients and their family members go through.

Before surgery starts, we say a quick hello to the patient, who by this point will have been checked a number of times by multiple people, including the admitting clerk, the operating room nurse, the anesthesiologist, any number of medical learners, and finally the surgeon doing the operation. The meticulous task of scrubbing or washing your hands thoroughly and then being "gloved and gowned" is routine for each surgery. By this time, the patient is lying on the OR table, anesthetized, waiting to be prepped and for the procedure to begin. There is a short OR pause when everyone in the room stops to ensure the right patient is present, reviews the procedure, and notes the start time. Then it all begins.

PATRICIA: AFTER THE SURGERY

When I awoke I was gasping to breathe. In coming out of the anesthetics I could not catch my breath properly. I found myself praying and reaching out to hospital staff to reassure me that I would be safe, and that this was sometimes a part of coming to consciousness after surgery. I remember a nurse attending to me. After we conversed for some time, she commented, "Oh, you're the woman who wants to take her uterus home." I responded that, yes, she was right. I told her I had an obligation to honour my own body parts by taking them home and providing them with a proper ceremony and burial, for without those body parts I would not have had the gift of my children.

I can truly say that I felt the hospital staff looked after me exceptionally well. I found the nursing staff very professional and friendly. Due to the nature of the surgery, I did not see the doctors often. The anesthesiologist came to see me and we shared walking stories. He was an avid walker and had gone on many walks worldwide. My specialist dropped by, along with the discharge physician. Overall, all of the medical staff were friendly and very helpful during my brief hospital stay. In addition to their professional duties, they took time to converse with me.

James: *nehiyaw* Ways of
Honouring the Female Body

In the gynecology rotations—which can include seeing patients who have undergone various gynecological procedures to remove cancers like ovarian cancers and cysts, cervical cancers, as well as full or partial hysterectomies—the surgeries can be long and tedious. While waiting and assisting with the surgery, the conversations within the OR can vary, but often focus on issues regarding the surgery itself. The OR nursing staff are almost always female and so are often personally familiar with the particular surgeries being performed as many have had such operations themselves.

During these conversations in the OR, I became privy to the general disdain that some women have toward their own bodies. I remember one conversation in which an OR nurse referred to her own hysterectomy, which she had for menorrhagia (heavy menstrual bleeding) and associated dysmenorrhea (painful menstrual periods), and how she wanted to "get that thing [her uterus] out of me!" During this conversation, we were performing a hysterectomy on another woman.

In the medical scientific world, many might think this is not important since the patient is unconscious; however, *nehiyawak* view themselves as spiritual beings and would therefore be aware of such conversation. Our *kihtehyak* remind us that we always must be mindful of our words as they can have unintended consequences that we may not foresee. I can understand how someone may be frustrated with the pain, inconvenience, and impact on the quality of life that her disease caused, but I had never heard female anatomy referred to as a "thing" before. At times some female patients coming into the OR would express similar feelings.

On a typical day, depending on what surgeries were scheduled, three to eight patients go through the OR. It was very mechanical in nature, down to a science of precision, and much like what I would imagine working in a factory conveyor-belt system might be like. But instead of assembling a product, we were removing women's female organs. Day in and day out, this is what would happen in the ORs on a gynecology surgery rotation. Often the same sentiments and beliefs about the female body would be expressed. After the female organ was removed, it would likely be sent to pathology for analysis. If the pathologist found nothing wrong, the organ would be sent to the incinerator or biohazard facility to be destroyed. There would be no thought or consideration for the importance of the organs as part of one's body and in all likelihood no ceremony to return them in an honourable way back to our *kikawinaw askiy* (Mother Earth).

Again, this language and process was in sharp contrast to the *nehiyaw iskwew* (Cree woman) teachings that I had grown up with, particularly around the reverence and respect we have for women as the life-givers, leaders, and foundations of our Nations. These are reflected in our *tipi* teachings, women's moon ceremonies, women's rites of passage, women's pipe teachings, *kokom/ nohtikwew* (grandmother/old woman) teachings, and *piyesewak* (Thunder-beings) who teach us about good child-rearing practices, etc. From this frame-work and understanding I knew why *nikāwiy* (my mother) had taken such extensive effort and preparation to ensure that she would be prepared for the entire process when she had her hysterectomy.

PATRICIA: RECONNECTING TO OUR MOTHER

Three days after my surgery I was discharged. When I got home from the hospital, I was tired and I went to bed shortly thereafter. That night as I lay in bed, I remember listening to nature as our bedroom window was open. It was peaceful, but I also remember that I could not hear the frogs; they were not singing. It was serene.

I dreamt that first night home. In my dream, I was in a big room with no windows. I was being swung around the room. I grabbed onto sweetgrass (a form of smudge) as I was being whirled around the room. As I hung onto the sweetgrass, the room opened up. Lying on the bed were my son, my mother, and my late grandmother. Their heads were covered up, and as I jumped onto the bed, I threw the blankets back and they were all happy. In my dream I heard a beautiful song that included the words "miracles are made." I awoke with tears. I could hear my dog sleeping outside our bed-room window—he stayed all night. This was my first night home after my surgery.

I remember that night was extremely quiet. Usually I can hear birds and frogs from my bedroom in the summer, but on this night I could not hear anything except for the beautiful silence of our Mother, the Earth.

In the days that followed while I waited to return to the hospital to pick up my uterus and ovaries, I prepared Grandmother prints (flowered broadcloth) and sage to wrap them in. I was not certain in what condition I would be pick-ing up my remains, but when we got to the hospital, the lab attendant wrapped them all in individual containers, and then placed them in a box. I wrapped the prints and sage around it, then gently placed the box into my bag. This was emotional as I was now taking my own body parts on their last journey home to bury them. My children and I were rather quiet. I guess we were all in our own spiritual space of taking our collective remains home.

When the time was right for all of us spiritually, my husband, son, daughter, and I went to a chosen site, prayed and sang *nehiyaw* ceremonial songs, and then took the remains out of the containers and put them back into our Mother, the Earth. This was an emotional moment for me, as we took the body parts out of the containers for burial. We all looked at the uterus and the two tiny ovaries. They were preserved in formaldehyde. We all looked at them, commenting on how these beautiful body parts had given us our family. The ovaries looked so tiny. The uterus looked thick. It had been cut open and we could see the thick walls. We all looked at the parts very quietly. I cried and gave thanks to my body parts aloud. We all prayed and sang in honour of the life-giving body parts. Afterwards, we all hugged.

JAMES: RECONNECTION FOR *NIKÂWIY*

Reflecting on the process our family went through to not only support *nikâwiy*, but to help her grieve part of the removal of her bodily organs was very powerful for me as her son, but also as a medical learner. It is hard to explain what medical school and residency is like to others who are not going through it themselves. People could not understand that it is possible to be awake and working for 33 hours straight while you are on call at the hospital, and that one shift would almost equal a week's worth of their daily full-time hours in their regular job. In this setting and learning environment, you need to really focus, prioritize, and turn off a lot of what makes you an *iyiniw* (human being) to be able to cope, survive, and make it through such a rigorous training program, not to mention having to deal with the trauma you are exposed to in the process.

One of the first times I remember facing this type of trauma was during our obstetrics and gynecology block in pre-clerkship, when we were encouraged to sign up for a medical elective called "A Hard Night of Labour." Here we were observers on a portion of a call shift on the obstetrics, labour, and delivery ward. Near the very end of my six-hour shift, a mother expecting twins and her partner presented to the ward with early signs of labour at the end of her second trimester. The resident on call assessed her, found her to be fully dilated, and immediately took her to a delivery room. The pediatrician on call was paged and while the woman was pushing, she was informed of all the complications that premature babies may be born with—blindness, seizure disorders, cardiovascular and lung problems, etc. All the while the mother kept on saying "No, no, no, they are not supposed to come yet," while the father looked dazed and confused, trying to comfort his wife, but not quite understanding what had just taken place in the 10 minutes since they arrived on the floor.

After the twins were born, they were brought back to the parents to hold before they passed away quietly in their arms. By this time, my shift was over. Not knowing what to do or how to process the situation that had just occurred, the staff left to return to their duties, and the resident looked at me, said farewell, signed my elective form, and we both parted ways. I drove home in the middle of the night in a state of shock, not having had an opportunity to reflect with another colleague on what had just happened, something that I had never witnessed before. I went home sad, confused, and traumatized, and although I talked to my partner, I could not tell the whole story. I smudged and prayed that night for the babies born too soon and for the expectant parents who had lost the two children they had only just met.

Although medical school attempts to integrate into its programs the humanistic qualities desired of physicians, it is difficult to do so when you need to turn off those very qualities as a survival mechanism to make it through the program emotionally intact. As an Indigenous medical learner, this was more challenging as I was away from my family, community, and ceremonial support network. To maintain these connections and to gather the strength I needed to complete the program, I would travel back frequently from Ontario to Alberta to participate in our *cihcihkewinah* (ceremonies). By maintaining this connection and through the prayers of our *kihtehyak*, family, and community, I was able to complete my six-year journey of becoming a family physician.

CONCLUSION

What stands out for me (Pat) in this surgical experience is how I was emotionally, spiritually, and physically able to deal with the loss of an aspect of womanhood. It was physically painful, but by spiritually preparing for the loss of these female reproductive parts, I was able to recover quickly mentally, emotionally, spiritually, and physically. I did not experience depression or significant sadness. In retrospect, I healed quickly, and I did not require a lot of the prescribed pain medication—in fact, I did not take any. In my opinion, I healed holistically because of the individual and family preparation we did around this surgical procedure. For many Indigenous women, these reproductive organs hold significant cultural sacredness.

As mom and son, this chapter provided us an opportunity to share a unique experience of a common medical procedure from the perspective of the patient and the practitioner. This sharing is a reminder that there is strength and resilience within a culture that allows people to honour their own ways of being, even inside the Western institution of medicine.

CHAPTER 20

Reflections of One Indian Doctor in a Town up North

Nadine Caron

As Thomas King once said, "The truth about stories is that that's all we are."

First and foremost, I am an Anishinabe woman who simply studied to become a physician. Since then, I have learned much from the individuals who come to me because of the initials after my name. Patients demonstrate incredible trust by telling their stories so that perhaps my medical knowledge or surgical scalpel can relieve their pain or treat their cancer. I left behind days of memorizing textbooks and preparing for examinations in exchange for days that are now filled with my patients' life stories. These stories help me to see things more clearly—or strive to do so when clarity escapes. That's who I am and what I do; the stories of my days merge with the stories of others and I learn from the two. I am lucky. I love what I do. I know why I do it.

"I Told You Indians Could Be Doctors"

As a young surgeon, I often travelled to schools in First Nations communities to talk to students and to share the joy and wonderment I found in the study of the human body. I brought with me pathology specimens to show what a liver cancer looks like, the difference between a smoker's and a non-smoker's lungs, or what a child's appendix looks like after that pain in the lower right belly is fixed with a surgeon's hands. These powerful physical examples grab the students' attention as they sit in wonderment. The face of an inspired child is a beautiful sight.

There is one particular afternoon that I will carry with me forever. After giving class presentations all day long, I walked back and forth carrying boxes of pathology specimens from the school building to my rental car. On each

219

trip I walked past two young girls sitting on the bottom steps of the school's front entrance. I can picture them clearly to this day. They were engaged in an increasingly heated discussion. As it escalated, I approached them to ask for assistance in the hopes of diverting their attention from the upcoming battle of fists. When I asked for their help with packing the boxes, I realized the younger girl was in the Grade 1 class I had talked to earlier that day. Her spontaneous debating partner on the step beside her turned out to be her sister, whose Grade 3 class I would talk to the next day. The younger sister asked excitedly, "You're the Indian doctor who talked to my class today, right?" I confirmed her statement while watching the mixture of joy, relief, and satisfaction on her face. "See!" She playfully slugged her sister on the arm. "I told you Indians could be doctors."

This was one of the most insightful moments in my career to date. It filled my heart with pride in the younger sister's resolution, but also with deep sadness for the older sister, who could not believe a Native person could be a physician without the tangible evidence of an Indian doctor standing before her. It is not the positive effect that I saw in the Grade 1 student that first comes to mind when I picture that scene on that autumn day. It is the degree of certainty her eight-year-old sister had that her six-year-old sister's ambitions were a sign of dire misunderstanding and frustratingly misplaced optimism. What could have happened in her eight years of life that made her so sure she couldn't do something? How could there be anything she could not aspire to be or do? Isn't that the time in our children's lives when ambitions are cultivated, shared, embraced as children explore the world? Who would keep her doors of opportunity open when the doors of her reality seemed to be locking behind her?

When our youth believe more in what cannot be accomplished than in what can, it is a crisis. We need them to believe in themselves so that they can pass on this self-confidence to those who watch, listen, and follow in their footsteps. Pursuit of academic dreams and the confidence that they will reach their aspirations will create the foundation for representation of Aboriginal peoples in the health care profession. But there are consequences to finding success in this world where we seek access, equality, and success.

MANAGING EXPECTATIONS WITH EYES WIDE OPEN

For some, simply being a First Nations surgeon with academic responsibilities to conduct research, teach, and provide leadership is accepted and supported. But as a First Nations person and a physician, the never-ending challenge is the question: In which world should one place one's feet? Western? Indige-nous? Why do we have to choose? How often can we move between these worlds? This has not been resolved. On one hand, Aboriginal individuals and communities lobby for more representation of Indigenous peoples in the health care professions, yet at the same time pass some judgment on those who tread the thin, challenging, and often moving line between Western aca-demia and Indigenous perspectives. While I have done both, I find great frus-tration and disappointment when those who pass judgment are not those who have been tasked with the role of working in two different worlds. Aboriginal health care providers have often accepted the challenge of fitting into two worlds, when advocacy and understanding in one may be threatened by similar objectives in the other. I don't regret it. I understand it, but I must say that "failure" can come in surprising costumes. And who to turn to?

Sometimes one turns to those whom others think they are supposed to help. I have learned much from my patients and their families. Recently an Elder, at the urging of his family, came to my office regarding abdominal pain he had suffered for some time. In our interaction, I found his history engaging. As our visit approached an end, I asked this quiet Elder, who had served in both World War II and the Korean War and walked with a limp as the result of an injury in the latter, "Do you think that my generation respects and thanks you and your colleagues for what you did for our country and its people in those wars?" He answered quickly and definitely, as he had through-out our conversation, "No, no I don't." I was shocked to hear what I had already suspected, and it hurt.

After a brief silence passed between us, he gently asked if he could change his answer. With no indication from me otherwise he went on, "Actually, yes—I guess the generations that followed do respect and thank us enough—given the world they live in now. How can I expect another to understand? You need to live through it to understand it. I cannot judge those who live in a world that didn't survive those years, those times." His answer reminded me of the importance of history and how our stories are what comprise it. I left the concept of residential schools, assimilation, and racism on the table, unquestioned at this time. I suspected I would come to learn much from him.

My memory of this kind, wise Elder, who may have seemed physically frail, reminds me that much of someone's hidden strength lies in what they have overcome. Even a large tree, with solid roots and healthy leaves, stands vul-nerable if alone in an open field. Isolated trees standing alone are different than the multitudes that lie within a forest, even when on the surface they appear to be the same species with similar underbrush. Within the health care profession, Aboriginal doctors are like those solitary trees. While one who is first to achieve some milestone or accomplishment is often celebrated, it is clear that there are too few. There is often pressure on Aboriginal health care professionals not to fail, yet "fail" is defined by those who have never been in our shoes. Are they like the sheltered trees in a forest that never really feel the impact of the wind and wondering why the trees in the open, facing the gale head on, have trunks that bend to the force of the wind?

Concluding Thoughts: Embracing Our Stories

If stories really are all we are, then I have even more reason to love my career in medical care, teaching, and research. My days are constructed of stories and the scripts for future tales. These stories are also the ammunition to advocate for the patients, students, and their communities. I keep going. I hope that my path helps those who follow to believe that Aboriginal Canadians like themselves will be the solution to our historic health challenges. The forest is growing. More and more Indigenous students are entering the health care professions. The wind sometimes doesn't seem as strong. We are not bending to the pressures. Our story of eliminating our health disparities and optimizing our health status will have an ending that we, as the script writers, have the power to control. I see great advances in our roles as a people to improve our health, health care, and leadership for both.

CHAPTER 21

Type 2 Diabetes in Indigenous Populations

Why a Focus on Genetic Susceptibility Is Not Enough

Fernando Polanco and Laura Arbour

Indigenous peoples of North America have undergone drastic social, cultural, and environmental changes since the colonization of the Americas. Displacement of whole communities, traditional diet suppression, and sedentary lifestyles are all factors that contribute to the disproportionate disease/chronic illness risk experienced by Indigenous peoples (Browne, Smye, & Varcoe, 2005; FNC, 2011; Reading, 2010). Diabetes mellitus (DM) is characterized by an inadequate uptake of glucose into the cells, resulting in increased levels of glucose in the blood (hyperglycemia). Insulin, produced by the pancreas, is the hormone responsible for the uptake. Type 2 diabetes (T2D) is caused by either inadequate insulin secretion from the pancreas, cellular resistance to insulin action, or both (Alberti & Zimmet, 1998). T2D has become a worldwide epidemic (Young et al., 2000) and by 2025 is forecasted to affect 300 million people worldwide (Taylor, 2006). In 2009, over 2 million Canadians were diagnosed with T2D (Health Canada, 2011). Notably, Aboriginal peoples in Canada are three to five times more likely to develop T2D than non-Aboriginal people (CDA, 2008; Health Canada, 2011).

For example, 17.2 percent of on-reserve and 10.3 percent of off-reserve First Nations peoples in Canada were diagnosed with T2D in 2009 (Health Canada, 2011) compared to a national rate of approximately 6.4 percent (Statistics Canada, 2010). In addition, the prevalence of pre-diabetes—as defined by blood sugar levels (Hemoglobin A1C of 5.7–6.4 percent)—has been reported to be as high as 11 percent in Aboriginal peoples of Canada (ADA, 2012; Ralph-Campbell et al., 2009). T2D is also considered one of the most common chronic diseases affecting Aboriginal children and youth (Health Canada, 2011), thereby reflecting lifelong disproportionate disease burden.

Although genetics, environmental, and social factors influence the development of T2D, the interaction remains complex (Macaulay et al., 2003). Traditional diet suppression, displacement of whole communities, natural resource exploitation, and increasing sedentary lifestyle environments are just a few of the shifts that Aboriginal peoples of Canada (and throughout the world) have experienced through colonialism (Smeja & Brassard, 2000; Browne et al., 2005; Reading, 2010). Consequently, research focused on T2D in Indigenous populations needs to be carried out in a balanced way, considering biological, social, and environmental factors, as well as a combination of all their effects in order to understand the high prevalence. This chapter will explore why a focus on genetic susceptibility as a priority is not enough to curb the epidemic.

Genetic Studies in Indigenous Populations

It seems intuitive that if there is an increased rate of a condition within families, and in relatively homogeneous communities, a genetic predisposition may be the explanation. The concept of the "thrifty gene" hypothesis, first published in 1962 (Neel, 1962), postulated that the reason why some modern Indigenous groups tend toward obesity and diabetes is because of a historically protective underlying genetic factor, allowing for metabolic adaptation to low caloric intake. This theory postulates that in the context of modern-day lifestyles, which include high-calorie diets and less exercise, these individuals would be predisposed to T2D and a range of other metabolic disorders (Campbell et al., 2012; Chakravarthy & Booth, 2004). In the search for the validity of the "thrifty gene" hypothesis, T2D genetic susceptibility studies have been conducted worldwide within Indigenous populations such as in the Pima Indians of the United States, the Oji-Cree of Canada, and certain Indigenous peoples in South America (Muller et al., 2010; Hegele et al., 1999b, 2000a; Campbell et al., 2012; Gutiérrez-Vidal et al., 2011).

Although genetic susceptibility likely plays a role in all populations, the identification of common susceptibility genes in Indigenous populations has proven elusive (Cornelis & Hu, 2012; Hegele et al., 1998). To establish whether a genetic marker is associated with a disease, genetic association studies are carried out (Lewis, 2002). Specifically, single nucleotide polymorphisms (SNP)—single base-pair changes that are common throughout the genome—are used as markers to ascertain whether there is an association of a gene variant with a particular disease (e.g., T2D) in a certain population

(Lewis, 2002). Although numerous genetic T2D association studies have been carried out, there have been no consistent genetic variants identified that might explain or support the thrifty genotype hypothesis (Southam et al., 2009). Furthermore, specific genetic associations, if found, are often not replicated in more than one community. The inconsistency of these T2D association studies demonstrates that even in Indigenous populations, as expected in mainstream populations, T2D is a result of complex factors, both genetic and non-genetic (Baier et al., 1995).

Susceptibility genes identified in non-Indigenous populations have also been explored. Peroxisome proliferator-activated receptor γ and α (PPARγ and PPARα) genes are considered candidate T2D genes. PPARγ plays an important role in glucose and lipid metabolism, insulin sensitivity, insulin-sensitizing drugs, and adipogenesis (Andrulionytè et al., 2004; Hegele et al., 2000a; Muller et al., 2003a, 2003b), and variants have been found to be associated with T2D (specifically the Gly482Ser variant) in Danish and UK populations. In the Pima Indians, the Gly482Ser variant was not associated with T2D (Muller et al., 2003a, 2003b); however, a positive association was present in the Oji-Cree population of Canada (Hegele et al., 2000a; Muller et al., 2003b). This exemplifies that important T2D predisposition variants may contribute to some risk in non-Indigenous and Indigenous populations alike, but the results are not generalizable to all, again calling into question the generalization of the thrifty gene hypothesis. Another example is the hematopoietically expressed homeobox gene (HHEX), which encodes transcription factors involved in developmental processes (Cai et al., 2011). In recent meta-analysis of variants within the HHEX gene, positive associations were found in Caucasian and Asian populations, conferring risk to T2D; however, in African American population studies there was no association detected (Cai et al., 2011; Rong et al., 2009). Furthermore, studies have been carried out in the Pima Indians and in Indigenous Mexicans (Teenek, Mazahua, Purepecha peoples); however, no association was evident (Rong et al., 2009; Gutiérrez-Vidal et al., 2011).

An unexpected direction of genetic T2D susceptibility has recently emerged. The KCNQ1 gene is well known for a high rate of Long QT syndrome (LQTS) Type 1 diabetes in northern B.C. First Nations peoples (Arbour et al., 2008; Jackson et al., 2011). KCNQ1 encodes for Iks (Slow Delayed Rectifier K+ current), an ion-channel responsible, in part, for the late repolarization phase of the cardiac action potential. LQTS is a condition predisposing individuals to irregular heart rhythm and risk of sudden cardiac death. Of relevance here, this gene is also expressed in the pancreas and has a role in insulin secretion (Yasuda et al., 2008).

Because of the importance of *KCNQ1* in insulin secretion, *KCNQ1* variants have been explored for T2D susceptibility in many populations. For example, Campbell et al. (2012) have shown that single nucleotide polymorphisms (SNP) within the *KCNQ1* gene are associated with T2D risk in an Antioquian (South America Mestizo-Colombia) population. SNPs in *KCNQ1* have also been reported to be associated with T2D in various non-Indigenous populations: European and Asian populations (Been et al., 2011; Dehwah et al., 2010; Unoki et al., 2008; Yasuda et al., 2008). Furthermore, the SNP associated with T2D in the Antioquian population is the same SNP associated with T2D found in a Japanese T2D association study (Campbell et al., 2012; Yasuda et al., 2008), suggesting altered insulin secretion because of the variant, which may influence the development of T2D. Whether there is a further relationship with insulin function, including insulin resistance, remains unclear (Masato, 2011; Yamagata et al., 2011). Research is underway to better understand a common genetic mutation found within the *KCNQ1* gene and risk for T2D in the First Nations peoples of northern British Columbia (Polanco, 2012).

Although genetic factors do indeed influence the development of T2D in any population, there is little evidence to support that genetic factors can explain the disproportionate degree that Indigenous populations around the world have been affected with T2D. Other complex determinants, including social and economic determinants, need to be considered in greater depth.

SOCIAL DETERMINANTS OF HEALTH

The complex social and economic environments in which Indigenous peoples live influence their health, including the development of chronic diseases (Ghosh & Gomes, 2011; Millar & Dean, 2012). Furthermore, the ability to adopt healthy behaviours is also influenced by equally complex factors (Health Canada, 2011). As such, factors affecting the development of T2D in Indigenous peoples are broad and diverse, and include Westernization of behaviours and lifestyles, and fluctuating stress levels (allostatic loads), which influence stress-hormone levels (McEwen, 2000).

Social determinants also affect the physical, mental, emotional, and spiritual dimensions of health in Aboriginal peoples of Canada (Reading & Wien, 2009; see also chapters 1 and 4). In a review of social determinants of Aboriginal health, Reading and Wien (2009) identify proximal determinants of health as healthy behaviours, physical environments, employment and income, education, and food insecurity; intermediate determinants as health care systems, educational systems, community infrastructure, resources and capacities, environmental stewardship, and cultural continuity; distal determinants as colonialism, racism and social exclusion, and self-determination (Reading & Wien, 2009). Specific determinants include poverty and social marginalization (Campbell, 2002); unemployment, education, and household income (Millar & Dean, 2012; Reading, 2010); traditional language and traditional beliefs (McIvor, Napoleon, & Dickie, 2009; Millar & Dean, 2012); connection between the land and traditional medicine (McIvor et al., 2009; Wilson, 2003); spirituality (Receveur, Boulay, & Kuhnlein, 1997); and access to health care (Booth et al., 2005). For example, as a continuum, low income has been linked to increased illness, which in turn decreases employment opportunities, which has an overall influence on increased poverty rates in Aboriginal communities in Canada (Marmot, 2005).

Although, by its nature, genetic predisposition to T2D development would have been present historically, it is important to note that the current epidemic came to light only in recent years. Increased T2D rates have coincided with lifestyle changes (Hegele et al., 1999a), diet shifts (Gittelsohn et al., 1998; Young et al., 2000), decreased physical activity (Lui et al., 2006), increased obesity (Reading, 2010; Wolever et al., 1997), and decreased socio-economic status (Campbell et al., 2012).

Increasing obesity in Aboriginal populations in Canada is an ongoing concern (Hegele & Pollex, 2005; Lear et al., 2007; Reading, 2010; Foulds, Bredin, & Warburton, 2011). Specifically, obesity is a major risk factor for chronic disease risk factors in general, such as metabolic syndrome (MetS), hypertension, and hyperlipidemia (Hegele & Pollex, 2005; Reading, 2010; Wang & Hoy, 2004). Although obesity is a strong indicator for a risk to develop T2D in Aboriginal populations, interestingly, studies concerning Inuit peoples have observed increased levels of obesity, but historically a low prevalence of T2D (Hegele & Pollex, 2005; Lemas et al., 2011). The term "healthy obesity" has been attached to Inuit populations: "healthy obese" individuals have increased body fat, yet this excess of fat does not seem to predispose individuals to T2D development (Wildman, 2009). It is speculated that their diet rich in n-3 polyunsaturated fatty acids (n-3 PUFA) may be a protective factor (Johnson et al., 2009; Lemas et al., 2011). Also, the shorter and less intense history of Western contact may provide an explanation for the decreased rates of T2D (and MetS) as Western lifestyle acculturation has been linked to adverse health outcomes concerning Aboriginal populations in Canada

(Hegele & Pollex, 2005). Although Inuit peoples may be an exception, the overall adoption of decreased physical activity and nutrient-poor foods has significantly contributed to the prevalence of T2D and overall health of Indigenous peoples worldwide, regardless of genetic background. How do adverse social determinants affect the development of risk factors, such as obesity?

Stress and the lack of control in coping with stress coexist with adverse social determinants such as poverty, lack of adequate housing, and lack of access to health care (Reading & Wien, 2009). *Allostasis* describes the mechanism by which the body deals with fluctuations and variability to maintain homeostasis (McEwen, 2000). An excessive allostatic load results in an excessive burden of stress that may affect the health of an individual (McEwen, 2000). Over a short period, the body's methods of handling stress can have beneficial or damaging consequences; furthermore, negative stress responses over long periods likely accelerate disease processes (McEwen, 2000).

Allostatic load affects stress regulation and the hormones associated with that regulation (McEwen, 2000). Glucocorticoids (GC) have been identified as key regulators/mediators of stress responses (i.e., GC are up-regulated in a stressful environments) and have been implicated in many important metabolic pathways, including gluconeogenesis, immune system regulation (specifically with immune system suppression), and transcription suppression/up-regulation (Tomlinson & Stewart, 2007).

The relevance here is that increased levels of GC as a result of stress have been reported to increase insulin resistance, hypertension, and many other adverse health outcomes (Kotelevtsev et al., 1997). Increased GC levels have been observed to increase appetite and food-seeking behaviour (Tomlinson & Stewart, 2007). In summary, the stress-mediated steroid hormone GC is up-regulated in cases of stress, which in turn contributes to adverse health outcomes. Over time, increased levels of GC can accelerate disease progression. Thus, the stressful environment dictated by adverse social determinants of health that Aboriginal peoples face contributes to increased GC expression, which may in turn influence the rates of T2D and other adverse health outcomes.

In short, current societal and historical factors need to be considered and addressed in concert with genetic determinants if rates of T2D in Aboriginal populations are to be reduced (Reading & Wien, 2009).

Epigenetics

Although a great deal of attention is paid to gene structure—i.e., the sequence of genes and its variations—the expression of genes (how and when genes are turned on and off) is arguably even more important. In this context, epigenetics is a term describing how genes can be functionally changed by surrounding environmental influences without a change in structure (Godfrey et al., 2007; Ptashne, 2007). For example, it has been suggested that the genome (all the genetic material [DNA] in an individual) can be considered as a conduit where environment plays a large role on resultant phenotypes reflecting health and disease (Franks, 2011). An example of an epigenetic effect is the "maternal effect." This concept suggests that environmental stresses on a mother can influence the expression of genes in her fetus, and the gametes of that fetus, therefore influencing at least two generations (Gluckman, Hanson, & Beedle, 2007).

In an attempt to better explain the epigenetic effect, the "thrifty phenotype" hypothesis describes further environmental influence on genetic material (Hales & Barker, 1992; Millar & Dean, 2012). The "thrifty phenotype" hypothesis stipulates that maternal malnutrition during pregnancy triggers "fetal nutritional thrift," resulting in underdeveloped β-cells, increased insulin resistance (both leading to hyperglycemia), and increased adipose tissue storage (Hales & Barker, 1992; Millar & Dean, 2012). The "thrifty phenotype" hypothesis suggests that obesity and T2D result from fetal malnutrition, combined with exposure to risk factors in later life such as physical inactivity and an unhealthy diet (Millar & Dean, 2012); therefore, those experiencing malnourishment in fetal life will be predisposed to negative lifelong effects if additional risk factors are also present during the life course (Hales & Barker, 1992).

Further to the "thrifty phenotype," the "developmental plasticity" concept proposed an explanation for the influence of environmental factors on fetal developmental, including intergenerational changes in expression of the genome (Gluckman et al., 2008; Millar & Dean, 2012). The "developmental plasticity" concept incorporates the ability of an organism to develop in various ways depending on its surrounding environment, and changes in the expression of the fetal genome (Gluckman et al., 2008; Millar & Dean, 2012). These changes in the expression of the genome may be permanent and passed on to the next generation. For the remainder of the organism's lifespan (and possibly its offspring's lifespan), chronic disease development therefore could be influenced by the direct health status of the mother (Gluckman et al., 2007, 2008; Millar & Dean, 2012).

Thus, a deprived developmental environment during prenatal and early postnatal life, followed by socio-economic transitions to a Western lifestyle high in caloric dense food and low in physical activity, increase the risk for diseases such as T2D (Godfrey et al., 2007). The "thrifty gene" hypothesis has yet to generate the genetic basis it describes (Campbell et al., 2012). However, it has been suggested that "developmental plasticity" seems a likely explanation for the relationship of T2D and low birth weights in Pima Indians (Gluckman et al., 2008; Millar & Dean, 2012).

Although there is some evidence for epigenetic influences on T2D development in Oji-Cree youth of Canada (Millar & Dean, 2012), by and large this area has been unexplored in Indigenous populations to date (Gluckman et al., 2007). T2D is a complex condition with various counterparts affecting its susceptibility, development, and prevalence. While genetic association studies are important for understanding susceptibility factors to T2D, the effect of current social and historical environments, as epigenetic response triggers, deserve proportionate evaluation in Indigenous populations worldwide if the epidemic is to be adequately addressed.

Conclusion

Although there has been considerable focus on genetic susceptibility for T2D in Indigenous populations, there has been little success in determining a genetic explanation for the high rate of T2D worldwide. The origins of T2D are complex, but there is evidence emerging that social, economic, and environmental influences act biologically in early developmental stages that shape disease risk later in life. The exploration of gene expression in response to environmental and social influences (epigenetics) may indeed provide insights into at least part of the mechanisms for increased rates of chronic disease in Indigenous populations (Godfrey et al., 2007). These components together influence how disease and wellness are manifested.

This chapter illustrates that genetic studies are insufficient as a primary focus of T2D prevalence and development. After years of study, it is apparent that a "genetics first" approach in Indigenous populations is not enough to turn the epidemic around. The relative paucity of positive and consistent genetic study results within populations disproportionately affected by T2D indicates the need for a broader understanding of the determinants of T2D susceptibility. This may be because it is the environment that is influencing gene function throughout the life course. It is not a question of "nature" versus "nurture" when considering T2D susceptibility, but rather how both intertwine to continue to unjustly affect Indigenous populations worldwide.

References

Alberti, K. G., & Zimmet, P. Z. (1998). Definition, diagnosis, and classification of diabetes mellitus and its complications. Part 1: Diagnosis and classification of diabetes mellitus provisional report of a WHO consultation. *Diabetic Medicine, 15,* 539–553.

American Diabetes Association (ADA). (2012). Position statement. Standards of Medical Care in Diabetes—2012. *Diabetes Care, 35,* S11–S63.

Andrulionytè, L., Zacharova, J., Chiasson, J. L., Laakso, M., STOP-NIDDM Study Group. (2004). Common polymorphisms of the PPAR-γ2 (Pro12Ala) and PGC-1α (Gly482Ser) genes are associated with the conversion from impaired glucose tolerance to type 2 diabetes in the STOP-NIDDM trial. *Diabetologia, 47,* 2176–2184.

Arbour, L., Rezazadeh, S., Eldstrom, J., Weget-Simms, G., Rupps, R., Dyer, Z., Tibbets, G., Accili, E., Casey, B., Kmetic, A., Santani, S., & Fedida, D. (2008). A KCNQ1 V205M missense mutation causes a high rate of long QT syndrome in a First Nations community of northern British Columbia: A community-based approach to understanding the impact. *Genetics in Medicine, 10,* 545–550.

Baier, L. J., Sacchettini, J. C., Knowler, W. C., Eadst, J., Paolisso, G., Tataranni, P. A., . . . & Prochazka, M. (1995). An amino acid substitution in the human intestinal fatty acid binding protein is associated with increased fatty acid binding, increased fat oxidation. *Journal of Clinical Investigation, Inc., 95,* 1281–1287.

Been, L. F., Ralhan, S., Wander, G. S., Mehra, N. K., Singh, J., Mulvihill, J. J., Aston, C., E., & Sanghera, D. K. (2011). Variants in KCNQ1 increase type II diabetes susceptibility in South Asians: A study of 3,310 subjects from India and the U.S. *BMC Medical Genetics, 12,* 1–10.

Booth, G. L., Hux, J. E., Fang, J., & Chan, B. T. (2005). Time trends and geographic disparities in acute complications of diabetes in Ontario, Canada. *Diabetes Care, 28,* 1045–1050.

Browne, A. J., Smye, V. L., & Varcoe, C. (2005). The relevance of postcolonial theoretical perspectives to research in Aboriginal health. *Canadian Journal of Nursing Research, 37,* 16–37.

Busfield, F., Duffy, D. L., Kesting, J. B., Walker, S. M., Lovelock, P. K., Good, D., . . . & Shaw, J. T. E. (2002). A genome-wide search for type 2 diabetes: Susceptibility genes in Indigenous Australians. *American Journal of Human Genetics, 70,* 349–357.

Cai, Y., Yi, J., Ma, Y., & Fu, D. (2011). Meta-analysis of the effect of HHEX gene polymorphism on the risk of type 2 diabetes. *Mutagenesis, 26,* 309–314.

Campbell, A. (2002). Type 2 diabetes and children in Aboriginal communities: The array of factors that shape health and access to health care. *Health Law Journal, 10,* 147–168.

Campbell, D. D., Parra, M. V., Duque, C., Gallego, N., Franco, L., Tandon, A., . . . & Ruiz-Linares, A. (2012). Amerind ancestry, socioeconomic status, and the genetics of type 2 diabetes in a Colombian population. *PLoSONE, 7,* e33570.

Canadian Diabetes Association (CDA). (2008). Canadian Diabetes Association 2008: Clinical practice guidelines for the prevention and management of diabetes in Canada. *Canadian Journal of Diabetes, 32,* 51–201.

Chakravarthy, M. V., & Booth, F. W. (2004). Eating, exercise, and "thrifty" genotypes: Connecting the dots toward an evolutionary understanding of modern chronic diseases. *Journal of Applied Physiology, 96*, 3–10.

Cornelis, M. C., & Hu, F. B. (2012). Interactions in the development of type 2 diabetes: Recent progress and continuing challenges. *Annual Review of Nutrition, 32*, 245–259.

Dalziel, B., Gosby, A. K., Richman, R. M., Bryson, J. M., & Caterson, I. D. (2002). Association of the TNF-alpha-308 G/A promoter polymorphism with insulin resistance in obesity. *Obesity Research, 10*, 401–407.

Dehwah, M. A. S., Zhang, S., Qu, K., Huang, H., Xu, A., & Huang, Q. (2010). KCNQ1 and type 2 diabetes: Study in Hubei Han Chinese and meta-analysis in East Asian populations. *Gene and Genomics, 32*, 327–334.

First Nations Centre (FNC). (2011). *First Nations Regional Longitudinal Health Survey (RHS) 2008/10—Phase 2: Preliminary results for adults, youth, and children living in First Nations communities*. Ottawa, ON: First Nations Centre at the National Aboriginal Health Organization.

Foulds, H. J. A., Bredin, S. S. D., & Warburton, D. E. R. (2011). The prevalence of overweight and obesity in British Columbian Aboriginal adults. *Obesity Reviews, 12*, e4–e11.

Franks, P. W. (2011). Gene × environment interactions in type 2 diabetes. *Current Diabetes Reports, 11*, 552–561.

Ghosh, H., & Gomes, H. (2011). Type 2 diabetes among Aboriginal peoples in Canada: A focus on direct and associated risk factors. *Journal of Aboriginal and Indigenous Community Health, 9*, 245–275.

Gittelsohn, J., Wolever, T. M. S., Harris, S. B., Giraldo, R. S., Hanley, A. J. G., & Zinman, B. (1998). Specific patterns of food consumption and preparation are associated with diabetes and obesity in a Native Canadian community. *Journal of Nutrition, 128*, 541–547.

Gluckman, P. D., Hanson, M. A., & Beedle, A. S. (2007). Non-genomic transgenerational inheritance of disease risk. *Bioessays, 29*, 145–154.

Gluckman, P. D., Hanson, M. A., Cooper, C., & Thornburg, K. L. (2008). Effect of in utero and early-life conditions on adult health and disease. *New England Journal of Medicine, 359*, 6–73.

Godfrey, K. M., Lillycrop, K. A., Burdge, G. C., Gluckman, P. D., & Hanson, M. A. (2007). Epigenetic mechanisms and the mismatch concept of the developmental origins of health and disease. *Pediatratic Research, 61*, 5R–10R.

Gutiérrez-Vidal, R., Rodríguez-Trejo, A., Canizales-Quinteros, S., Herrera-Cornejo, M., Granados-Silvestre, M. A., Montúfar-Robles, I., Ortiz-López, M. G., & Menjívar, M. (2011). LOC387761 polymorphism is associated with type 2 diabetes in the Mexican population. *Genetic Testing and Biomarkers, 15*, 79–83.

Hales, C. N., & Barker, D. J. P. (1992). Type 2 (non-insulin-dependent) diabetes mellitus: The thrifty phenotype hypothesis. *Diabetologia, 35*, 595–601.

Hanley, A. J. G., Harris, S. B., Mamakeesick, M., Goodwin, K., Fiddler, E., Hegele, R. A., ... & Zinman, B. (2005). Complications of type 2 diabetes among Aboriginal Canadians: Prevalence and associated risk factors. *Diabetes Care, 28,* 2054–2057.

Harris, S. B., Gittelsohn, J., Hanley, A., Barnie, A., Wolever, T. M. S., Gao, ... & Zinman, B. (1997). The prevalence of NIDDM and associated risk factors in Native Canadians. *Diabetes Care, 20,* 185–187.

Health Canada—Public Health Agency of Canada. (2011*). Diabetes in Canada: Facts and figures from a public health perspective.* Ottawa, ON. Retrieved from http://www.hc-sc.gc.ca/fniah-spnia/diseases-maladies/diabete/index-eng.php

Hegele, R. A., & Pollex, R. L. (2005). Genetic and physiological insights into the metabolic syndrome. *American Journal of Physiology—Regulatory, Integrative, and Comparative Physiology, 289,* R663–R669.

Hegele, R. A., Cao, H., Harris, S. B., Hanley, A. J. G., & Zinman, B. (1999a). Hepatocyte nuclear factor-1 alpha G319S. A private mutation in Oji-Cree associated with type 2 diabetes. *Diabetes Care, 22,* 524.

Hegele, R. A., Cao, H., Harris, S. B., Hanley, A. J. G., & Zinman, B. (1999b). The hepatic nuclear factor-1α G319S variant is associated with early-onset type 2 diabetes in Canadian Oji-Cree. *Journal of Clinical Endocrinology & Metabolism, 84,* 1077–1082.

Hegele, R. A., Cao, H., Harris, S. B., Zinman, B., Hanley, A. J. G., & Anderson, C. M. (2000a). Peroxisome proliferator-activated receptor-γ2 P12A and type 2 diabetes in Canadian Oji-Cree. *Journal of Clinical Endocrinology & Metabolism, 85,* 2014–2019.

Hegele, R. A., Harris, S. B., Zinman, B., Wang, J., Cao, H., Hanley, A. J. G., Tsui, L., & Scherer, S. W. (1998). Variation in the AU(AT)-rich element within the 3-Untranslated region of PPP1R3 is associated with variation in plasma glucose in Aboriginal Canadians. *Journal of Clinical Endocrinology & Metabolism, 83,* 3980–3983.

Hoy, W. E., Kincaid-Smith, P., Hughson, M. D., Fogo, A. B., Sinniah, R., Dowling, J., ... & Bertram, J. F. (2010). CKD in Aboriginal Australians. *American Journal of Kidney Diseases, 56,* 983–993.

Jackson, H., Huisman, L., Sanatani, S., & Arbour, L. T. (2011). Long QT syndrome. *CMAJ, 11,* 1272–1275.

Johnson, J. S., Nobmann, E. D., Asay, E., & Lanier, A. P. (2009). Dietary intake of Alaska Native people in two regions and implications for health: The Alaska Native dietary and subsistence food assessment project. *International Journal of Circumpolar Health, 68,* 109–122.

Kotelevtsev, Y., Holmes, M. C., Burchell, A., Houston, P. M., Schmoll, D., Jamieson, P., ... & Mullins, J. J. (1997). 11 beta-hydroxysteroid dehydrogenase type 1 knockout mice show attenuated glucocorticoid-inducible responses and resist hyperglycemia on obesity or stress. *Proceedings of the National Academy of Sciences, 23,* 14924–14929.

Lear, S. A., Humphries, K. H., Frohlich, J. J., & Birmingham, C. L. (2007). Appropriateness of current thresholds for obesity-related measures among Aboriginal people. *Canadian Medical Association Journal, 177*, 1499–1505.

Lemas, D. J., Wiener, H. W., O'Brien, D. M., Hopkins, S., Stanhope, K. L., Havel, P. J., ... & Boyer, B. B. (2011). Genetic polymorphisms in carnitine palmitoyltransferase 1A gene are associated with variation in body composition and fasting lipid traits in Yup'ik Eskimos. *Journal of Lipid Research, 53*, 1–30.

Lewis, C. (2002). Genetic association studies: Design, analysis, and interpretation. *Briefings in Bioinformatics, 3*, 146–153.

Liu, J., Young, T. K., Zinman, B., Harris, S. B., Connelly, P. W., & Hanley, A. J. (2006). Lifestyle variables, non-traditional cardiovascular risk factors, and the metabolic syndrome in an Aboriginal Canadian population. *Obesity, 14*, 500–508.

Macaulay, A. C., Harris, S. B., Lévesque, L., Cargo, M., Ford, E., Salsberg, J., ... & Receveur, O. (2003). Primary prevention of type 2 diabetes: Experiences of 2 Aboriginal communities in Canada. *Canadian Journal of Diabetes, 27*, 464–475.

Marmot, M. (2005). Social determinants of health inequalities. *Lancet, 365*, 1099–1104.

Masato, K. (2011). KNCQ1, a susceptibility gene for type 2 diabetes. *Journal of Diabetes Investigation, 2*, 413–414.

McEwen, B. S. (2000). Allostasis and allostatic load: Implications for neuropsychopharmacology. *Neuropsychopharmacology, 22*, 108–124.

McIvor, O., Napoleon, A., & Dickie, K. A. (2009). Language and culture as protective factors for at-risk communities. *Journal of Aboriginal Health, 5*, 6–25.

Millar, K., & Dean, H. J. (2012). Developmental origins of type 2 diabetes in Aboriginal youth in Canada: It is more than diet and exercise. *Journal of Nutrition and Metabolism, 2012*, 1–7.

Muller, Y. L., Bogardus, C., Beamer, B. A., Shuldiner, A. R., & Baier. L. J. (2003a). A functional variant in the peroxisome proliferator-activated receptor $\gamma2$ promoter is associated with predictors of obesity and type 2 diabetes in Pima Indians. *Diabetes, 52*, 1864–1871.

Muller, Y. L., Bogardus, C., Pedersen, O., & Baier, L. (2003b). A Gly482Ser missense mutation in the peroxisome proliferator-activated receptor γ coactivator-1 is associated with altered lipid oxidation and early insulin secretion in Pima Indians. *Diabetes, 52*, 895–898.

Muller, Y. L., Hanson, R. L., Bian, L., Mack, J., Shi, X., Pakyr, R., ... & Baier, L. J. (2010). Functional variants in MBL2 are associated with type 2 diabetes and pre-diabetes traits in Pima Indians and the old order Amish. *Diabetes, 59*, 2080–2085.

Neel, J. V. (1962). Diabetes mellitus: A "thrifty" genotype rendered detrimental by "progress"? *American Journal of Human Genetics, 14*, 353–362.

Pérez-Bravo, F., Fuentes, M., Angel, B., Sanchez, H., Carrasco, E., Santos, J. L., Lera, L., & Albala, C. (2006). Lack of association between the fatty acid binding protein 2 (FABP2) polymorphism with obesity and insulin resistance in two Aboriginal populations from Chile. *Acta Diabetologica, 43*, 93–98.

Polanco, F. (2012). Type II diabetes and KCNQ1 mutations in First Nations people of northern British Columbia (master's thesis). Victoria, BC: University of Victoria. Retrieved from https://dspace.library.uvic.ca:8443/handle/1828/4245

Ptashne, M. (2007). On the use of the word "epigenetic." *Current Biology, 17,* R233–R236.

Ralph-Campbell, K., Oster, R. T., Connor, T., Pick, M., Pohar, S., Thompson, P., . . . & Toth, L. E. (2009). Increasing rates of diabetes and cardiovascular risk in Métis settlements in northern Alberta. *International Journal of Circumpolar Health, 68,* 433–442.

Reading, C. L., & Wien, F. (2009). *Health inequalities and social determinants of Aboriginal peoples' health.* Prince George, BC: National Collaborating Centre for Aboriginal Health. Retrieved from http://ahrnets.ca/files/2011/02/NCCAH-Loppie-Wien_Report.pdf

Reading, J. (2010). *The crisis of chronic disease among Aboriginal peoples: A challenge for public health, population health, and social policy.* Victoria, BC: Centre for Aboriginal Health Research, University of Victoria.

Receveur, O., Boulay, M., & Kuhnlein, H. V. (1997). Decreasing traditional food use affects diet quality for adult Dene/Metis in communities of the Canadian Northwest Territories. *Journal of Nutrition, 127,* 2179–2186.

Rong, R., Hanson, R. L., Ortiz, D., Wiedrich, C., Kobes, S., Knowler, W. C., Bogardus, C., & Baier, L. J. (2009). Association analysis of variation in/near FTO, CDKAKL1, SLC30A8, HHEX, EXT2, IGF2BP2, LOC387761, and CDKN2B with type 2 diabetes and related quantitative traits in Pima Indians. *Diabetes, 58,* 478–488.

Smeja, C., & Brassard, P. (2000). Tuberculosis infection in an Aboriginal (First Nations) population of Canada. *International Journal of Tuberculosis and Lung Disease, 4,* 925–930.

Southam, L., Soranzo, N., Montgomery, S. B., Frayling, T. M., McCarthy, M. I., Barroso, I., & Zeggini, E. (2009). Is the thrifty genotype hypothesis supported by evidence based on confirmed type 2 diabetes- and obesity-susceptibility variants? *Diabetologia, 52,* 1846–1851.

Statistics Canada. (2010). *Diabetes, 2010.* Retrieved from http://www.statcan.gc.ca/pub/82-625-x/2011001/article/11459-eng.htm

Taylor, A. (2006). The genetics of type 2 diabetes. *International Journal of Diabetes & Metabolism, 14,* 76–81.

Tomlinson, J. W., & Stewart, P. M. (2007). Modulation of glucocorticoid action and the treatment of type-2 diabetes. *New Therapies for Diabetes, 21,* 607–619.

Unoki, H., Takahashi, A., Takahisa, K., Hara, K., Horikoshi, M., Andersen, G., . . . & Maeda, S. (2008). SNPs in KCNQ1 are associated with susceptibility to type 2 diabetes in East Asian and European populations. *Nature, 40,* 1098–1102.

Wang, Z., & Hoy, W. E. (2004). Body size measurements as predictors of type 2 diabetes in Aboriginal people. *International Journal of Obesity, 28,* 1580–1584.

Wildman, R. P. (2009). Healthy obesity. *Current Opinion in Clinical Nutrition & Metabolic Care, 12*, 438–443.

Wilson, K. (2003). Therapeutic landscapes and First Nations peoples: An exploration of culture, health, and place. *Health & Place, 9*, 83–93.

Wolever, T. M. S., Hamad, S., Gittelsohn, J., Hanley, A. J. G., Logan, A., Harris, S. B., & Zinman, B. (1997). Nutrient intake and food use in an Ojibwa-Cree community in northern Ontario assessed by 24 h dietary recall. *Nutrition Research, 17*, 603–618.

Yamagata, K., Senokuchi, T., Lu, M., Takemoto, M., Fazlul, M., Go, C., . . . & Song, W. J. (2011). Voltage-gated K+ channel KCNQ1 regulates insulin secretion in MIN6 β-cell line. *Biochemical and Biophysical Research Communications, 407*, 620–625.

Yasuda, K., Miyake, K., Horikawa, Y., Hara, K., Osawa, H., Furuta, H., . . . & Kasuga, M. (2008). Variants in KCNQ1 are associated with susceptibility to type 2 diabetes mellitus. *Nature, 40*, 1092–1097.

Young, T. K., Reading, J., Elias, B., & O'Neil, J. D. (2000). Type 2 diabetes mellitus in Canada's First Nations: Status of an epidemic in progress. *Canadian Medical Association Journal, 163*(5), 561–569.

CHAPTER 22

Determining Life with HIV and AIDS

Sherri Pooyak, Marni Amirault, and Renée Masching

When HIV was first identified in the early 1980s, no one really knew what to do; doctors and patients were learning together, and often the patients were more knowledgeable than their care providers. This early relationship dynamic still influences HIV prevention, care, treatment, support, and research today. As staff of the Canadian Aboriginal AIDS Network (CAAN), a membership-driven organization of Aboriginal AIDS organizations and Aboriginal peoples living with HIV and AIDS (APHAs), we are well positioned to apply our knowledge and lived experience in order to take up groundbreaking leadership roles. The preparation of this chapter led us to reflect on how the social determinants of health (SDoH) come to life through our own experiences and those of our friends and colleagues.

In Canada, Aboriginal peoples comprise 4.3 percent of the Canadian population (Statistics Canada, 2013), yet a 2011 report from the Public Health Agency of Canada (PHAC) estimated that 8.9 percent of all prevalent HIV infections were Aboriginal peoples living with HIV (PHAC, 2012). In fact, "Aboriginal peoples in Canada are many times more likely to be diagnosed with HIV compared to White Canadians; across all age groups and among both sexes" (Ogunnaike-Cooke, Halverson, & Archibald, 2011, n.p.). Within the Aboriginal population, the people who are most affected by HIV and AIDS are women, youth, people who use injection drugs, as well as transmission through heterosexual contact (PHAC, 2010).

HIV 101

HIV is transmitted through blood, bodily fluids, and breast milk. The most common forms of HIV transmission are through unprotected sexual contact (such as vaginal or anal sex) and/or the sharing of unclean needles or injection drug–use equipment. Other forms of HIV transmission include using unsterilized needles for tattooing, skin piercing, or acupuncture; vertical or mother-to-child transmission during delivery; and/or occupational exposure in health care settings.

Human immunodeficiency virus (HIV) is a lot like other viruses, including those that cause the flu or the common cold, but with one important difference: once infected with HIV, the body cannot get rid of the virus. HIV attacks the immune system, leaving HIV-positve people vulnerable to opportunistic infections and cancers. Over time, HIV destroys so many healthy cells that the body isn't able to fight infection any longer. This is when HIV progresses and is referred to as acquired immunodeficiency syndrome (AIDS).

New treatment regimes have reduced the number of pills a person has to take each day. There have been significant advances in research toward a cure. For most people, HIV can be treated well enough that a standard test will no longer detect the virus in the blood. All of this is hopeful for a future when those living with HIV are physically well and the risk of transmission is very low.

REFLECTING ON OUR STORIES

We are part of the community of Aboriginal peoples who live with HIV and AIDS. Collectively our lives are affected by the complexity of the virus, by our drive to respond, by our passion for the people we work alongside, and the members of the First Nations, Inuit, and Métis communities that we represent. Individually, drawing on insights based on the varying lengths of our involvement within the Aboriginal HIV and AIDS community, we offer our own stories to give voice to the lived experience of working in the context of HIV and the SDoH. None of us is HIV-positive. Each of us joined the HIV community at different times: Renée, a First Nation woman from Six Nations, in 1993; Marni, an Acadian Nova Scotian woman with strong ties to the East and West coasts, 2009; and Sherri, a Cree woman from Saskatchewan, in 2011.

RENÉE'S STORY

I have held various roles within the community of Aboriginal peoples responding to HIV and AIDS over the past two decades: project staff, executive director, committee member, board member, executive committee or chairperson, facilitator, student, manager, researcher, etc.

As I reflect back, I experience two things simultaneously: people's faces start flashing in my mind with the Eagles' song "Hotel California" as a soundtrack. There are so many who were trailblazers and left footsteps for us (for me) to follow. I am fond of the expression "we stand on the shoulders of giants"—truly there is great humility in the scope and depth of the contributions to be made toward health and healing grounded in response to HIV and AIDS in the hope that others will continue to follow us.

When an advocate friend spoke about the moment when he stopped dying of AIDS and began living with HIV, he taught me about the spirit of our work. A response to HIV cannot occur without responding to a person's whole being. Living well requires care to address the physical impact of the virus in a person's body, but even more, living well with HIV is about mental, emotional, and spiritual health. It is striking how effectively the SDoH can be applied to capture the power of healing as well as the roots of poor health. There are the positive influences of culture: Aboriginal teachings, HIV community culture, traditional ceremonies, and ceremony shared among individuals. There are the beautiful physical environments where we live and work, and the personal and professional environment created by family and colleagues. There is the peace that comes with a deeper understanding of the historical forces that impact our lives and shape our journeys. The multiple determinants that swirl around us create a challenging, sometimes heartbreaking and utterly compelling reality in the response to HIV and AIDS.

—Renée

In the early years of responding to HIV within the Aboriginal community, before thinking about SDoH became influential in government policy, the Atlantic First Nations AIDS Task Force, where Renée worked, delivered week-long training programs about HIV and AIDS based on medicine wheel teachings brought home to the Atlantic region from the West. Using the *Healing Our Nations* manual, we taught the basics of HIV—what a virus is; how it is transmitted; the care, treatment, and support options and needs of an APHA. Then we would spend days discussing the links between HIV, mental health, substance use, and child development. We fundamentally understood that HIV had come to our community in relationship with many other factors that "determined" our health and well-being.

In the face of an emerging epidemic, we were racing to make as many people as possible aware of the complexity of HIV and AIDS and understand that this infection was often the outcome of circumstances greater than the individual person, and that stigma and discrimination would feed the virus and strengthen its hold in our communities. We were talking about social determinants of health before we knew the academic language to describe what we had already learned through the medicine wheel.

MARNI'S STORY

Early one morning in November 2012, I was in a cab on my way to the airport. The taxi driver was chatty and he asked the typical kinds of questions cab drivers ask: Are you coming or going? Where are you headed? Is it for business or pleasure? When I told him I worked for a national Aboriginal organization and was headed to Chicago for a conference on HIV and AIDS, he stopped talking. "Look at that beautiful moon," I mused aloud, testing the waters after a few moments of silence. Those were the last words spoken between us until we arrived at the airport.

Later when I told the customs agent where I was going and why, she eyed me coolly. "Is that what you do for a living?" she asked. It took everything in me not to say "Yeah, I 'do' HIV for a living."

Often people will share the one or two experiences they've had meeting Aboriginal peoples. They'll nod and say, "Yeah, that's [HIV] a big problem, isn't it, in the Native community?" As a non-Aboriginal, white, middle-class woman who has been working in and with Aboriginal communities in Canada since 2001, I am blown away by the degree of stereotyping that still exists. Add to that the stigma many people face because of their HIV status and sometimes I wonder how people manage to get through the day. But they do.

I have had the privilege to work alongside and learn from some pretty amazing people in the time I've been with CAAN. This is what I try to convey to the cab drivers and others I encounter on a daily basis who exist far beyond this world of Aboriginal HIV and AIDS research. My colleagues, friends, and mentors are so much more than the stereotypes related to Aboriginal or HIV status; they are people with healthy families, stable jobs, rich and rewarding lives—certainly much more than the limits of a stereotype-bound imagination might allow.

—Marni

The federal government began referencing the SDoH model in requests for applications for project funding in the late 1990s. In the years that followed this transition to a "new" policy framework, our ability to tell the story of HIV and AIDS within the Aboriginal community in a way that others, and we ourselves, can understand has also changed. It has changed how we engage our leadership, how and when we design prevention strategies, who we partner with, and who will partner with us.

Perhaps of most value is the shift in how the story of living with HIV has changed. For the Aboriginal community as a whole, we have a framework to understand the roots of the HIV and AIDS epidemic within the broader context of the living legacy of colonization and how our collective healing journey is linked to the end of the epidemic. Most profoundly, however, is the shift for individuals living with HIV and AIDS. A life story evolves to include the SDoH factors beyond personal control that contribute toward the time(s) of possible HIV transmission and ultimately HIV infection. In this evolution, a person can put down the burdens of blame and internalized stigma and by doing so, be freed to pursue a path toward healing.

SHERRI'S STORY

In the early 1990s I lived in Whitehorse, Yukon. During my first long, cold winter in the North as a newcomer, I was often called a "greenhorn," a term used to describe people without much experience or knowledge. I think this term accurately reflects my experience in working with APHAs, those affected by the virus, and with CAAN. Working at CAAN has meant that I have had to learn about viral loads, medications, the impact of HIV and AIDS on individuals, families, communities, and so much more. My learning curve has been steep and yet so incredibly rewarding.

I remember my first HIV conference a little over two months into my job. I was introduced to a colleague whom I have since come to admire and see as one of the knowledge keepers within the Aboriginal HIV and AIDS movement. I was lucky to sit beside him in the large conference area while waiting for the event to start. As we waited, he shared his knowledge by pointing out to me who he knew. This may sound odd, but within the Aboriginal community it is often customary to identify who you are and who you are related to. Although he wasn't related to anyone by blood, he shared who he knew, and how he knew them in the context of the HIV movement and in some cases what they had looked like the year before. Some of the people he talked about had been gravely ill, although I would not have known this had he not shared this information. This is the complexity of HIV or AIDS. A person can be healthy one year, then gravely ill, and then well again. I am grateful to the knowledge keeper for sharing his knowledge of community, people, his life (his list of meds), and his spirit—this was a gift and valuable lesson.

In the year and half since we sat together, I am still only beginning to understand the complexities that Aboriginal peoples experience in the context of HIV and AIDS. Part of what I have come to understand is that these complexities include a lack of prevention strategies specifically for Aboriginal peoples, a lack of education for rural and remote areas (such as reserves), and a lack of stories of resilience—although these are being told more and more.

—Sherri

CONCLUSION

Our work is guided by community need on the one hand and influenced by government strategy and policy on the other. We have learned to be flexible and creative, to conduct ourselves in a good way and ensure that we stay true to the multiple priorities laid out before us. In the years of our collective involvement in the response to HIV within the Aboriginal community, the SDoH have been applied strategically in different ways. Each of us has our own stories about our journey with HIV and AIDS, lessons we have learned about ourselves, our families, and our community. With over 20 years of direct HIV experience and more than 40 years of involvement in Aboriginal community health, we have come to respect the virus as a teacher.

The end of AIDS will come when our circle is strong again. Every day we engage with Aboriginal peoples living with HIV and AIDS who are resilient, strong, knowledgeable, outspoken role models who can have a sense of humour about their illness. In understanding the roots of disease, we also discover the roots of healing—as individuals, as families, as communities, nations, and as proud Aboriginal peoples.

REFERENCES

Barlow, J. K. (2003). *Examining HIV/AIDS among the Aboriginal population in Canada: In the post-residential school era.* Retrieved from http://www.ahf.ca/publications/research-series

Canadian Aboriginal AIDS Network. (2009). *Our search for safe spaces: A qualitative study of the role of sexual violence in the lives of Aboriginal women living with HIV/AIDS.* Vancouver, BC: Author.

Canadian Aboriginal AIDS Network. (2011). *International strategic plan on HIV & AIDS for Indigenous peoples & communities from 2011–2017.* Vancouver, BC: Author.

Ogunnaike-Cooke, S., Halverson, J., & Archibald, C. (2011). *HIV and AIDS among Aboriginal peoples in Canada: An epidemiological overview.* [PowerPoint presentation]. Canadian Aboriginal AIDS Network Annual General Meeting. Quebec City, QC, June 7–9, 2011.

Pearce, M., Christian, W., Patterson, K., Norris, K., Moniruzzaman, A., Craib, K., Schechter, M., & Spittal, M. (2008). The Cedar project: Historical trauma, sexual abuse, and HIV risk among young Aboriginal people who use injection drug and non-injection drugs in two Canadian cities. *Social Science & Medicine, 60,* 2185–2194.

Public Health Agency of Canada (PHAC). (2010). *HIV/AIDS epi updates.* Ottawa, ON: Author.

Public Health Agency of Canada (PHAC). (2012). *Summary: Estimates of HIV prevalence and incidence 2011.* Ottawa, ON: Author. Retrieved from http://www.phac-aspc.gc.ca/aids-sida/publication/survreport/estimat2011-eng.php

Statistics Canada. (2013, May 8). 2011 National Household Survey: Aboriginal peoples in Canada: First Nations people, Métis, and Inuit. *The Daily.* Retrieved from http://www.statcan.gc.ca/daily-quotidien/130508/dq130508a-eng.pdf

CHAPTER 23

Medicine Is Relationship

Relationship Is Medicine

Leah May Walker and Danièle Behn-Smith

We consider ourselves blessed to be translators and learners. We're very grateful to have a unique bicultural perspective of several interfaces—Aboriginal/non-Aboriginal, Western medicine/Indigenous medicine, practitioner/patient, inside/outside. We've chosen to work and live in a tension-filled space where we are tasked with honouring two divergent world views. This task is particularly problematic because of the legacy of colonization and ongoing colonial dynamics that dismiss and undermine Indigenous world views. We endeavour to privilege Indigenous knowledge and create space for it to be heard.

Prior to the arrival of the first Europeans, we as Indigenous peoples had our own medicines and medical systems. The systems of care, medicines, and ceremonies are specific to our families and communities and are deeply contextual and relational. Our systems of care prior to colonization were highly effective—we lived in harmony with the world around us. Since colonization, powerful dynamics have undermined our own medicines and medical systems and have privileged the Western medical system. This has been such a dramatic shift that in many Western medical arenas there isn't even space to recognize "other" systems. Evidence-based medicine and the reliance on Western science as truth have made it difficult to have a balanced conversation about barriers to Indigenous health. The invisibility of our own systems of care to the larger Western medical system is in itself a negative determinant of health.

THE MEDICAL SYSTEM AS A DETERMINANT OF HEALTH

We know that the Western medical system has often been a determinant of ill health for Indigenous peoples (Nelson, 2012). The history has been well documented in many literatures, and in particular the report of the Royal Commission on Aboriginal Peoples (RCAP). The RCAP report tells many stories of the effects of the colonizing practices of well-intentioned physicians and field matrons who wanted to save our relatives from whatever afflicted them, but, through their work, ended up contributing to even poorer health outcomes (Indian Affairs and Northern Development Canada, 1996).

Currently, the forces of colonization are barely recognized in our health system. Although health disparities are very well documented, we have a hard time believing that our health system is set up to be inequitable (Adelson, 2005; Waldram, Herring, & Young, 2006; Reading & Wien, 2009). Yet, the barriers for Indigenous peoples are many and complex, and include the contributing forces of the Indian Act, wherein only status Indians have access to certain health benefits, and where health services are often located far away from reserves (Fiske, 2006). We hear about health care providers who won't provide a necessary service unless the patient can pay up front as the health system bureaucracy takes too many months to reimburse providers for health services. This is clearly a barrier for an Indigenous person living in poverty. We also know that Indigenous peoples lack access to many health services that are available to other Canadians. For example, equal care and access to services for First Nations children are still being fought for in struggles to ensure application of Jordan's Principle, a child-first principle named in memory of Jordan River Anderson that stipulates governments of first contact must pay for vital life-saving services and seek reimbursement later (Lett, 2008). The Canadian government recently appealed the Supreme Court ruling of the case of Jeremy Meawasige, and disputes it should pay costs to keep him with his mother at home in Pictou Landing, Nova Scotia (MacDonald, 2012).

Our relatives tell us how the structures of colonization are visible in hospitals in that they look like and remind them of residential schools. The invisible structures are no less daunting and dominant: Western medicine and knowledge are a hierarchy, in which Indigenous medicine is not valued or considered inferior. The "evidence-based" biomedical model implicitly renders Indigenous medicine and knowledge as less scientific and therefore dubious. We also hear too often of the explicit racism that Indigenous peoples face in schools and in health care settings, such as the emergency departments at hospitals (Browne, Smye, Rodney, Tang, Mussell, & O'Neil, 2011). While there seems to be a real willingness in some settings to address this issue by providing culturally appropriate spaces, Aboriginal navigators to help patients understand and access the medical system, and education in cultural competency for health care providers, there are also too many instances where we hear Aboriginal peoples say that they feel it is "unsafe to go" to the hospital or clinic, or that they'll "only go there to die" (Makokis & Steinhauer, 2012).

There is a cultural clash in how we define what health is and what medicine is. Spend time with an Elder. The medicine is specific—the sage and sweetgrass smudge, for example. But medicine is also the stories, the ceremony, the witnessing, and the honouring of the relationships. This is one thing that we seem to forget in Western medical practice, where medicine is reduced to the very specific chemical makeup of a pill and the proper administration of it. Often, anything else around it—the bigger process of healing, relationship making with our relatives, with each other, with the planet—is neglected or forgotten. We acknowledge that both systems have powerful medicine and can contribute to Indigenous peoples' health and well-being. We need to work together to navigate the tension-filled space between these systems in order to move forward in a good way. The conversation that follows, one between two Indigenous health care educators, is reiteration of that theme. Our Indigenous relatives are asking for a commitment to the whole relationship, and we want to share what makes us well.

WHAT MAKES US WELL: A CONVERSATION BETWEEN TWO INDIGENOUS HEALTH CARE EDUCATORS

We sought to honour our relationships and our Indigenous world views through our creative process as encapsulated in a series of conversations. These conversations focused on the concept of medicine as a determinant of health in the context of our work as a physician/medical educator and a health researcher/medical educator. We transcribed and analyzed our initial conversations and developed categories, which we coalesced into themes. We returned to our initial conversation and explored in greater detail the stories that best illustrated key themes. The guiding questions that provide purpose and direction to our work are as follows:

- What have we witnessed that is colonizing about our Western medical system?
- What enables decolonization of our Western medical system?
- What have we witnessed or experienced as the possibility for repairing a relationship?

Our final conversation is a mosaic of teachings, stories, and insights that lend clarity and intention to our work. We humbly share our conversation with you.

DANIÈLE BEHN-SMITH: Unfortunately, my medical training and early practice were marked by a series of colonizing experiences in which I was at
times the colonizer and at other times the colonized. The relationship between the Western medical system, myself as an Indigenous physician in
training, and the Indigenous individuals whom I saw as patients was (and is)
complex. I was a young physician and was also at a very early stage of consciousness about what it means to be an Eh Cho Dene/French Canadian/
Métis woman. As a result, I embarked on my training with a naive desire
to help improve Aboriginal health, but without the necessary critical eye
and personal grounding to withstand the powerful colonizing forces at
play. What I saw and experienced of the Western medical system as a determinant of health for Indigenous peoples can be illustrated by sharing the
following story. This story is not one of which I'm proud. In fact, it still
brings me to tears to think of how I treated this Cree man. I share it today
in the hope that by telling it, we can all help to co-create a new narrative
that will prevent this story from being re-enacted again.

    This story took place during my first year of family practice residency.
I was in the middle of an internal medicine rotation that was very busy
and demanding. I was working at a large, inner-city, tertiary-care hospital
in Winnipeg. This same hospital became infamous years later when an
Aboriginal man died in the waiting room of the ER after spending many
hours being overlooked. There is no question that racism runs deep in this
institution and influenced my training.

    I was on a team with four other medical learners and a lead physician.
Between us we were caring for about 30 patients who were all admitted for
serious illnesses. A Cree man was admitted for a leg infection. It started
because he had chronic venous stasis ulcers, and he had those because he
had poorly controlled diabetes. In the Western medical system's eyes, he
was a non-compliant Indian. His condition suggested he wasn't taking
care of himself, and now our team was responsible for making him better.
We (or the system) started this process of "healing" him by flying him out
of his home community, pumping him full of medications, running lots
of different tests, and taking various different measurements throughout
the day and night—heart rate, blood pressure, oxygen saturation. All of
these things were part of our tools to make him better.

    When I met him the first morning, I barged into his room at some
ungodly hour to expeditiously do my rounds. I needed to get all the "right"
information about his progress so that I could report back to the team and

we could deliberate on what the next step in his care should be. Our conversation went something like this:

ME: How are you this morning?

CREE PATIENT: You know damn well how I'm doing!

ME: No, I don't, that's why I'm asking.

CREE PATIENT: Well, I'm stuck up in here. Can't get around. That's how I'm doing.

ME: How is your pain?

CREE PATIENT: What do you care? All you see is some dumb Indian sitting in here.

ME: I take offense to that! I'm Native too, and I'm here because I want to help.

CREE PATIENT: You might be Native, but you're trained white man's way.

ME: Well, I don't know what other options I had!

Shortly after that exchange, I stormed out of his room. I felt sad, angry, attacked, and defeated. The whole reason I had gone into medicine was to improve Aboriginal health and here I was, getting into an argument with my only Aboriginal patient. There was no way I was going back into that room, so I promptly asked one of my colleagues to take over his care. I made up some excuse about having too many patients on my list, but the truth was I was afraid. I didn't know what had gone wrong or how to fix it, and quite honestly my patient was right—I didn't have the energy to care.

All these years later, I still feel sad about that encounter. My anger and offence have since turned to shame and grief that I was hurtful instead of helpful. Thankfully, I've had many teachers and teachings that have helped me to understand what actually happened that morning so many years ago. They have gifted me with a different way to approach my work so as to avoid repeating this traumatic scenario.

LEAH MAY WALKER: This is the challenge we have before us, isn't it? In so many ways we feel powerless in the system we have created. And so you are both playing parts in the medical system that have been played before in other realms: the Cree man is given little choice in how he is cared for in an environment that is set up in a way to make him entirely helpless and dependent, and you as a wise physician are playing the part of the saviour, knowing best how to make him better. He has to play by your rules, with your timing, no matter what the hour. You're doing it in his best interest, of course. Ultimately these roles trap both of you. The systemic colonization becomes personally colonizing. It becomes moot that you are an Indigenous physician caring for an Indigenous man.

The medical system doesn't see itself as colonizing, though. I think it's a challenge for a medical practitioner to see how a structure that is intended to provide the best evidence-based care as efficiently and effectively as possible is a colonizing system.

If you could go back in time, what would you do differently?

DANIÈLE: I'm so grateful to say that now, in most instances, I approach my role differently and the result is much better. As you have brought to light, the parts that we play are so critical to how clinical encounters unfold. Today I'm far more aware of the part I am choosing to play. At that stage in my life and career, I was blindly following the examples set before me, which were for the most part paternalistic, hierarchical, and without a doubt positivist to the core. The flip side of this is that the role of saviour is wildly seductive and hypnotic. The illusion of control is a powerful drug, and I must admit that the "power" that came with my credentials probably kept me from examining my role in any great depth until the pain of encounters like these became too much to bear.

Through a lot of prayer and seeking, I was introduced to various Elders and medicine people, who helped me to understand myself as an Indigenous woman and helped me to reframe my role within Western medicine as a helper or midwife rather than a saviour. In an instant my burdens were lifted! I no longer carried the weight of "healing" every person I met, but rather I could be there to support him or her on a healing journey. If I could go back to that morning so many years ago, I would have focused on being a supporter rather than a saviour, and I would have tried to develop a positive relationship with this man. In order to do that, I would have started that meeting by asking permission.

ME: Good morning, Mr. Charlie. Is now an OK time for me to come in and meet with you?

If he was OK with me entering his space—physical, emotional, spiritual—I would have introduced myself, where I'm from, what my roots are, and my intention for being there in his room. I would have clarified my intention to try and help him in the way that *he* wanted to be helped, not to feed my ego. Then I would have gently asked him to share something about himself, his home, and his personhood outside of his "diagnosis" so that I could come to know him rather than his illness. In this way, the encounter could have been about trying to create an ethical space: treating him with respect, demonstrating reciprocity, and tending to our budding relationship. Above all else, I would endeavour to respect the law of non-interference and constantly check in to make sure that what I was doing was truly helpful in the way that he was requesting.

Outside of our encounter, I would have advocated for him within the system. I would have tried to share the greater context of his narrative and illness with my team, so that they might shift their understanding of the "non-compliant Indian." I would have gone to bat for him against the barriers of non-insured health benefits (NIHB) system, dysfunctional discharge planning, and jurisdictional loopholes that can leave Aboriginal clients high and dry and unsupported. I would have tried to take the time to examine my reactions to him and his story and not attack him if he were to uncover my insecurities and vulnerabilities as he so aptly did that morning so many years ago.

This Cree man was one of my greatest teachers, and I can't even remember his name. I regret that our paths crossed at a time in my personal development when I didn't have the benefit of knowing what I do now. The result of our meeting was harmful rather than healing. If I could do it all over again, I would do it very differently.

LEAH: My best learning about decolonization is the research process I'm privileged to participate in with some First Nations communities in northern British Columbia. A few years ago, the health director of one small community and I were having a conversation about the state of the relationship between her people and some of the health professionals who worked there. She was dismayed that community members felt disempowered, felt like second-class citizens, and didn't get the care they should. As an educator in the medical school, I was interested in how to practise cultural safety and find ways to rebuild relationships between First Nations communities and health providers. It became obvious we would find a way to work together. We created a team that included community members and a mentor and colleague who had practised in that community and was trusted by the people there. We wrote and were awarded a grant. Our research was to discover what people's experiences were with the health care system and what recommendations they would make in training health care professionals.

On the day we were to hold focus groups with community members, the health director asked if people from a neighbouring community could join in the focus group conversations. The state of the relationship between the other First Nations community and health professionals was pretty grim as well, and epitomized by security guards recently being brought into the hospital. Since this was a community process as much as a research one, food and focus groups in the form of sharing circles grew to include members from both communities. We honoured community research protocols by beginning with prayer and acknowledgement of Elders and territory, as well as having participants sign consent forms. A community health researcher (CHR) asked the research questions and beautifully facilitated the process in a way that respected the stories and recommendations of the community members.

I felt privileged to be there. It was extremely moving for me to bear witness to the stories, and in the process of listening to them, healing as well. I was impressed with people's resilience despite a history that resulted in health disparities and emotional and spiritual wounds. The research team transcribed the notes, we worked together to analyze and organize into themes, and we checked our findings with participants in each community. We brought a final report back in a formal ceremony. It was a lengthy process, but important to pay attention to the relationships and follow protocols to ensure we were working in a good way.

We are now working together on a second project. The research question has changed. Rather than focusing on the health care professional relationship, the question is about the people's relationship with health and wellness. How do they take care of themselves? Their answers have everything to do with self-determination and decolonization. In the current project, there are some of the same people from the first project, as well as many new faces, willing to share and trust because of what went before. After the focus group circles, our research team spent time deconstructing the process and reflecting on what we were learning personally, as well as what the stories and data were telling us. We felt it was critical to reflect on the process and ourselves in order to ensure that we were gathering stories in a culturally safe way for participants, as well as for ourselves. It has been incredibly powerful to be part of this research. This ongoing research project, to me, feels like a spiritual process: we are all invested in sharing knowledge and stories—deep listening.

Recently, one of the participants, whose parent was also part of the circles, told me that her mom for the first time had a great experience at the hospital. Rather than being treated poorly, dismissed, and feeling disempowered, she felt taken care of. Her mom actually hugged the nurse at the end of the appointment! What a long way from the disrespect she received before! The only difference between the past and what had recently happened was that her mom participated in these focus group circles. There was no intervention, there was no pill. She attributes that hug to the circles that supported her community's values and wellness. The process was the medicine. The process was a catalyst that improved her relationship with herself and then changed the relationship she had with the health professional.

Despite the colonial legacy, these First Nation communities are resilient. They have the courage to look at their relationships with others, each other, and themselves in such a way that so few of us do. They really are leading the way in creating their own decolonized terms of engagement. They are advocating and determining their own present and future in ways that I think will result in improved relationships and ultimately health. And it's not a straight line, but a continual process of reflection and renewal that is inspiring. I hope I can continue to learn with them and to share this learning in ways that helps others.

CONCLUSION

What have we witnessed or experienced as the possibility for repairing relationships? Ultimately, transformation of our approach to supporting Indigenous health and wellness needs to occur at several intersections. The first intersection is personal. We need to make space to know our own selves and each other. We need to create opportunities to listen, to ask permission, and to articulate what wellness means. We need to make space for and honour Indigenous ways of being, knowledges, and medicines. We see a remarkable opportunity for individuals working within the medical system to acknowledge and honour relationships as one of the key medicines for Indigenous peoples.

The second intersection is the medical system. Providing physicians, nurses, and health staff with the opportunity to increase their knowledge about Indigenous and non-Indigenous shared histories, to challenge their own attitudes/

beliefs, and to incorporate culturally safe ways of being into their practice is critical; however, that alone is not enough. We see fee-for-service payments, the emphasis on acute care, differential service, and lack of access for Indigenous peoples in a medical system that serves few and perpetuates continuing colonial dynamics. In our experience, it is an unsustainable system that leaves medical practitioners and Indigenous peoples deeply dissatisfied and with limited options. The medical system must transform to be able to support practitioners in relationship making as the first step toward improved health and wellness for Indigenous peoples.

A third intersection is the area of health governance. We believe that the formation of the First Nations Health Authority in British Columbia, an Indigenous-governed wellness system, is an incredible opportunity to repair relationships. The experience of the Southcentral Foundation (SCF) in Alaska has demonstrated that when Indigenous peoples assume responsibility for our own care, we can determine the direction of our health services. The SCF Nuka Model of Care recognizes "the core product (being) about human beings and relationships—messy, human, longitudinal, personal, trusting, informing, respecting and accountable relationships. . .partnering to make a difference over time" (Gottlieb, Sylvester, & Eby, 2008, n.p.). Indigenous-led health and wellness systems allow us to place respectful, reciprocal, and healthy relationships as the foundation of our work. Governing with the wisdom of our Elders for the benefit of our future generations sets us up for success rather than failure. The mandate of the B.C. First Nations Health Authority is to support individuals, families, and community members coming together to create health and wellness plans, deciding on how services will be delivered, articulating challenges and strengths, and supporting traditional medicine. This is a remarkable indicator of progress. If we all accept responsibility for our part in these personal, systemic, and leadership transformations, we will undergo sustained, meaningful, and satisfying shifts in our experience of the health and wellness system as both Indigenous and non-Indigenous peoples.

ACKNOWLEDGEMENTS

We acknowledge the Coast Salish territory on which we gathered to collaborate on our contribution to this text. We acknowledge all of our relations and the countless teachings that have helped form our understanding of medicine as a determinant of health. We have been blessed to receive teachers in many forms—Elders, family members, medical learners, friends, colleagues, communities. We do not identify the insights we share in this chapter as being proprietary or our "own." We present teachings that have been passed on to us through oral traditions and are authentic and unchanged. We share ideas that have been shaped and influenced by our experiences and myriad relationships. Finally, we humbly offer our thoughts in the form of a dialogue that's been ongoing for many years. This dialogue has been fuelled by our shared desire to improve the health care of Aboriginal peoples through medical education.

REFERENCES

Adelson, N. (2005). The embodiment of inequity: Health disparities in Aboriginal Canada. *Canadian Journal of Public Health, 96,* S45–S61.

Browne, A. J., Smye, V. L., Rodney, P., Tang, S. Y., Mussell, B., & O'Neil, J. (2011). Access to primary care from the perspective of Aboriginal patients at an urban emergency department. *Qualitative Health Research, 21,* 333–348.

Fiske, J. (2006). Boundary crossings: Power and marginalisation in the formation of Canadian Aboriginal women's identities. *Gender and Development, 14,* 247–258.

Gottlieb, K., Sylvester, I., & Eby, D. (2008, January). Transforming your practice: What matters most. *Family Practice Management, 15,* 32–38. Retrieved from http://www.aafp.org/fpm/2008/0100/p32.html

Indian Affairs and Northern Development Canada. (1996). *Final report of the Royal Commission on Aboriginal Peoples.* Ottawa, ON: Author.

Lett, D. (2008). Jordan's Principle remains in limbo. *Canadian Medical Association Journal, 179,* 1256.

MacDonald, N. (2012). Aboriginal children suffer while governments ignore Jordan's Principle. *Canadian Medical Association Journal, 184,* 853.

Makokis, J., & Steinhauer, D. (2012, June). *They only go there to die: Experiences of nehiyawak seeking out health-care in rural Alberta: Results of a talking circle.* Paper presented at the Department of Family Practice Resident Research Day, University of B.C., Vancouver, BC.

Nelson, S. (2012). *Challenging hidden assumptions: Colonial norms as determinants of Aboriginal mental health.* National Collaborating Centre for Aboriginal Health. Retrieved from http://www.nccah-ccnsa.ca/Publications/Lists/Publications/Attachments/70/colonial_norms_EN_web.pdf

Reading, C., & Wien, F. (2009). Health inequalities and social determinants of Aboriginal peoples' health. Prince George, BC: National Collaborating Centre for Aboriginal Health. Retrieved from http://www.nccah-ccnsa.ca/Publications/Lists/Publications/Attachments/46/health_inequalities_EN_web.pdf

Waldram, J. B., Herring, D. A., & Young, T. K. (2006). *Aboriginal health in Canada: Historical, cultural, and epidemiological perspectives* (2nd ed.). Toronto, ON: University of Toronto Press.

CONTRIBUTORS

WARNER ADAM is a member of Lake Babine Nation and the chief executive officer for Carrier Sekani Family Services (CSFS), serving 11 First Nations in the northwestern region of British Columbia. As chief executive officer of CSFS, he administers several projects related to professional senior managers in health, social development, education and child welfare programs, alternate dispute resolution, and youth cultural camps. He also has been conducting research on youth suicide prevention in partnership with the University of Northern British Columbia and the Canadian Institutes of Health Research, and is involved in research on implementation of a child and youth mental health program for northern British Columbia. Mr. Adam is the co-chair for the First Nations Health Council and founding president of the Aboriginal Child Care Society of British Columbia. He has also served on numerous community boards, federal, provincial, and First Nations committees, including the Carrier Sekani Tribal Council executive board, the Lake Babine Nation Council, and treaty tables.

MARNI AMIRAULT has a master of arts in cultural anthropology from the University of Alberta. Her academic background is focused on issues surrounding the representation of Aboriginal peoples in Canadian media: stereotypes, self-representation, and media control, for example. She has worked with First Nations, Inuit, and Métis on community-based research projects. Moving to Halifax after receiving her master's introduced her to issues regarding sexual health and HIV and AIDS. She currently works with the Canadian Aboriginal AIDS Network as a community-based research manager for eastern Canada. She lives in Halifax with her husband and their cat, Fennel.

LAURA ARBOUR is a professor in the Department of Medical Genetics at UBC at the UBC Island Medical Program in Victoria, British Columbia. Her clinical practice and research focuses on northern and Aboriginal health issues as they pertain to genetics. Trained as both pediatrician and clinical geneticist, her work includes maternal-child health issues and the understanding of the genetic component in Aboriginal health of all ages, such as congenital heart defects in the Inuit of Nunavut, Long QT syndrome in northern British Columbia, and the potential association of CPT1A P479L and infant mortality in northern populations. Currently she is also division head of Medical Genetics for the Vancouver Island Health Authority in British Columbia and is co-director of the B.C. Inherited Arrhythmia Program.

CHERYL BARTLETT is a retired professor of biology and former Tier 1 Canada research chair in integrative science at Cape Breton University (CBU). She completed her MSc and PhD at the University of Guelph for research on nematode parasites of wild animals and served several years as assistant editor for the international *Journal of Wildlife Diseases*. She was originally hired at CBU to teach biology and then transitioned into integrative science, working with Mi'kmaw Elders Murdena and Albert Marshall to bring together Indigenous and Western scientific knowledges and ways of knowing for science education using Two-Eyed Seeing as a guiding principle. The initiative later expanded to science and health research, applications, and youth outreach. In recognition of her work, Cheryl was appointed as a member of the Order of Canada in December 2011. Cheryl is of newcomer lineage; she grew up in southern Alberta, in the traditional territory of the Blackfoot Confederacy.

DANIÈLE BEHN-SMITH is French Canadian/Métis from the Red River Valley on her mother's side and Eh Cho Dene from Fort Nelson First Nation on her father's side. She is a family physician who had the remarkable opportunity to travel around the world and learn about traditional medicine from Elders and medicine people as part of a documentary series entitled *Medicine Woman*. She is honoured and privileged to incorporate Indigenous approaches to health and healing in her personal and professional life. She is the site director for the UBC Aboriginal Family Practice Residency site, which has a unique mandate to train family physicians with dedicated interest in providing culturally safe care to Aboriginal peoples, families, and communities. She is committed to transforming the experience of Western medical practice and training to be a healing rather than harmful journey by using approaches grounded in Indigenous teachings.

MARLENE BRANT CASTELLANO is a Mohawk of the Bay of Quinte Band and professor emerita of Trent University, where she provided leadership in developing the emerging discipline of Indigenous studies (1973–1996). She has served as co-director of research with the Royal Commission on Aboriginal Peoples and editor and writer with the Aboriginal Healing Foundation. Recently her writing has focused on research ethics and respectful treatment of Indigenous knowledge. Honours received included LLDs from Queen's, St. Thomas, and Carleton universities, a National Aboriginal Achievement Award, and the Order of Ontario. In 2005 Dr. Castellano was named an officer of the Order of Canada.

NADINE CARON is an Anishinabe general and endocrine surgeon, assistant professor at the University of British Columbia's Northern Medical Program and associate faculty at Johns Hopkins University's Center for American Indian Health. As the first female First Nations student to graduate from the UBC medical school, she won the Hamber Gold Medal as the top graduating student and was named one of Maclean's "One Hundred Canadians to Watch." During surgical residency, she completed her master's degree in public health from Harvard University and was awarded UBC's Top Student Award. She serves on numerous committees, including the Governing Council for the Canadian Institutes of Health Research, the Board of Directors of the Michael Smith Foundation for Health Research, and is co-director for UBC's Centre for Excellence in Indigenous Health. Through role modelling, speaking engagements, and committees, Dr. Caron shares her passion to optimize the health and wellness of Indigenous peoples.

MICHAEL J. CHANDLER is professor emeritus, working at UBC's Department of Psychology. His ongoing program of research features an exploration of the role that culture plays in constructing the course of identity development, shaping young people's emerging sense of ownership of their personal and cultural past, and their commitment to their own and their community's future well-being. These efforts, along with more than 150 published books, articles, and book chapters, have earned Dr. Chandler the Izaak Walton Killam Memorial Senior Research Prize, the Killam Teaching Prize, and being twice named a Peter Wall Institute for Advanced Studies Distinguished Scholar in

Residence. His research and scholarly efforts have also resulted in his appointment as Canada's only Distinguished Investigator of both the Canadian Institutes of Health Research and the Michael Smith Foundation for Health Research.

SARAH DE LEEUW is a human geographer and creative writer. Author of five literary texts, a two-time recipient of a CBC Literary Award in creative nonfiction, and a recipient of the 2013 Dorothy Livesay B.C. Book Prize award for the best book of poetry in the province that year, she has also published more than 45 research-based academic journal papers and book chapters. She is northern British Columbia's first recipient of a Michael Smith Foundation for Health Research Partnered Scholars Award and held a Fulbright postdoctoral fellowship with the University of Arizona between 2007 and 2008. Teaching and undertaking research about medical humanities and health inequalities between Indigenous and non-Indigenous peoples, she is an associate professor in UNBC's Northern Medical Program (NMP), an arm of UBC's Faculty of Medicine in Prince George. Sarah grew up in northern British Columbia, on Haida Gwaii, and in Terrace, which from an early age inspired in her an interest about relationships between place and people's well-being.

MADELEINE DION STOUT, a Cree speaker from the Kehewin First Nation in Alberta, graduated with an MA from the Norman Paterson School of International Affairs at Carleton University and a BA from the School of Nursing at the University of Lethbridge. She has been appointed to the boards of the Aboriginal Nurses Association of Canada, the National Forum on Health, the Mental Health Commission of Canada, and the First Nations Health Authority, and serves on a number of health-related advisory committees across the country. Madeleine has worked as a community health nurse, civil servant, and assistant professor. Now self-employed, she adopts a Cree lens in her ongoing research, writing, and lectures.

WILLIAM L. DUNLOP is an assistant professor of personality and social psychology at the University of California, Riverside. He received his PhD in developmental, personality, and social psychology from the University of British Columbia in Vancouver. In his research, which has appeared in the *Journal of Personality*, the *Journal of Personality and Social Psychology*, the *Journal of Research in Personality*, and the *International Journal of Behavioral Development*, he explores the development and nature of identity, social cognition, character, and personality coherence. Professor Dunlop examines these topics using both variable and person approaches. His research pursuits have been recognized by both the Society for Research in Identity Formation and the Canadian Psychological Association.

MARGO GREENWOOD is an Indigenous scholar of Cree ancestry with more than 25 years of experience in the health and well-being of Indigenous children, families, and communities. She is the academic leader of the National Collaborating Centre of Aboriginal Health, is a professor in both the First Nations studies and education programs at the University of Northern British Columbia, and was appointed in June 2013 as vice-president of Aboriginal Health for the Northern Health Authority in British Columbia. She is recognized regionally, provincially, nationally, and internationally for her work in early childhood care and education of Indigenous children and public health. She received the Queen's Jubilee Medal in 2002 in recognition of her years of work to promote awareness and policy action on the rights and well-being of Aboriginal and non-Aboriginal children, youth, and families, and was honoured in 2011 with the National Aboriginal Achievement Award for Education.

SARAH HUNT has worked for the past 15 years as a researcher and community-based educator on issues of sexuality and gender, sex work, justice, violence, and exploitation in communities across British Columbia. She has also pursued academic interests in Indigenous research ethics, Indigenous methodologies, and decolonial praxis. Sarah's doctoral research, for which she received a Governor General's Gold Medal, focused on intersections of law and geography in investigating strategies for addressing the normalization and expectation of violence in "Indian space" within colonial relations in British Columbia, Canada. This work explored the diverse ways that violence is being addressed at a local level within Indigenous peoples' relationships, families, and communities, emphasizing initiatives that are grounded in culturally specific Indigenous legal principles. Dr. Hunt is a member of the Kwagiulth Band, Kwakwaka'wakw Nation, as well as of Ukrainian and English ancestry.

KAREN ISAAC, a Mi'kmaw from the Gaspé region of Quebec, has been involved in Aboriginal children's issues since 2000 and is currently the executive director of the B.C. Aboriginal Child Care Society (BC ACCS), a non-profit organization established in 1995 by the First Nations Summit to administer British Columbia's $12 million allocation of the First Nations/Inuit Child

Care Initiative. Between 1996 and 2000, the society helped oversee the creation of 800 new licensed child care spaces in 57 B.C. First Nations communities throughout the province. Today BC ACCS continues to support First Nations and other Aboriginal communities and early childhood educators in British Columbia by providing culturally focused early childhood education and care resources, training, networking, and research.

MARILYN IWAMA is a grandmother of Cree/Saulteaux/Métis/Mennonite descent who published her first volume of poetry, *Skin Whispers Down* (Thistledown) in 2003. Convinced that Indigenous and mainstream ways can thrive together, she joined the team at Cape Breton University's Institute for Integrative Science and Health. Marilyn has helped articulate two guiding principles for integrative research and living. One involves Mi'kmaw Elder Murdena Marshall's linguistic teachings on the "healing tense" in Mi'kmaw language. The second, Two-Eyed Seeing, is a principle that Elder Albert Marshall developed as a means for using the strengths of both Indigenous and Western knowledges and ways of knowing. Some of this work appears in *I Got It from an Elder: Conversations in Healing Language* (Gaspereau Press, 2007) and "Two-Eyed Seeing and the Language of Healing in Community-Based Research" (*Canadian Journal of Native Education*, 32(2010), 3–23). These days, Marilyn interweaves in Okinawa, Japan.

KATHLEEN JAMIESON trained as a researcher at the National Library and Archives of Scotland after graduating from the University of Edinburgh with a master's degree in history and philosophy. She spent six years working as a volunteer with young children in South America before immigrating with her family to Canada, where she pursued graduate studies in sociology and anthropology at Carleton University in Ottawa and then Simon Fraser University in British Columbia. She worked as a writer and researcher with the Canadian Advisory Council of the Status of Women, which published her report on First Nations women and the Indian Act as a book. She was employed as director of consulting services by the Social Planning and Research Council of B.C. for six years. She has worked as a research consultant with Aboriginal women across Canada for many years and with the B.C. Aboriginal Child Care Society since 2002.

ELIZABETH JONES is faculty emerita in human development at Pacific Oaks College in Pasadena, California, where she taught for 50 years. She has participated with Margo Greenwood and Alan Pence in the development of programs for Indigenous children in western Canada, serving as a member of the Advisory Board for the Meadow Lake Tribal Council Childcare Initiative at the University of Victoria. She has also worked with programs for Indigenous children and teachers in Australia and New Zealand, and served as a consultant on the Navajo reservation. Her publications include *The Play's the Thing* (with Gretchen Reynolds), *Playing to Get Smart* (with Renatta Cooper), *Emergent Curriculum* (with John Nimmo), and *Teaching Adults: Active Learning for Early Childhood Educators.*

ROBERTA KENNEDY's Haida name is Kung Jaadee. It means "Moon Woman." She lives on Haida Gwaii (the Land of the People, formerly the Queen Charlotte Islands, British Columbia). She has travelled across Canada performing traditional Haida Raven stories to audiences of all ages for 22 years. She has travelled to nearly every province and territory in Canada, telling her stories at schools, conferences, and festivals. She tells Yaahl, or Raven, stories—the Haida Nation's Trickster/Creator. Kung Jaadee's favourite activity is baking treats for her loved ones. She loves walking in the rain, in her slicker gear, and falling asleep to the 100 kilometre-an-hour winds during the fall and winter. Kung Jaadee is most grateful for her blessed and beautiful life.

JAMES LAMOUCHE is Cree/Métis from northern Alberta. He has experience working as an educator developing science curriculum that respects Indigenous knowledge and attempts to engage Indigenous students more fully. His research experience includes the Pulmonary Research Institute at the University of Alberta and the Dana Farber Cancer Institute in Boston, Massachusetts. James also served as coordinator of the Four Directions Summer Research Program at Harvard Medical School. The focus of his work with the National Aboriginal Health Organization was the protection and promotion of traditional healing practices and medicines for the improvement of the health of Indigenous peoples. To this end, James has worked with, and in, numerous communities across Canada, the United States, Colombia, Brazil, and Suriname with the Cree, Lakota, Haudenosaunee, Anishinabe, Ingano, Waura, Siona, Kofane, and Trio peoples, among others. James is the director of research at Blue Quills First Nations College.

NICOLE MARIE LINDSAY is a doctoral candidate in the School of Communication at Simon Fraser University. Her research is focused on the emergence and evolution of discourses of responsibility and sustainability in the mining industry, with an empirical focus on Canadian companies operating in Mexico and Latin America. She is a past research associate at the National Collaborating Centre for Aboriginal Health and former associate faculty at Royal Roads University.

BRENDA MACDOUGALL, appointed as the chair of Métis research at the University of Ottawa in 2010, has worked with a number of Métis communities documenting their cultural history through the stories of families. She is the author of several articles, and her first book, *One of the Family: Métis Culture in Nineteenth-Century Northwestern Saskatchewan* (2010), was awarded the Clio Prize for Prairie history by the Canadian Historical Association. Recognized as one of the foremost scholars on the Métis, she is invited to speak at community, government, industry, and academic events, sits on a number of national and provincial committees, and oversees a number of significant research grants.

JAMES MAKOKIS, born and raised on Saddle Lake Cree Nation, Alberta, graduated from medical school at the University of Ottawa in 2010. He completed his residency in the Aboriginal Family Medicine Program (Victoria, British Columbia) in 2012, and is currently a family physician at the Saddle Lake Health Care Centre. Dr. Makokis also holds a master's degree in health science-community nutrition from the University of Toronto. From 2007 to 2009, he was the national spokesperson for the National Aboriginal Health Organization's "Lead Your Way" youth role model program, promoting healthy lifestyles among Indigenous youth and communities across Canada. As a committed volunteer, Dr. Makokis has been involved in a number of community programs, including those that support gays, lesbians, and two-spirited Indigenous youth. He was the 2007 National Aboriginal Achievement Award youth recipient, and received the Queen's Diamond Jubilee Medal in 2012. His medical interests involve working with traditional Indigenous knowledge holders to provide more holistic patient care.

PATRICIA MAKOKIS resides on the Saddle Lake Cree Nation in northeastern Alberta with her husband, Eugene, and occasionally adult children, Janice and James, and grandson, Atayoh. Pat intentionally focuses on serving the community, always remembering that she is a "servant" of the people. She received her doctorate of education from the University of San Diego in 2000, specializing in leadership studies. Since then she has developed and taught leadership and health courses in First Nations college settings and now co-teaches in the Faculty of Extension at the University of Alberta. Pat currently works for a family-owned company that does work in the oil and gas industry. At present, she co-leads the development of an industry credential for the Circle for Aboriginal Relations and the University of Alberta (Faculty of Extension) designed to enhance better relationships between Indigenous peoples, government, and industry. Pat is very proud of this work, believing it will contribute significantly to better relationships.

MURDENA MARSHALL AND ALBERT MARSHALL are both much-loved and deeply valued Elders from the Mi'kmaw Nation. They live in Eskasoni First Nation in Unama'ki (Cape Breton), Nova Scotia. Murdena is retired from her position as associate professor of Mi'kmaw studies at Cape Breton University, but continues to be very active in projects locally and nationally. She is a fluent speaker, reader, and writer of the Mi'kmaw language and a highly respected holder of Mi'kmaw traditional knowledge. Albert is also a fluent speaker and a passionate advocate of cross-cultural understandings and healing and of our human responsibilities to care for all creatures and our Mother Earth. He is the designated voice with respect to environmental issues for the Mi'kmaw Elders of Unama'ki, and he sits on various committees that develop and guide collaborative initiatives and understandings in natural resource management that serve First Nations' governance issues or otherwise work toward ethical environmental, social, and economic practices. Moreover, Albert is the person who coined the phrase "Two-Eyed Seeing"/*Etuaptmumk* as a guiding principle for collaborative work that encourages learning to see from one eye with the strengths of Indigenous knowledges and ways of knowing, and from the other eye with the strengths of Western knowledges and ways of knowing, and learning to use both these eyes together for the benefit of all. In 2009, Albert and Murdena were awarded honorary doctorates of letters by Cape Breton University for their work seeking the preservation, understanding, and promotion of cultural beliefs and practices among the people of the Mi'kmaw Nation.

RENÉE MASCHING is a First Nation woman originally from southern Ontario. Renée has dedicated her professional energies to working with Aboriginal peoples and health-related programs. Her formal involvement in the Aboriginal HIV and AIDS movement in Canada began in 1995 and Renée has been honoured to contribute with dedication and determination. Contributions have included: providing support to community-based HIV and AIDS organizations; serving as a board member with national organizations; assisting with the development of government policy in the Atlantic provinces and federally; working with numerous committees; and working directly with Aboriginal peoples living with HIV and AIDS. Formal education achievements include bachelor and master of social work degrees from McMaster University. Renée's research interests are focused on community-based research frameworks, Indigenous knowledge, and community health with an emphasis on self-care and HIV and AIDS. Renée lives with her husband, sons, and a menagerie of pets by the ocean in Nova Scotia in Mi'kmaw Territory.

FERNANDO POLANCO is a native of Guatemala and raised in northern British Columbia. He completed his bachelor of science in microbiology at Vancouver Island University with a focus on community-associated infectious diseases and global health, and completed a master of science from the University of Victoria with a focus on medical genetics (medical sciences) and Aboriginal health (Centre for Aboriginal Health Research) through the Social Dimensions of Health program. Fernando is past recipient of the Kloshe Tillicum-CIHR-IAPH Masters Scholarship, and has worked internationally in Peru, Ecuador, Tanzania, Guatemala, and throughout Canada (British Columbia–focused) for health care initiatives with Indigenous peoples at the front line and policy level. Fernando is currently a project coordinator at the South Okanagan Similkameen Division of Family Practice.

SHERRI POOYAK has a master's in social work from the University of Victoria, and is of Cree descent from Saskatchewan. Sherri's academic background has focused on areas of Aboriginal child welfare, Aboriginal sex-worker issues, and family resilience. Since 2007 Sherri has been involved in the area of Aboriginal health research, and welcomes her recent transition to focusing on HIV and AIDS. Working in the field of community-based research since 2009 has given her a greater understanding in supporting and assisting with relationship building between communities and academics as they embark on conducting community-based research.

CHARLOTTE READING is a professor in the School of Public Health and Social Policy, Faculty of Human and Social Development, University of Victoria; director of the Centre for Aboriginal Health Research (UVIC); and editor of the *International Journal of Indigenous Health*. Dr. Reading has undertaken research and published in the areas of Aboriginal health inequities, Aboriginal HIV/AIDS, social determinants of Aboriginal health, racism and cultural safety, cancer among Aboriginal peoples, Aboriginal ethics and research capacity building, as well as the sexual and reproductive health of Aboriginal women. Her research partners have included individual First Nations communities, as well as regional and national Aboriginal organizations (e.g., Canadian Aboriginal AIDS Network, National Aboriginal Health Organization, Assembly of First Nations) and provincial non-government (e.g., Cancer Care Nova Scotia) and national government stakeholders (e.g., First Nations Inuit Health, Public Health Agency of Canada).

CHANTELLE RICHMOND is an Anishinabe scholar from Pic River First Nation. Her research is framed by community-based approaches that aim to understand how Indigenous health is affected by processes of environmental dispossession. Through this work, she seeks to aid in the preservation of Indigenous knowledge and the implementation of strategies that may foster environmental repossession efforts in affected communities. Chantelle is an associate professor at the University of Western Ontario, where she is director of the Indigenous Health Lab, and co-director of the Indigenous Health and Well-Being Initiative. Chantelle co-wrote and produced a 60-minute documentary, *Gifts from the Elders*, which focused on the preservation of Indigenous knowledge among Anishinabe communities on the north shore of Lake Superior. Her research is supported by a CIHR New Investigator Award and an Ontario Early Researcher Award. Chantelle lives in London, Ontario, with her husband, Ian, and children, Maya and William.

DIANA STEINHAUER, Cree, from Saddle Lake, is an educator with 29 years of experience in teaching and administration in K–12 schools and post-secondary institutions. Most importantly, she is a mother and first teacher of her two children, Alexis and Ty. Diana completed her doctorate in *iyiniw pimâtisiwin kiskeyitamowin* (Indigenous peoples' knowledge) at Blue Quills First Nations College, where she coordinates and teaches in the master of education and bachelor of education programs. Her MEd and BEd degrees were completed at the University of Alberta. She is particularly grateful to the Elders and knowledge keepers who have guided and mentored her in Indigenous knowledge and ways of being as a *nehiyaw iskwew*. Recognizing the value and worth of *iyiniw pimâtisiwin*, Diana's work as a change agent in language, education, and research is grounded upon her late father's adage, *pimâtisîtotetân kimiyikowisiwininaw*, let us live life the way our Creator intended us to live.

SHIRLEY TAGALIK is an educator who has lived in Arviat since 1976 and worked at all levels in the school system. In 1999 she joined the new Government of Nunavut as manager of early childhood and school services within the Curriculum Division. Her main task was to redesign the educational system within a framework of Inuit knowledge and to begin the rewriting of the curriculum to fit this framework. She worked extensively with Inuit Elders to document their cultural knowledge, Inuit Qaujimajatuqangit. Shirley lives in Arviat with her husband, children, and grandchildren. She helped establish the Arviat Wellness Centre, which delivers programs promoting wellness and healing. She continues to research with Inuit Elders, write curriculum grounded in Inuit Qaujimajatuqangit, and support program development promoting cultural and linguistic revitalization through her business, Inukpaujaq Consulting. She and a team of Elders are currently writing a book on Inuit cultural knowledge and belief systems.

TERRY TEEGEE is a registered professional forester and the tribal chief of the Carrier Sekani Tribal Council since July 2012. Terry also served three years as vice tribal chief from 2009 to 2012. Prior to his political endeavours, Terry was the forestry coordinator for his community of Takla Lake First Nation from 2005 to 2009. In 2005 Terry graduated from the University of Northern British Columbia (UNBC) with a bachelor of science degree in forestry. Terry has also completed his diploma in forest resource technology from the College of New Caledonia in 2001. Terry was born in Saikuz Territory (Vanderhoof, British Columbia) and raised in Nakazdli Territory (Fort Saint James, British Columbia). Terry currently resides in Lhiedli Tenneh (Prince George, British Columbia) with his wife, Rena, and their two children, Rylie and Rowan. Terry is part of the Laxgibuu (Wolf) Clan and is of Carrier, Sekani, and Gitxsan ancestry.

RICHARD VAN CAMP is a proud member of the Dogrib (Tlicho) Nation from Fort Smith, Northwest Territories. He is the author of two children's books with the Cree artist George Littlechild: *A Man Called Raven* and *What's the Most Beautiful Thing You Know About Horses?* He has published a novel, *The Lesser Blessed*, which is now a feature film with First Generation Films.

His collections of short stories include *Angel Wing Splash Pattern, The Moon of Letting Go and Other Stories,* and *Godless but Loyal to Heaven.* He is the author of three baby books: *Welcome Song for Baby: A Lullaby for Newborns, Nighty Night: A Bedtime Song for Babies,* and *Little You* (now translated into Cree, Dene, and South Slavey), and he has two comic books out with the Healthy Aboriginal Network: *Kiss Me Deadly* and *Path of the Warrior.* You can visit Richard on Facebook, Twitter, or at his website: www.richardvancamp.com.

LEAH MAY WALKER is of Danish, English, and Nlaka'pamux descent and has kinship ties with the Sto:lo Nation at Seabird Island. She studied theatre, literature, youth and adult education, and has a background that includes being a legal assistant, driving a coal truck, teaching high school English, theatre, and filmmaking. In 2001 she joined UBC and is currently the associate director for education at the newly formed Centre for Excellence in Indigenous Health. Leah is passionate about developing educational opportunities that enable health professionals to create culturally safe practices and genuine partnerships that improve health and well-being in Indigenous communities. She teaches Indigenous health sessions and courses, such as an Aboriginal health elective, which situates health professional students in Indigenous communities to work with and learn from the local people. She feels honoured to lead Summer Science for high school students and other initiatives at UBC, including the UBC Learning Circle.

INDEX

Page numbers followed by n *refer to notes*